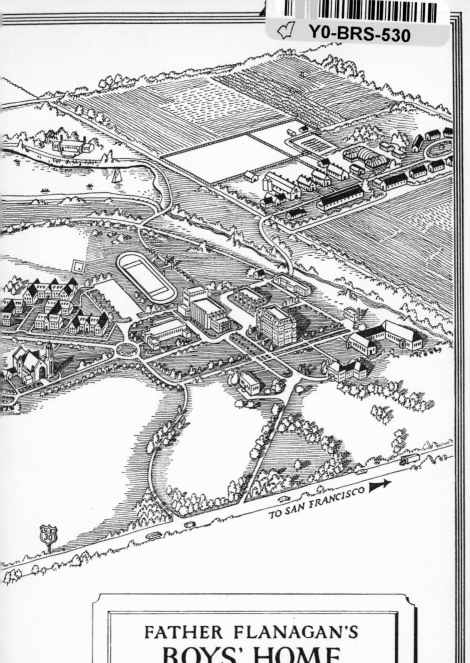

TO SAN FRANCISCO ➤

30

FATHER FLANAGAN'S
BOYS' HOME
BOYS TOWN, NEBRASKA

FATHER FLANAGAN
OF BOYS TOWN

Fulton Oursler *and* Will Oursler

Father Flanagan

OF BOYS TOWN

Doubleday & Company, Inc.

GARDEN CITY, N.Y.

To all children who hunger for love—may they find it in that fullness of Christian charity that distinguished the life of our friend Father Edward Joseph Flanagan.

THE AUTHORS

Authors' Note

Much of the information from which this book was written was obtained from many lengthy conversations which the authors had with Father Flanagan and, after his death, with those closest to him in his family, including his sister Nellie and his brother, Monsignor Patrick A. Flanagan. In addition we talked with many of his associates in Omaha, Nebraska, and with many former friends and associates in the Church.

We consulted also scores of scrapbooks at Boys Town itself and hundreds of case histories on record there, in addition to firsthand interviews with numerous officials on the Boys Town staff whose assistance was invaluable. Available to us also and of great assistance were the speeches and letters of Father Flanagan, covering the many years since Boys Town was founded, a first-person history of Boys Town dictated by Father Flanagan while recuperating from an illness, and an unpublished biography of Father Flanagan prepared by Gilson Willets.

We are grateful for these many sources of information which were open to us and which were of such help in the preparation of this book.

THE AUTHORS

Foreword

The lives of all great, magnanimous people instill into our hearts a deep admiration and a warm feeling of gratitude. We breathe a prayer of thanks to Almighty God for having given them to the world. There are many so great that even though no written record of their deeds and worth were left to posterity, they would continue to influence the lives of numberless persons long after death as their stories passed from mouth to mouth through the ages.

However, there have always been—and it is hoped ever will be—gifted writers who have recorded for future generations the biographies of the great. Regardless of time or field of service, the outstanding leaders have never wanted for talented pens to write and rewrite their lives. Now Fulton Oursler and Will Oursler—father and son, and two of the most accomplished of our contemporary writers—present the life and deeds of a man who for twoscore years was not only well known but loved and respected throughout the world: Father Flanagan.

In this book the authors narrate the life of Father Flanagan with such clarity and with such simplicity that they have caught the very spirit of the man, and the reader will feel his presence on every page. The reader will absorb the kindness, generosity, sympathy, and understanding that welled in the heart of Father Flanagan.

Each page bears witness to Father Flanagan's love for and unshaken confidence in the American boy. His life proves conclusively that boys from broken, shattered homes, even those who have early run afoul of the law, can, with proper environment, with a solid religious education, with instruction in natural and moral law, and with love, make good. The proof of the pudding lies in the eating thereof: Thousands of boys who came under his benign influence are useful, happy citizens today.

The authors of this book deserve the thanks of all who knew and admired Father Flanagan, and indeed of all the world. They have captured in their own style the humility and the simplicity of Father Flanagan, and just as it was his strength, so is it the strength of this book. The appealing story of the man and his work, the unforgettable lessons he taught, and the recognition he so widely received are told here fully and readably for the first time so that all the world may know this man.

FATHER NICHOLAS H. WEGNER
Director, Father Flanagan's Boys' Home

Boys Town
Nebraska
June 1, 1949

Contents

Contents

Illustrations

Illustrations XV

Shaping unhardened clay.

Shoemaker's shop.

Learning to swim.

Boys Town teams in all sports compete with the best in the country— but informal play is important too.

Boys get the best in medical care.

School's out.

In addition to his other presents, every boy received one personal gift from Father Flanagan at Christmas.

Informal prom.

Soloists of the Boys Town Choir at practice.

After chapel.

Although no dog ever replaced the original Carlo, pets are still popular. This is one of the many animal pets given by Boys Town friends in recent years.

The farm and part of the herd.

Father Flanagan in Ireland, 1946.

Miami Beach, 1946.

Japanese children besiege him for autographs, 1947.

Father Flanagan found these boys "housed" in a Manila jail. His efforts won them a fresh start.

Father Flanagan just before he sailed for Germany and Austria, 1948.

Nellie Flanagan, Father Wegner, Father P. A., and Father Flanagan watching a Boys Town basketball game.

The last picture: Arriving at Tempelhof Airfield, Berlin, May 14, 1948. Father Flanagan was fatally stricken that night and died the next morning.

Book One

CHAPTER ONE

Father Somebody from Somewhere

For the better part of the first half of this century Edward Joseph Flanagan, a Roman Catholic priest, was the most beloved clergyman in the United States. His millions of devoted admirers were not of his faith only; Jews and Protestants actually contributed to his work as much as his own people.

That work, as the world knows, was the education and care of unfortunate boys. Not, as generally supposed, merely of delinquents whom the police and courts were glad to get rid of. Because he sheltered some young thieves and killers, a popular impression grew up that Father Flanagan worked only with adolescent malefactors.

Actually, the highest percentage of juvenile offenders ever studying and living in Boys Town at one time was only 20 per cent. Primarily the place is a home for the homeless, a family for the fatherless—from whatever source they may come.

No restrictions of color or creed have ever been imposed in the incorporated town for luckless youngsters which Father Flanagan established ten miles west of Omaha, Nebraska. Chinese and Negroes plant its fields, work at its shop benches, and sit in its classrooms as companions with Baptists and Jews.

Nor are those who come from the police segregated from those who become homeless because of desertion, or illness, or death. There is no difference, because the courthouse minority are soon most curiously and agreeably transformed into good citizens. Wild lads they may be when they arrive; audacious, defiant of restraint, bitter with an insolent and seemingly incorrigible obstinacy. They have known the feculence of that most degraded of all American public institutions, the county jail; and the foulness, mental and physical, of its prisoners. They are veterans of back-alley wars and in battle would not hesitate to gouge out an enemy's eye with a broken beer bottle. Worse, and invariably, the minds of such children have been polluted and defiled almost from birth.

Some are little wanderers who, until they came to Boys Town, had never slept in a bed; one helped to rob a bank, another—that bright-faced honor pupil over there—killed his stepfather with a pitchfork.

They will never again steal or kill. Nor are they likely to run away from this self-contained, self-earning village that has no fences, gates, locks, or bolts. They are content to stay here, submitting to a rigorous discipline; they buckle down like other boys to book lessons and shop instruction and practical apprenticeship in scientific farming. And every one of them is being individually coached in personality; in learning the lessons of sportsmanship, in getting along with people.

The basic purpose of Father Flanagan when he bought the farm was to make it a training place for good character. That he succeeded, not only with the 80 per cent who had never been in police trouble but also with the 20 per cent looked upon as beyond redemption, is an indication that he had something good to offer his boys. In the midst of an almost constant and quite frightening increase in crimes committed by youths, the prowess of this Irish-born priest with young souls, his ability to transform the toughest of juvenile delinquents, so-called, into co-operative and socially adjusted young men of contented integrity, shines like a beam of light in a darkened scene.

Experts in many fields were baffled at his results, and some still are. The intellectuals were deeply grounded in psychology and psychoanalysis and psychiatry and neuropsychiatry; fortified with statistics from a hundred, no, a thousand surveys and inquiries and scientific studies. But for a long time they did not understand Boys Town. The secret of its techniques seemed to remain an abstruse mystery.

That befuddlement was largely due to the simplicity of the explanation which Flanagan freely gave to them. His theory seemed inadequate to cover the facts; his rationale of such startling skill in rehabilitation seemed sentimental, even, perhaps, a little childish. Therefore many scientists cross-examined him in friendly jousts, trying to probe beneath this simplicity, not realizing it was deep as the universe itself. Father Flanagan confided all that he knew. There was nothing doctrinaire about his opinions and he listened respectfully to modern theories—though with a certain reserve. In his heart he distrusted scholastic theory, but only because generally God was left out of it.

But he also distrusted the flatulence and windiness and vanity and blindness of many sermons, preached to all faiths, criticizing the younger generation.

Boys, he said, had more need of models than of critics!

Indeed, Father Flanagan had a vast respect for the native wit and discernment and innate decency of even the roughest lads, agreeing with Emerson that boys can detect truth from counterfeit as quickly as any chemist. They can perceive weakness and hypocrisy in your eyes before you even open your mouth and remove all doubt.

So, while some types of reformers denounced the children of this age and experts failed to explore beyond motor and sensory impressions tests, Binet charts and I.Q.s, Flanagan, simple pastor that he was, in his simplicity spoke of love.

"It is not enough," he told us, "to see that what has been called an underprivileged child is given good food, warm clothing, and a clean bed. An army commissary can do as much. No! More than food, clothes, and shelter, what these lads have been deprived of is mother's tenderness, and father's wisdom, and the love of a family. We will never get anywhere in our reform schools and orphan asylums until we compensate for that great loss in such young lives.

"And what does that mean? It means you will have to develop a new class of social workers, not merely distinguished for their professional training, but, more important, consecrated to the great, the soul-lifting task of bringing tenderness and solicitude and understanding and motherly interest, if you please—a doting interest, if you don't mind—to the little affairs of desolate children."

That is a precise statement of what Flanagan himself had been doing up until his last day alive. The greatest fact about him was that he knew how to love; that was why he was beloved by so many different kinds of people. A full-handed, generous offer of affection was his invincible technique. He was not only filled up with its power, he was expert in its control and direction, certain that it was the supreme medicine for body, mind, and soul.

That was a hard lesson for some of the experts to learn.

Into the service of such love Father Flanagan called unhesitatingly for a wide variety of tools and techniques—from chocolate candy to psychiatry. He insisted that he got results out of all those devices because he used them with spiritual perception and unremitting prayer. And that was even harder on the experts.

Nor was it merely that Father Flanagan loved others as he loved himself. That admonition to Christian neighborliness is often quoted by rationalists as if it were all the doctrine anyone needs for the good life. But invariably Father pointed out that it was only a half quotation. In hearty voice, blue eyes kindling, he would repeat the whole verse:

"And thou shalt love the Lord, thy God, with thy whole heart, and with thy whole soul, and with thy whole mind and with thy whole strength . . . *and* thy neighbor as thyself."

Anything less was putting the cart before the horse.

Father Flanagan told us that that love must, therefore, begin in the heart, and for the Father in heaven. His was a simple, unquestioning, utter devotion to that Father, Who, he felt, was ever beside him, nearer than breathing, closer than hands and feet. Because he was a child of that Father, all other human beings must be a part of his family, his brothers and sisters. That was the animating spirit of his thinking and feeling and working, a sense of kinship that passed all barriers and beheld his Master in every eye.

Since there is no human loss greater than not to know love, and since it was that ingredient he found consistently missing from the experience of boys whom communities called bad, he set out to supply the lack. No one knew him but to receive some of that warmth for himself. That was his way of life, and because he lived it faithfully, ministers of widely different pulpits hailed him as a saint.

II

Thus the Rev. Dr. Daniel Poling, Protestant editor of the *Christian Herald,* wrote:

"Father Flanagan of Boys Town has gone to his coronation. He is immortal now—indeed, his immortality began long ago, began when he said 'there is no such thing as a bad boy.'

"In that statement is more than a man's faith, for it possesses the secret of his success. He knew that personality is divine and that the spark of divinity cannot be put out by either a human act or an inherited human weakness. His authority was love—God's love. This is the only ultimate power, and Father Flanagan demonstrated that while its fulfillment is beyond time and space, it also wins with boys here and now.

"This man was the universal friend. He loved and served beyond the barricades of faith and race. The crypt in which his body lies is covered by a slab on which these words are engraved in gold: 'Father Flanagan, founder of Boys Town, lover of Christ and Man.'

"He was loyal to the royal in himself and he respected the loyalty of every other person. However a boy prayed, the important thing was that he should pray. The complete catholicity of Father Flanagan's spirit was demonstrated when he identified himself with the American Christian Palestine Committee. Firmly he stood with Jew and Protestant for the new Zion. He loved freedom with a passion, and he wanted every group, every minority, every person to be free —free to conquer an evil inheritance; free to develop a worthy character; free to choose; free to be a man in God's image.

"This man did not know how to retreat. He was on the march, and when last seen by mortal eyes, he, too, was going forward. There is something prophetic in the fact that he died in Germany, where a new world must be born. As his wish was fulfilled and his body was borne across the continents to its last resting place in Boys Town, the thoughts of men were turned not only to him but to the cause that to him was incarnate. He lived and died to redeem and glorify human personality. In this he was like his Master with Whom he is now forevermore alive."

Another Protestant minister, Rev. Dr. Thomas R. Niven, pastor of First Presbyterian Church in Omaha, was able, close at hand, to watch the work, and he wrote:

"A great Christian has been in our midst. As a representative of the Protestant clergy, I know I speak the mind of all my brethren when I say we have no greater example in the last fifty years of American life of a great Christian, a statesman and gentleman and social worker than this priest of the Roman Catholic Church. The world will long look to Boys Town as a center where a great man interpreted the life of Christ."

And Rabbi Edgar F. Magnin, of Los Angeles, spoke for the Jews:

"Like Abraham, he sat at the door of his tent to welcome these strangers passing by, freckle-faced boys with torn trousers and dirty shirts. He reached out his arms, took them to his bosom. Some were black. There were Jews, Catholics, and a variety of Protestants, and those who called themselves by no name and knew no God because they had never been taught there was a God until they met Father Flanagan.

"The simple motif was always present: the love for wandering waifs, the driftwood of an ugly, cruel society; the little Cains wandering over the earth with no place to lay their heads—except Boys Town.

"Out of this place emerged stalwart, wholesome citizens who became an asset to society rather than a drain. The country was saved millions of dollars that would have gone to try them and to incarcerate them in prison, and only the good Lord knows how many human beings were saved from becoming the victims of criminals.

"The world is poorer for the passing of Father Flanagan. But in another sense the world is richer than it was before he entered it, for he will live on in the hearts and minds of Americans, in ages yet to come."

And from the Negroes came this stirring editorial in the Los Angeles *Sentinel:*

His haven of refuge is open to all youth . . . An abandoned Negro youth is just as welcome as an abandoned Irish Catholic.

The June issue of *Ebony* magazine carries a feature on Pfc. Chester W. Oden of St. Paul, Minn., for his perfect score in the army's grueling paratrooper physical test. His name flies on a pennant atop the Airborne Training School at Fort Benning, Ga., in honor of his unusual achievement.

Pfc. Oden, the first of any race ever to make the perfect score of 500 in the army's strenuous paratrooper test, was a four-letter man at Father Flanagan's Boys Town. He is only one of dozens of Negro youths who have made good in life through the teachings of this devout Catholic priest.

Social workers who have labored among youth in the West have been keenly aware of the lack of facilities for saving unfortunate boys and girls who are victims of broken homes and poverty-stricken families. The institutions which do exist, unlike Boys Town, do not admit Negro youth into their precincts.

In the face of such racial discrimination as is commonly practiced here in America, Monsignor Flanagan, with bold courage and a true Christian spirit, preferred to follow . . . his church by opening his institution to all races. This fact should win for him a place in American history as a man of saintly zeal and devotion to the cause of humanity.

America was founded upon the philosophy that every man deserved his chance to contribute his talents to make the country great. But America has yet to learn by the example of this humble disciple of Christ that the phrase "all men" truly includes the white, the brown, and the black.

III

In his simplicity, Father Flanagan was harmless as a dove, but in the service of his Master he was also wise as a serpent. Over the years he won many a conflict with official and unofficial foes, being as astute in tactics as he was gentle and forgiving in victory or defeat. No one who crossed swords with him ever went away without a deep respect for his qualities, and a full realization that he battled with consuming emotion for the Lord.

In his fine book, *The Belief in a God,* Professor J. B. Pratt says: "In our safe and sane and sober fear of emotionalism and sentimentality, we seem to disown the spiritual nature which is part of our human heritage." Day and night, in courtrooms and classrooms, in lecture halls and on the radio, in Japan and in Austria, when he counseled with homeless boys of our defeated enemies, Flanagan proclaimed that heritage. Without an appeal to the spiritual nature, he declared, you would get nowhere with boys.

"Some of the *soi-disant* high-brows tell me I deal in platitudes," he mused one winter night by the fireside in his study at Boys Town. "But in reply I quote them another: 'A platitude is an immortal truth become so familiar that we have forgotten its meaning.' "

Far into that deep February night he chatted about his work. And the more he talked, the clearer it was that he meant literally there was no such thing as a bad boy. He could palliate any boyish deed and make it appear less offensive. Yet there was nothing namby-pamby or weakly insipid in this attitude; he was a man of hard common sense, outspoken, bold of speech, sometimes painfully frank, but always fervent and full of ardent feeling. To him the admonition "Love one another" was not a pathetic appeal to our better nature; it was a fiat, a positive and authoritive and very difficult command from the Lord God of Hosts, and as a good Christian he had to obey it. This was his catholicon, his universal panacea, not only for wayward boys but for the world; the only leaven in a heathen age that could cause a general change. With stoutheartedness and intrepidity and, as we shall see, with the boldness of perfect faith, he carried out the Master's orders. He did love, and the results at Boys Town were the product of that devotion.

We shall always be glad that it was with Father Flanagan as dragoman that we saw his village. There could be but one better way to see it: the way that a small boy saw it after he ran away from home.

On his last day in America, Father told us of this boy.

"Put Stubby in the story," he urged, "because he's typical. No one will ever spot him, because I've changed it around. But it's all, every bit, true!"

IV

The small boy whose nickname was Stubby was in a boxcar, hooking a ride. All night he had sat crouched in one corner of the rattling freight, and not until the morning light came through the slatted walls did he discover that another passenger was riding with him.

At first he had been glad of the light; it had been cold and lonesome on this first night of being away on his own. Seeing the old man in the other corner made him afraid all over again; afraid and ashamed of being afraid, too, because after all he was twelve years old. He should be able to take whatever came along, to feel and act just like a man.

"What do you think you're gawking at?" the old man growled. A shrill, harsh screech of the engine obliterated the boy's answer.

"You're scared, kid." The ragged stranger laughed, opening his toothless mouth. "Come over here. I'm as friendly as an old shoe and smell just about the same. What's your name?"

"Stubby. What's yours?"

"Harry. Running away from home, Stubby?"

"That's my business."

Something admiring and grotesquely paternal flickered in the bleak eyes, dull and dimmed.

"What you running away for?" he persisted.

"I'm afraid to tell anybody. If the cops ever find me, I'll——"

"Aw, the cops can't track an elephant in four feet of snow. And people like us never turn in a pal, Stubby. Mosquitoes don't bite each other."

"My pop died."

"Uh-huh."

"And Mom got married again."

"Yep?"

"And then Mom died too."

"Ya don't have to tell me any more, Stubby," groaned the old man and seemed to mumble curses in his stiff little beard. "Where you heading for?"

"Anywheres."

Upon that answer Harry pondered through many swaying, rattling miles. His soiled and wrinkled countenance was contracted in a tormented reflection of unaccustomed mental struggle. Slowly back and forth he shook his shaggy head.

"It's no good," he declared at last. "You're too nice a kid to be a bum. Take it from me——"

"I don't want to be a bum, either," said Stubby. "But I've got it figured out there's nothing else for me to be—not yet awhile anyhow. If I get caught they'll send me back, and that's worse than being a bum. Or else I'll be sent to a reformatory——"

"Stubby," said Harry, "listen to me. I've got an idea."

He scratched his head with both hands in deep exasperation.

"I can't remember the guy's name," he snarled. "You'd think the way I hate him—to this very minute I hate him—I'd at least remember his name."

"Who?"

A priest, Harry explained. Father Somebody from somewhere. He couldn't remember. A Roman Catholic priest who once had done him in the eye. Years ago it had happened, when the man who buttoned his collar in the back was running some kind of free hotel for guys without money. A "hotel-de-gink," Harry called it. Upstairs there were beds for drifters. Downstairs were beds for drunks and dope addicts and such——

"Such as me," admitted Harry, spitting largely. "I may inform you, Stubby, that I am an alcoholic. I remember the night I went in there—I could have killed him, just with my hands. Why? Because he smiled at me so sweet and I told myself, here's an easy touch. He misled me!

"He asked me if I had any liquor left on me and I said no. Then he patted me all over, frisking me as smooth as any dick. But he didn't find anything. So I started for the stairs, feeling very proud and smart, when all of a sudden he ups with the back of his hand and knocks my brown derby right off my head. And with it he knocks out a full half pint of good booze. It fell on the floor and broke and every last drop was lost."

Stubby's gaze had wandered; what had all this to do with him? He was beginning to feel hungry. Then he saw Harry peeling open a newspaper from around a ham sandwich; he broke it in half and they ate together.

"But he wasn't really a bad guy," Harry conceded. "He meant well and he did his darnedest to get me to quit drinking and go to work.

He don't have that hotel any more, so I heard. Opened up a new place—just for kids."

"Another industrial school," said Stubby with poisonous scorn.

"Not the way I heard it. It's a town just for boys. It's got a big dining room, with plenty of hot food all the time! And a ball field. And a swimming pool. And graphophones and moving pictures— and swell rooms to sleep in——"

"You're drunk right now!" suggested Stubby.

"No such luck. I'm giving it to you straight. It's a place for guys like you, with no friends and no place to go, where they can learn things and play, like other boys."

"On the level, Harry?"

"On the level!" the old man avouched.

"What's its name?"

"Boys Town!"

There was silence, while Stubby thought it over. The story sounded like a fairy tale, the kind Mom used to tell him.

"Where is Boys Town?" he asked warily.

Old Harry shook his head with a dismal sigh.

"Brains all gone," he confessed. "I just can't remember. But you could find out—any priest ought to know. Pretty soon we'll be pulling in. Our next town is Harrisburg, Pennsylvania. You just scram, kid, and ask your way to Father——"

Helplessly, he shook his head.

"Father Somebody. Boys Town," said Stubby. "Thanks, Harry. Maybe I will. What have I got to lose?"

v

Across several states Stubby, the boy pilgrim, trudged and thumbed his way. He was thin and dusty, and his hair was disheveled, his shoes in collapse. Only inexhaustible curiosity and hope had kept him on his long journey; goaded him on the roads, over the mountains, and across the Mississippi and now the rolling Missouri. By dint of begging and stealing, of asking questions and dodging other questions, he had got to Omaha. With cautious eye he had circled the Douglas County Courthouse until, on Farnam Street near the First National Bank, he had been stopped by a policeman:

"Where do you think you're going?"

"I'm on my way to Boys Town. Is it near here?"

"Straight out Route Number 30," pointed the officer; this was not the first unkempt child he had directed that way.

After long hours Stubby began slowly to climb a long hill. Since early afternoon he had been walking from Omaha. They had told him it was only ten or eleven miles. It had seemed like a hundred. At last, as the sun was streaking red and orange and splashing gold on the Nebraska fields, he stopped in his tracks. This must be it.

At the foot of the hill, in plain view of his eyes, was a ball field— full of boys screaming like wild Indians. And all around were broad, verdant fields still green with vegetation and trees. And great buildings and schoolhouses, and cottages with red roofs, blue roofs—and a church with a tower and swinging bell that now began to peal out the sunset hour.

"It's not like any town I've ever seen," reflected Stubby. "No Main Street. No juke-box joint. Bet those guys on the diamond are sure having a good time."

It was a stupendous, an unnerving sight. He was tempted to turn and go back. What if they would not take him into this prodigious spread of houses and fields, with its broad arch of entry, its sign that blazoned in great stone letters the words "Boys Town"!

There was no gate; just the open arch. Old Harry hadn't mentioned that. No fences, no outer doors, no bars, and no locks. You could run away, easy enough, if you wanted to! But those boys on the baseball diamond didn't look as if they wanted to run away.

Stubby could not put into words all that he was feeling of hope and fear and the nearness of deliverance. But these were his Elysian fields where everything seemed supremely blessed and happy. He had never heard, and to this day has probably not heard, of the last will and testament of Charles Lounsbury, yet what that romantic lawyer bequeathed to all the boys of the earth was now—if they would only let him in—his heritage too:

"I devise to boys, jointly, all the idle fields and commons where ball may be played, all pleasant waters where one may swim, all snow-clad hills where one may coast, and all streams and ponds where one may fish, or where, when winter comes, one may skate, to have and to hold the same for the period of their boyhood. And all the meadows, with clover blossoms and butterflies thereof, the woods with their appurtenances, the birds and squirrels and echoes and strange noises, and all distant places which may be visited, together with the adventures there to be found."

VI

A big man in green blazer and brown corduroy trousers, standing near the archway, beckoned to Stubby and asked him what he wanted.

"Are you a cop?"

No, he was just Larry Kennedy, and worked around the place; besides, this town had no policeman and no jail. And Mr. Kennedy grinned.

"Can a fellow like me stay here?" was Stubby's next question.

As to that, Mr. Kennedy couldn't say. His job was to supervise traffic and visitors, of which there were sometimes, in the midst of summer, two thousand a day. However, he would escort Stubby over to the Administration Building. On the way Larry Kennedy explained that he was once a boy citizen here himself; he was in the first high-school class ever to graduate from Boys Town.

"Did you play baseball?"

"I used to pitch. Won twenty-four games in a row for our team."

"Gee whiz! I'll bet the big leagues were trying to get you."

The next few hours were like a dream to Stubby. Behind glass doors of the office building he was led before a priest with a face unbelievably flushed and young—Father Edmund C. Walsh, chief assistant of the administration. Father Walsh was kind but not overkind; he did not flatter a young runaway's ego by getting excited. He took Stubby's arrival as a matter of routine, inquired his name, where he came from and why. Having listened to Stubby's carefully invented autobiography, he brushed it all aside and with a fast grin demanded the truth.

"I want to stay here. If I tell you the truth, you'll send me back," pleaded Stubby.

Then Father Walsh explained that thousands of boys wanted to come there. Only a very few could be taken; Father Flanagan must decide that. Meanwhile Stubby could remain as a transient, a temporary guest, while the conditions back home in West Virginia could be investigated. If the situation was as bad as Stubby made out—well, there might be some hope. The thing to do while waiting was to pray.

"I haven't done that since I was a kid," said Stubby. "And there's something else. I'm no Catholic. When Mom was living she took me to the Baptist church."

"You can go to a Baptist church here too. And that reminds me— how would you like a bath? Larry, take him over to Apartment Four."

It wasn't a real apartment house, not like the kind you would see in a city. It was a large red brick house with a green slate roof, and there were a number of others like it set around in a sort of court.

An uproar of shrill voices came through the opening door: a herd of boys talking all at once, with a phonograph screaming a new ditty.

A young man supervisor took Stubby in charge and led him through pandemonium to a dormitory with twenty-five beds. Soap, towel, shower, a complete new outfit of clothes, toothbrush, comb —and come on now, Stubby, or we'll be late for chow.

Old Harry of the boxcar had been far righter than he knew. There was plenty of hot food, all right; you could smell it. And you didn't line up and march, either, into the dining hall. It was like a big, cheerful, noisy cafeteria: long gleaming counters with food piled up and steaming. The boy beside him warned: "Don't take more than you can eat. You're supposed to eat all you take and you can always go back for more."

Tonight it was frankfurters, beans, and fried potatoes, plenty of milk, with cookies and pie for dessert. Suddenly all the boys were at table, standing behind their chairs and facing the eastern wall, on which was suspended a crucifix. They bowed their heads, then exploded into noisy chatter as they all sat down.

Irish school days: Somewhere in this group of pupils is a youngster named Flanagan.

*Membership card of Edward Flanagan, theological student, in the German and
Austrian Mountain Climbing Club.*

In the colorful costume of the Tyrol.

A moment of relaxation for future theologians. Young Flanagan has one foot on the step of the cart.

Young Flanagan, third from left in middle row, with classmates, soon to start on his life's mission.

The boys around Stubby asked him a few questions. When he reluctantly told them of his mother's death, they had heard enough. Stepfather trouble, eh? Lot of that kind here, all right. But he hadn't been in any jail trouble? Good. For the first time Stubby realized that some of these boys had been young criminals.

In his astonishment at this extraordinary news, he turned to Eddie, the boy on his right, and asked:

"They have any guards around? I don't see any guards."

"This isn't a prison."

"Don't they even have somebody in charge?"

Eddie pointed to a table in one corner: all grownups there, two men in street clothes and several priests.

"That one on the end," Eddie said, "that's Father Kuhn. He directs most of the Boy Scout work. And you can't get away with much around him."

"Pretty strict?"

"He knows all about it—used to be a boy here himself. When he was made a priest he was ordained right here in the chapel."

Other boys, instead of eating, were cleaning up the tables; was that the way they punished you? Eddie said no. Work of this kind was something to be proud of. You got paid for it.

"Cash?" gasped Stubby.

Surely! You had your account in the Boys Town Bank. Everything you earned went into that account and you could spend a small part of it for things you needed.

"You don't need much, anyway," the other boy explained. "If you want, you can let what you earn pile up so when you're ready to leave—well, when some fellows leave here they have maybe a couple of hundred dollars to take with them."

The meal was almost over. They had gone back for seconds on their franks and now were finishing pie. Stubby asked his friend in a low voice: "That business we did before we sat down—facing the cross. What was that all about?"

"Saying grace, that's all."

"I know—but they didn't say it—they didn't say nothing. They just stood there."

"They were saying it to themselves. We got guys here with all kinds of religions. So they say it different, to themselves."

A little later the boys pushed back their chairs. Once again they went through that moment of standing in silence as they faced the Cross. This time Stubby understood. As he bowed his head he began to feel like one of the group.

VII

As a transient, Stubby remained four days, suspended between hope and despair, while Boys Town officials got in touch with his late mom's second husband and also with local social-service agencies in West Virginia. The runaway had no idea how free he had been of pursuit. His stepfather had not even bothered to report his disappearance to the police. The kid was sure to come back when he got hungry. Anyway, in his eyes, this stepchild was nobody's bargain.

As for social-service workers, they agreed with Stubby's argument that the stepfather's house was no place for him, but they had nowhere better to send him. They were overburdened, understaffed, and broke. No one in town really cared whether or not Stubby came back.

Poor Stubby was spared this cynical demonstration of the indifference of the world. Every day of the transient's refuge had increased his desire to become a permanent resident and quickened his fear of law and in-law; the more he saw of Boys Town, the more ardent became his hopes.

He watched a basketball game in a big gym, first he had ever entered, crowded and noisy with excited Towners and a visiting team, from Beatrice, Nebraska, who brought along girls, too, including cheerleaders in festive yellow dresses.

The Boys Town team, Negroes and white boys, wore blue leather jackets with white letters across the chest. As they sprang into practice, handling the ball with belligerent precision, they were watched by a long, lean man with fighting face. "That's Skip Palrang. He's our coach. Football, too. He even wrote a book about the T-formation——"

From the balcony came voices of cheering women during the game, one rising impetuously above the others: *"Come on, Tommy. That's a boy, Tommy——"*

Nuns! One end of the gallery was crowded with Sisters in black-and-white habit, all rooting for the home team.

Hopeful dreams came to Stubby as he slept in new green-and-white pajamas; every boy seemed to be wearing a night suit of different design; no uniformity even in the dormitory! The signal for lights out silenced pillow fights and radios as the boys knelt for the good-night Our Fathers.

Next morning Stubby began to understand his surroundings. It was Saturday and a busload of boys was going into Omaha for a day's holiday. But Eddie would stay behind and show Stubby the home-town sights; he got into the city often enough, anyway, because he was a commissioner.

That sounded official.

Well, of course! He was one of the official commissioners of Boys Town. The government was not a make-believe but the real thing; the town had its own post office; in fact, the third largest in the state of Nebraska.

It was a most attractive world that unfolded before Stubby's eyes. First, a forest of orange-painted steel: girders of many rising buildings.

"Over there's going to be the new field house for athletics. A hundred universities won't have anything as big."

Big was not the word; it was already colossal. Eddie was recounting: "It'll have half a dozen basketball courts and handball courts and squash——"

Another steel skeleton beyond the field house would be the new auditorium, for assemblies and shows. "A movie once a week," Eddie told Stubby.

Some of the new buildings were virtually finished; among them, a handsome one-story dining hall for older boys, and, next to it, a long, low house with big glass windows, the new high school.

There were groups of English-style cottages, just like the homes of well-to-do people in West Virginia. Inside, the walls and drapes and rugs were bright, furnishings and leather florid and gay. Comfortable armchairs, where you could sit by a window and read or study. And basement game rooms with sixteen ping-pong tables, every one turned out by boys in the metalwork shop.

Upstairs, a new type of sleeping quarters, four boys only to a room. Each bed projected from a separate corner, pointing toward the center of the cubicle, where a single pillar was provided with four private cabinets for clothes and keepsakes.

Most startling of all was the new Trades School building, covering an area vast as an automobile factory, all steel, concrete, and glass. In these cement acres would soon be housed an auto electric shop, a ceramic department, woodworking, electrical, machine, and print shops, bakery and barbershop.

Past the lake the two boys wandered. Beyond the infirmary and the maintenance buildings they followed a winding road to the farm. Like an agent bent on a sale, Eddie showed off to Stubby the green-and-white barns, the dairy building, cannery, slaughterhouse, and the laboratory where young student farmers pasteurized their own milk.

Last of all they entered the chapel, a hymn of frozen white stone gleaming in morning sun. The light streamed in through the stained glasses of high, thin windows.

"When there's a service here, there's a Protestant service in another chapel. Jewish boys are driven into Omaha for their services Friday and they stay overnight with some family."

At the Welfare Department in the Administration Building, Stubby took some educational tests and finally met Dr. Franz Plewa. The chief psychologist was a small, snowy-haired man who because he had studied and worked with the famous Alfred Adler was cast out of Germany by the Nazis. Father Flanagan brought the exile to Boys Town, and now Dr. Plewa proceeded to find out a great deal about Stubby and about his stepfather too. Not long after the psychological interview, word came that Father Flanagan was ready to talk with Stubby.

VIII

Cumbered with a dizzying burden of insecurity and hope, Stubby entered the study of Father Flanagan: a rather small office with a great desk set at a catercorner angle. Multicolored casement windows gave to the room a slightly sacerdotal air, but other pictures and curios smacked of a boyish interest in the odd and the picturesque and the memorable. Stubby's blanched face looked wildly around, then turned to meet the steady blue eyes of the man behind the desk.

A tall figure he made, looming and erect even when seated. The pink edging of his clerical vest marked him of monsignorial rank, one honorably chosen as a special servant of the Holy Father in Rome. Of that distinction, of course, Stubby knew nothing; but he did know that everybody called this man Father.

And Stubby could see and appreciate the power in the pale and rugged face. There was a granite look to him, as if the great brow and long jaw and straight nose had been carved from rock of great strength. And yet, with that visible and unmistakable masculine force and power, there was an almost womanly luster in the soft blue eyes. When necessary, this man could be father and mother both. With a glance up and down at his miniature visitor, the priest asked a laconic question:

"Stubby, do you like candy?"

"Sure, Father," with a gulp.

Father Flanagan moved breviary and rosary aside, opened a drawer, and pulled out a box of chocolates.

"Try some—dear!"

The word of affection, thrown casually at him, stunned the child. Who ever heard of calling a boy dear? Yet the cadence, the modulation of tone was thrilling and winning; it had a harsh, dry pleasantness, like unsweetened chocolate; in its vibrant resonance sounded the grown-up echo of a boy who had also once been twelve years old. Stubby's mouth was stuffed with an oversized Fanny Farmer cream as Father Flanagan, having glanced briefly through a little stack of reports, fixed the candidate with eye and finger.

"Stubby," he began, "we've got more than four hundred boys in this town. And did you see all the new buildings going up? Soon we'll have room for maybe four hundred more. But do you want to know something else? There's thousands and thousands who want to come here—and deserve to come, too. But we've no room for them. So you see why we have to pick and choose?"

"Sure, Father!"

"You do understand now, don't you? We have to take the boys that need us most? The ones we can help the most?"

"I guess so, Father!"

"Stubby, don't look so hopeless. I'm reminded that St. Paul told fathers not to irritate their children, or they may lose heart. I didn't want to irritate you or cause you to lose heart, but I did want to see how you could stand up to things. Have another coconut cream. Maybe I will too."

Boy-and-man talk, now. About the toughness of life and the need to have stoutness of heart, to do the will of the good Father in heaven and how a man comes to enjoy it, because habit makes it pleasant. And boys like himself were very important. When Jesus was on the earth he had called little children to Him, for of such was the Kingdom of Heaven. Wouldn't it have been a great thing to be alive in those days?

It was as if Father Flanagan were becoming younger and Stubby growing up in this twilight get-together. Stubby must help and encourage less fortunate lads than himself as time went on. Were there boys worse off than he? Much worse! Boys from jails and prison farms, with the police stigma, the mark of infamy, the token of disgrace upon them, their names down in the book. Father Flanagan could weep easily over matters like that.

And then, suddenly, the relief of nervous strain was too much for Stubby. At a most inappropriate time he began to grin and then to titter, his voice getting ever shriller and sobs not far off.

"What's so funny?" demanded Father Flanagan, but Stubby could only shake his head and squeak that he didn't dare tell.

"Wouldn't it be impolite for you not to tell?" Father Flanagan asked in a lenient tone.

So Stubby, now weeping for shame, confessed how, suddenly, in the ease and release and promise of this conversation, he had got to thinking of old Harry of the boxcar and his brown derby hat and how Father Somebody had upped with the back of his hand and knocked down the bottle.

Father Flanagan's bracing, invigorating yelp of laughter shivered the ceiling. He didn't remember Harry, but he did enjoy the joke; their laughter together sealed their friendship.

"You're in, Stubby! Here to stay, to love and be loved. You've got a home again. And a father!"

Hand on Stubby's shoulder, benison in his eyes, the priest turned the boy around so that he could see, across the desk, the blue porcelain figure of a woman, hands folded together at her breast in an attitude of prayer.

"That was made right here in our ceramics department, by some of our boys," confided Father Flanagan. "Mary—you know, the mother of Jesus. And always ready to mother anybody. Good night, Stubby—dear!"

IX

Yes, Stubby's would have been the most exciting way to see Boys Town and to meet Edward Joseph Flanagan. But we who are recording his memories can never forget our own stay in his incorporated village of youth, nor our hours in Father's company. By firelight, and with voices of a rehearsing choir rising and falling in the distance, we listened and asked questions. The more he talked, the more poignant seemed the firmness of his purpose, his gentleness, and goodness of heart. But we also saw at first hand the depth of his indignation against outrages which he saw society inflict on its young: the selfishness of men, their indifference, their ignorance, their worship of some profit-bestowing and immeasurable Moloch demanding human sacrifice in the form of small boys.

When Father prayed, as he did all day long, it was for those victims. In the penetralia, the sanctuary of his heart, they were the chief treasures. No work was of greater importance than doing for them.

"Remember," he said to us, "the words of Jesus to his disciples?" and he quoted from St. Matthew:

" 'For I was hungry, and you gave me to eat; I was thirsty, and you gave me to drink: I was a stranger, and you took me in:

" 'Naked, and you covered me: sick, and you visited me: I was in prison, and you came to me.

" 'Then shall the just answer him, saying: Lord, when did we see thee hungry, and fed thee; thirsty, and gave thee drink? . . .

" 'And the King answering, shall say to them: Amen I say to you, as long as you did it to one of these, my least brethren, you did it to me.' "

His father in Ireland had first taught him those great words. And in the deep February night he looked back and remembered Ireland and his father and mother and the eleven brothers and sisters and his own boyhood and his dreams.

CHAPTER TWO

A Shepherd Boy with Bleeding Hands

Affection and duty ruled the Flanagan home, nourished the whole family like food and drink, and he was to miss them bitterly when he had to go away. Any boy who had not known such familiar love and guidance was the immediate friend of Father Flanagan—as was every weakling and every little dreamer and every lonely youngster, for he had been all of these.

Of a large and rugged Flanagan family, Eddie was the least robust; a fragile prospect for manhood when he was born on Tuesday, July 13, 1886. That was in the year of the anarchist Haymarket riots in Chicago, and only a few months before the unveiling, to a million spectators, of the Statue of Liberty holding up the light for newcomers to America. It looked doubtful then whether the baby, baptized Edward Joseph, would ever grow up to see that torch of freedom.

When he was only a few weeks old Eddie had a convulsion; his tiny body turned purple and blue, and his sister Nellie, later one of the hardest workers at Boys Town, told us how in her firm opinion prayer miraculously saved the new little brother.

From that moment on it seemed as if he were set apart. While his childhood was wholly without remarkable incident, yet it was full of spiritual adventure; he was one to sit in silence and look far away. From that infant recovery, Eddie, they knew, was different.

He whose adult life crackled with action remembered himself as a thoughtful child, pensive and with that inexplicable touch of sadness; a sobersides, happiest when alone beside a sheet of still water, calm and unruffled, reflecting the clouds. He loved the open world with a dreamlike seeking for the broadness of nature and the seclusion of protracted silence long before he could put such thoughts into words. Most often he looked back on an Ireland out-of-doors; fog over the green fields and hills where he tended the heavy-fleeced Shropshire sheep, forty feeding as one.

Because he was small and thin, the boy from four years on was kept by his father's side in the fields of the rolling farm called Leabeg, of which the elder Flanagan was manager for an absentee landlord. Here they all lived together, father, mother, children, and grandfather in a great white-walled house.

Near by, across the shaded river Suck, was the town of Ballymoe where they went to church. A few miles off, in Drimatample, was the school—one of the "national schools" set up in this part of Ireland by the English. Ten miles distant was the village of Roscommon, where they would drive in the cart for supplies. Still farther was Castlereagh, a larger town where the girls in the family would be taken sometimes to shop, in the trap or the sidecar.

Even after he started school at Drimatample, Eddie continued to spend his free time in the fields, doing chores with his father. They called Eddie the bookworm of the family, because as he minded the animals he would always have with him some novel of Scott or Dickens or possibly some work of Macaulay.

Did he never get into scrapes like other boys? Now here is the curious answer to that question: the priest who could understand the waywardness of child thieves, gunmen, and murderers, boys who slew father with shotgun and stabbed mother to the heart, was in his own first years guilty of three offenses:

(A) Climbed an apple tree in the orchard of Sir Nicholas O'Connor, former ambassador to Turkey. Caught by caretaker before he got one apple. Case reported seriatim to brother (Patrick), father (John), and finally to Nora Flanagan, who was his mother, and "very like to Martha in the Bible."

(B) Smoked an old clay pipe behind the barn. Crime never discovered but fully punished by three hours of abdominal heebie-jeebies.

(C) Fought a bully and licked him. This was an undeniable case of self-defense; his only fight.

That was all the mischief he ever got into—the man who understood more about juvenile mischief than anyone else of his time!

II

From earliest years he learned about farm animals from his father. A deeply religious man, John Flanagan would often quote from the Bible: "Feed my lambs! Feed my sheep!" from St. John, or: "The good shepherd giveth his life for his sheep."

And John Flanagan would admonish him: "The animals know you are their friend. They all trust you. You can never betray them!"

But one afternoon little Eddie grew angry. All day his father had been laboring over sick cattle, some afflicted with distemper or the more dreaded maggots. It was part of the child's job to fend back grazing herds from bogs toward which they blundered easily, browsing among the flowering heather and getting themselves trapped in the quagmire. Now, suddenly, as if moved by one will, the cows started pell-mell for the swamp.

"Bad cows!" screamed Eddie. "Wicked, bad cows."

But his father shooed them all back. He laughed at his young son's moral indignation:

"Eddie, there is no such thing as a bad cow. They only don't know any better!"

III

He also had to learn to keep the sheep out of the briers.

Boundaries of those Irish fields were marked off by trenches, and around the ditches grew the briers. Sometimes a heavy-coated, fat-tailed sheep would wander toward the thorns and, before you could head him off, would be enmeshed. One day, when Eddie was no more than six, he was alone with his father's sheep as the stillness was shattered by the mad bleating of a snared young ram. Eddie began slowly and tenderly to work it free, knowing he had not only to rescue the animal from the briers but also to save the wool. Soon his hands were bleeding as he yanked out the briers one by one. At last he had the bloodstained sheep clear of the entanglement, and hoisting it up, heaving it on the back of his little shoulders, he staggered off to display his trophy.

But when Eddie came to a little clearing in the midst of the south woods, he found John Flanagan on his knees, rosary in hand. The father had been an unseen witness and was offering decades of thanks that his little son had already learned to be a shepherd.

IV

He remembered the mist in the dooryard, before nightfall came to Leabeg House, and himself in the inglenook, under great-grandfather's blackthorn shillalah which was suspended above as an ornament, a souvenir of other days. A great teakettle swung on the hob and simmered over the fire, the water boiling gently with a singing sound. Hot tea was always ready in that kitchen.

From nails spiked into the plaster wall, next to a florid calendar of the insurance company, hung in orderly array coats and caps and outdoor gear of fourteen in family here, counting Grandpa—four boys and seven girls.

From the middle of the ceiling depended a family treasure, the large oil lamp of crinkled blue glass, its spotless chimney held in the clutch of four brass prongs. Holy pictures were tacked to the oak paneling above the fireplace, and the mantelpiece was crowded with photographs of immigrant uncle and cousins in the misty, distant fairy-tale city of New York, the "cabinet portraits" standing against a painted fan from the county fair.

The boarded floor was warm, the room homelike, and there was always an extra hunk or cooky in the breadbox. Eddie soon realized that the Flanagans were more fortunate than many of their friends; not every boy he knew had a kitchen like theirs, or such a house. Most were floored in flat stones from the field; they had only a turf grate, never burning wood or coal, and often there were two beds or more against the wall; by local standards, the Flanagans were well-to-do.

The flames played over the open pages of the boy's book while Nora, his mother, kneading dough or fussing over supper, would hum a derry-down, some sweet old meaningless refrain, or a lully-lullay for the youngest baby while his father talked with a neighbor about rumors of the Sinn Fein underground in Roscommon.

Dinner was in the candlelit dining room, around a huge oak table always heaped high with enough, and plenty to share. Nellie Flanagan remembers how her mother taught the girls cooking, knitting, spinning, and quilt making. And how Grandfather Patrick Flanagan, a veterinary, would care for sick livestock of other farms as well as the Leabeg beasts. He could cure the neighbors' nags of glanders, "but the poor owners rarely paid him for his cures," Nellie recalls.

Father Flanagan liked to think of his boyhood home as a matrix, a pattern for Boys Town, with each member of a large family playing a useful part to keep things going; a self-sufficient unit. Like Boys Town, too, there was always music and singing: in their house was a piano, an accordion, a violin, and a flute. Often, just before prayers, they would have an evening concert and the girls would play. Young Eddie Flanagan had a rich and sympathetic baritone, which he raised with gusto, a voice that in later years was to ring out in pleading before many a judge.

Sometimes in a glow from the ceiling lamp, again in the fluttering light of hearth fire and swealing candles, while the tallow melted and ran, but every night of Eddie's boyhood the Flanagans prayed, aloud and together, lifting their voices in the sixty-five prayers of the joyous, the sorrowful, or the glorious decades of the rosary; the Apostles' Creed, the Our Fathers, the Hail Marys, and the Glorias.

Another who helped us in piecing together fragments of boyhood was Father Flanagan's older brother, Monsignor Patrick A. Flanagan, of Holy Angels Church, Omaha, whom many affectionately call "Father P. A."

Father P. A. coached Eddie in spare time for many years and remembers his apt quickness of mind as well as his habit of falling into long spells of contemplation. Through his older brother's coaching, Eddie later was able to skip three grades. And when Patrick set off to prepare for the priesthood in a Dublin seminary, Eddie turned to a new tutor, the pastor of Ballymoe, with whom he began the study of French, Latin, and Greek, all on the same day.

Almost too alert and too restrained for his own health was this lengthening, paling Eddie Flanagan who had been snatched from baby-death by a prayer and had spent most of his time dreaming and studying ever since.

"He's sure marked to be something special," his aunts would say.

"Yes—but what?" asked his cousins.

Eddie paid such speculation no heed at all. He was astounded when a family council was called to discuss his future. In his mind it had all been decided, finally, one long-ago morning when he was a very little boy. His mother had taken him with her to Mass at the church in Ballymoe. Afterward she lingered to speak a moment with Father Featherstone. The old cleric, who always had difficulty in recalling the names of the Flanagans, asked: "And which one of your brood is this thoughtful lad?"

"He's Eddie," Nora Flanagan replied.

The priest placed his hands on the child's overplentiful light hair.

"Someday," he predicted, "Eddie will be a priest."

The little boy and his graying mother had looked at each other with a solemn expression, but they did not exchange one word on the subject. Nor did either mention the prophecy as they left the church and started back across the bridge to Leabeg House. Since then they had never spoken of it, but neither forgot as the years flowed on with their changes.

Those years had left their marks on the big family in Leabeg House. Grandfather Flanagan had died. Eddie's older sister, Nellie, had gone to America and was living with cousins in New York City. Two other sisters, Mary Jane and Kate, were married.

Now Pat was home for tonight from Dublin and there was a family council in the front parlor. From the outset Eddie spoke his mind; his future, he averred, was already settled upon: he was to be a priest. As it turned out, no one opposed the idea. All agreed with Nora Flanagan:

"It was meant to be. He's that kind of boy. Father Featherstone knew the will of God. Eddie was born to be a priest."

That night it was decided that Eddie was to leave home to begin his formal academic studies at Summer Hill College, where his brother Patrick had studied before him, in the bleak old town of the northwestern coast called Sligo.

There he would begin his long preparation for the most austere calling among men. For all his talents, Eddie Flanagan possessed no inner eye for reading the future; leader and pathfinder he might be, but never prophet. For not the slightest suspicion did he have that night of the traps that lay before him and the bitterness of frustration. Few men, before him or since, have had such a long, hard series of seemingly impossible obstacles between aspiration and ordination.

CHAPTER THREE

Lock Step

It was in college years that Eddie Flanagan first came to understand the kinship of poverty and evil, and how desperate a criminal the boy with a hollow stomach and desolate heart could be. The young freshman did not realize it, but he was to get most important education for his future work, not so much in Summer Hill College itself as in the slums of Sligo.

Now Sligo today is a strange sort of town, and it was even stranger on that far-off afternoon in the year of the turn of the century. Playground for rod and gun, a sportsman's holiday rendezvous, it was also a region of legend and history, bleakness, poverty, crime, of fog and rain. The timid and awkward fourteen-year-old Eddie Flanagan, in blue reefer jacket, long tweed pants, and oblong gray hat, trudged out of the railroad station, valise in hand, and looked around him with wonder.

Thomas Street and its rickety bridge were swathed with fog from off the nearby Atlantic that September afternoon; the white veil felt like a cold hand against the new boy's chapfallen face. He shrank from the noisiness of the crooked cobblestone streets, rumbling wagons and hacks and jarveys, the whistles of long-skirted policemen called "peelers," and the cries of hucksters with their two-wheeled donkey carts laden with "Cockles and mussels, alive, alive, O!"

Father Flanagan in after years would sometimes sigh for Sligo. Beauty was there, in lakes and mountains. Although no one knew then, it was already the home of a great poet; here Yeats lived most of his youth and drank in the folklore, the old wives' tales, which lent such a mystical quality to his later work and brought about the

Celtic revival of Irish literature. Later Eddie Flanagan would often go to Lough Gill and stand on the shore, gazing out to Lake Isle, about which Yeats wrote: "I will arise and go now, and go to Innisfree. . . ."

History, too, was here to greet him, and the majestic ruins of the abandoned abbey whose moss-covered square stone tower dates back to 1253. The schoolmaster of Ballymoe had coached Eddie about Sligo; he knew that in centuries past, pirates had raided the seacoast settlement many times and carried off the menfolk as slaves. Often the town had been sacked and burned. Battles had been fought here in the long history of Ireland's struggle for freedom. The earth was thick with old blood and demoniac folklore and religious shrines; a Celtic city not only of God-fearing seafarers and fishermen but also many a superstitious soul, as it remains to this day.

But all of it, to the diffident lad from Leabeg House, where there were inexhaustible cheeriness, love and humor and music, had a haunted, desolate air. There were fine buildings and fine streets, but also dreary lines of hovels and urchins fighting in the rain; ragged lads and underfed. To a boy who had known only the rolling freedom and clean air of a great Irish farm these purlieus were shocking. His first impression was that Sligo was the great world and that there was much more wickedness in such a place than there could ever possibly be back home.

The buildings of Summer Hill College seemed grim and forbidding as he plodded up the hill. Tears of loneliness gathered in his eyes as he knocked at the front door of the red-bricked main building. An old porter fetched an assistant principal.

"You are a new boy," this master began. "I am sure you will get along all right. But take my advice and learn the rules at once. You will not escape punishment for any offense merely because you do not know the rules."

The new boy's mind flashed back to that green glen at home where he had spent so many peaceful hours reading the tales of Dickens. What he remembered now, as he beheld his dour adviser and welcomer, was Mr. Squeers: that emphatic, boy-driving Mr. Squeers in *Nicholas Nickleby* who exclaimed:

"Damn that boy! . . . He's always up to something."

To which his wife replied:

"I say it's obstinacy. I'd beat it out of him."

II

It was not that Summer Hill was a bad school, or that its governors were cruel. By the standards of the time, it was far better than average, the teachers good and wise custodians of youth. But solicitous love for sensitive children away from home was not a part of their goodness or wisdom.

It was the memory of his homesick loneliness, the deprivation of mother's and father's tenderness that remained more vividly in his memory of Summer Hill than all the formal lessons he was taught. That lonely time was always in his mind when he would counsel the helpers and teachers of youth to remember: "The simple fact is that nothing earthly can fill the void in the human heart."

In those days, of course, there was no Boys Town or anything comparable anywhere in the world. Management of children, even those whose way was paid by loving, sacrificing parents, was still a stern affair. The attitude generally was that boys were a constant prey to the instigation of the devil. All you could do with headstrong lads, stubbornly bent on having their own way, was to put them under such discipline that their evil tendencies would be extirpated. And better start the discipline before the tendencies appeared. If a boy persisted in disobedience, then, of course, he had to be "put away."

Institutions to which such children were sent, reformatories and occasionally orphanages as well, were centers of stupidity and brutality, even bestiality, run by misfits, political hangers-on, and often enough sadists. Whip them! Birch them! Strike them with a lash!

One night in Boys Town a visitor referred to such practices as if they were ancient history. But Father Flanagan exclaimed in a voice neither of us will ever forget:

"God help the boy in the United States today who gets himself a court record—he's doomed to be mistreated and he's tagged for life!"

Passionately he insisted there had been little improvement down through the years. Tragic conditions could be found today, in hundreds of so-called reformatories of many American states. Brutal punishments persisted, sordid conditions abounded, and it was still axiomatic that sending a youth to reform school was the surest way to make him a confirmed criminal.

And he quoted to us a statement once made by a former boy bandit, Ralph Fults, the only member of the Clyde Barrow-Bonnie Parker robber gang to survive:

"When I was fifteen years old, I was sentenced to reform school. They paid the help poor wages there and would hire anybody. Corporal punishment was permitted and those guards were brutal. I received worse punishment in 1925 at the reform school than I ever received in any penitentiary."

This outlaw eventually became an evangelist, and the rest of his life was lived in his church. He confirms, as do a thousand other witnesses, the attitude of Father Flanagan on reform schools:

"No race that does not take proper care of its young can survive —or deserves to survive."

In some states, of course, there have been great advances. But in those days when Eddie studied in Sligo not even a start had been made. Everywhere man clung to the shocking folly of "corporal punishment," as it was called, and to mental and spiritual tyranny. Even in Summer Hill College.

Life at Summer Hill was an undeniable shock to him; his introduction to a lock-step existence in which every deviation, even when unintentional, meant reprisal. Because he was so earnest and studious, he kept clear of trouble; his grades were excellent. But he was getting his first taste of soulless institutional life.

There was the night when he found a classmate, a boy called Mac, packing up. Mac had sneaked out behind a building and had a puff on a cinnamon cigarette. They were sending him home in disgrace. Eddie remembered his experience with the old clay pipes. Had John Flanagan known about that escapade it would have meant a spanking for Eddie, but it would have been no major crime. To be sent home from school, like Mac, was an earthquake in a boy's life.

Other boys were sent home, the black mark of expulsion against their record, for even lesser offenses; so strict were the rules that the boys lived in constant terror of making a mistake. Young as he was, the thoughtful Eddie felt sure it was wrong for boys to live in fear.

The thoughts of that lonely time, the heartache of days without affection, the alley sights of hungry boys swiping garbage from back yards of prosperous Sligo houses, were to haunt him. He knew what hungry children looked like and how they acted. Remembering them all the rest of his days, he was not to be frustrated by the sometimes tarnished majesty of the law. It was such a Sligo memory that, years afterward, animated him in the case of two American children, Donald and George.

III

George was seven and Donald was nine. The parents of the two boys had lived in bickering and quarrels, and at last—shortly after the birth of a third child—the father had deserted. For a while the mother tried to carry on, but how can you hold down a job and care for children as well? After a while she gave up trying and took to drink. Often there was no food in the house, as on one evening when the boys, wandering down an alley, caught a sudden whiff in the air —apples and onions and freshly baked bread. They had arrived at the rear of a grocery store, back door left partly open. Hungry Donald and famished George grabbed boxes of crackers, tore them open, and, standing in the middle of the shop, began to stuff themselves—until a night watchman collared them.

At the police station they were booked on the charge of "breaking and entering." A few days later Donald and George, aged nine and seven years, were tried and convicted in an American courtroom and sentenced to an indeterminate stay in juvenile prison.

For months they were in a jailhouse before word of their plight reached Father Flanagan in Omaha. Once again he wept over the civic madness of putting children of tender years in a criminal institution, to be in daily contact with older youths hardened in crime.

Father Flanagan wrote to the governor of that Southern state urging that the children be removed from unwholesome environment. The governor replied courteously that his hands were tied. The "accused had been found guilty of a serious crime." It was against the laws of the state to allow them to mingle with, and possibly corrupt, decent children.

But Father Flanagan refused to be balked; righteous wrath echoed in his second letter to the governor entreating him to reconsider:

". . . These lads are now in a place where criminals are kept. According to the facts set forth by yourself, these boys cannot be sent to the Orphan's Home because of some technicality in the law. Don't you think that in the interests of humanity, and for the sake of giving these mere children a better chance, some way can be found to overcome this technicality?

"These little children are not criminals at heart, neither are they, I feel, inclined to criminality. Environment will have a great deal to do with the future success or failure of these children. They are now conscious of the fact that they are being held in an institution for criminals. That fact is becoming impressed more deeply upon their minds each day. I say punish the criminal every time, and with his just punishment a lesson will be taught to those criminally inclined. But for the sake of all that is sacred and noble in our citizenship, save the child and give him an opportunity to make good."

One further suggestion! If the laws of the state were so exacting, would the governor consider sending the two culprits to Father Flanagan's Home for Boys, on the priest's guarantee to turn them into fine, outstanding citizens?

The governor, in reply, thanked him for the offer. But nothing could be done. So the boys were still kept in the jailhouse, slave cages where depravity was a commonplace.

Abhorring the very thought of surrender, Father Flanagan next wrote to every official who had anything to do with the case, to anyone and everyone in the state who might conceivably have an interest in human salvage. Before he was through, the newspapers had got wind of the story and were printing it in headlines.

Even so, there were long, wearying months of delay and excuses, but at last the combined efforts of Father Flanagan, the press, and

aroused public opinion had effect. The State was forced to act in
the matter of these two desperadoes, aged seven and nine. They
were taken out of the juvenile prison and sent to an orphanage.

IV

The deep sympathy that brought about that victory was born in
Flanagan in those days of Summer Hill College in Sligo, when indignation at the mistakes and follies of those entrusted with children
was fomenting within him even while he was burning midnight oil
over Latin and Greek.

His marks at Summer Hill placed him at the top rung of his class.
For sports, in his freshman year, he started out for track, but sprained
an ankle which had always been weak, since he had twisted it years
before in the fields back of Leabeg. So he returned to his one favorite sport—handball.

What few hours of spare time he had were spent on the handball courts, or reading, or walking around Sligo. In search of solitude
he would sometimes go down to Rosses Point, where the deep-sea
fishing smacks tied up and captains smoked their long pipes and
reviled the English. On Quay Street was the City Hall, a bare, grim
bit of gingerbread architecture where he occasionally went for a
concert in the auditorium. Here one night he heard the first public
concert given by an upperclassman at Summer Hill College—a
young singer named John McCormack. Years later, in Chicago,
Father Flanagan met McCormack after the great tenor's last concert in America. At Sligo one was a senior and the other a freshman,
but while under the same roof they did not meet.

One friend he made in Sligo was a certain P. G. MacDermott,
an auctioneer, who had a side line as steamship-ticket agent. Flanagan would put on his best store suit, purchased in Sligo at Lyons,
famous for Donegal tweeds and Irish homespuns, and walk into
town for a chat with MacDermott about the latest voyagers to
America and the success others had found overseas.

"Now there was Timmy Rourke," MacDermott would say. "I
sent him across with hardly sixpence in his pocket. And what now?

He owns a barroom of his own, thank you. And quite a figure in politics there he is, in a small way, and he'll be somebody, too, before he's finished."

The ticket agent loved to tell such stories, taking vast credit to himself for the prosperity of his customers.

"It's the greatest land on earth, America is," MacDermott would tell him. "Outside of Ireland, of course."

Eddie was getting letters, too, from his sister Nellie in New York, breathlessly full of marvels. His talks with MacDermott and the letters from his sister began to light new fires in his mind.

Summer vacations he spent home in the fields, tending sheep with Dad, whose beard was graying now. This was the sum of Eddie's life for four hard-studying, rather uncomfortable years.

v

He was eighteen when he was graduated with high honors from Summer Hill. In his college years he had grown quickly; he was more than six feet tall now, a rawboned, light-haired boy with far-seeing intense blue eyes.

Earlier in the year his brother Patrick had been graduated from the Dublin seminary and ordained as a priest. As his first assignment he had received a far-distant call to help build up a new parish in the cornfields of a community called Omaha, state of Nebraska, U.S.A.

It had been expected that Eddie, too, would go on to Dublin and complete his preparation for the priesthood at the same seminary. But the plans were suddenly and radically changed, largely because Nellie Flanagan came back from New York for a visit to Leabeg.

A shining, self-assured young woman, this older sister now. Excitement danced in her eyes as she told John and Nora Flanagan, and the others gathered around the dining-room table, of the wonders of New York. Nellie was agitated with ideas. Why go to the seminary in Dublin? Why not let Eddie come to America with her now and finish his studies there?

John Flanagan and his wife talked many a night about that. The children now were all almost grown up, the family gradually breaking apart. It was hard to think of young Eddie also going off. And yet the advantages were unquestioned. It was the thing to do. John Flanagan spoke the family decision.

There was nothing extraordinary, in that year of 1904, for an Irish boy to decide to try his luck in America. But to Eddie Flanagan it had unusual meaning, for already he had a glimmering of purpose. Nellie had not spoken only of the glittering and grandeur of the new land. Even more eloquently she had told of the unspeakable slums of the greatest city of the New World; the children with the run of the streets, like outlaws. Misery, hunger, crime, very visible. Young sheep in the briers.

CHAPTER FOUR

Pearls and Rubies

It was a dazzling, intimidating new world he was exploring; avenues of grandeur, just as Nellie had reported, and byways of hunger and vice from Mulberry Bend and the wretched old Bowery to the tenements of Rivington Street.

When Eddie Flanagan joined his sister in New York there was still a red Indian with green tomahawk on a pedestal outside of every cigar shop. Behind the milky glass of stationers' windows lay rows of five-cent Tousey and Street and Smith novels for boys— *Jessie James, Secret Service,* with Old King Brady and Young King Brady (who was not his son); *Young Wild West, Buffalo Bill,* and *Nick Carter,* and, for girls, the sloppy love tales of Laura Jean Libby and Bertha M. Clay. Some people said such trash was the ruination of the young, but Flanagan, explorer in New York streets, already suspected there might be other reasons.

The hurdy-gurdies were playing "In the Shade of the Old Apple Tree" and "Meet me in St. Louis, Louis," for this was the summer of the brilliant Louisiana Purchase Exposition in St. Louis; time of long skirts for women, broad-brimmed straw hats with yellow-and-purple bands for the men; excursion boats to Coney Island; and also a time of war.

The boys were playing "Japs and Russians"; big boys called themselves Admiral Togo and General Kuroki while they chased other boys—the undersized, the unliked, and the backward—shouting *"Nippon!"* and *"Banzai!"* The tall, skinny Irish youth, only recently arrived on the S.S. *Celtic,* stood among the pushcarts and watched in dismay. He had seen hoodlums in Sligo and even in Roscommon, but never so many as here, never so fierce, so unregarded.

No one seemed to mind that a miniature battle was turning bloody with sticks and stones.

"Give it to 'em, Joey! His old man's a Russiansky——"

The fight had spumed up out of nothing at all. One boy spat an oath at another and, after blasphemous repartee, like so many squirming imps, rival gangs on the street were at each other's necks, grappling on the sidewalk, rolling over and over into the gutter. Other boys came rushing in from distant blocks, raising obscene cries of Gophers and Hudson Dusters and Gas Houses. From behind a pushcart one dirt-smeared face peered out, cursing with such foulness as to crunch the ears of piety. Rocks, bricks, and pieces of lead pipe began to fly. A boy fell, bleeding from the head. Women craning out of tenement windows screamed advice above the yelps of homeless dogs:

"Cheese it! The cops!"

By the time the police arrived in their horse-drawn Black Maria, all the combatants had disappeared. Thoughtfully, Flanagan started back uptown to the house not far from Gramercy Park where he was boarding for a time with Sister Nellie and some cousins.

"I looked at the street boys with a sadness," he was to recall. "Like all children, even poorly fed ones, they had too much energy. And what outlet had these poor boys for that energy? No place to play but that crowded, filthy street. Nothing to do but to get into deviltry —no proper direction. Is it any wonder they turn to wrong? And don't make the mistake of thinking things are much better today. Improvement, yes—but not nearly enough."

Not then, or ever, could he blame children. The fault lay with parents who denied them love, with society which exhibited no concern, and with an environment which offered temptation and evil example simultaneously. It was a heathen setup. The remedy must be democracy, the great experiment implementing Christianity in political terms; the social structure resting firmly upon the foundation of the worth of each individual soul. And he was well aware even then, as a gawping youth, that many among the influential and the powerful disagreed with his simple remedy.

For days he walked the streets. He saw his first Jew, an immigrant like himself; his first Chinese and his first Negro.

II

His mother's brothers, the Larkins, were well established in New York and they were able to bring him directly to one of the eminent prelates of the Church—to "little Archbishop Farley," as he was called. Flanagan remembered the good-humored friendliness of his reception—and the cold water dashed on the furnace of his hopes. The archbishop, in the front room of the residence behind St. Patrick's Cathedral, listened attentively to the young man's appeal.

"So! You are anxious to study for the priesthood, be ordained as soon as possible, and then promptly make over the world? Well, it needs making over. How old are you, Edward?"

"Eighteen, Your Excellency."

"Do you have a degree?"

"No, Your Excellency!"

Archbishop John Farley was shaking his head dolefully.

"Very young," he murmured, "to study at Dunwoodie. But perhaps not too young to start preparation for it."

The archbishop had in mind a college called Mount St. Mary's, in Emmitsburg, Maryland: "A fine school. Go there first, my son. Get your bachelor degree. By that time—you may be ready for Dunwoodie."

From the archiepiscopal verdict there was, of course, no appeal. One of Eddie's uncles, Michael Larkin, a contractor, offered to pay the expenses at St. Mary's. So once again the lad from Roscommon packed up and boarded a train for school; three more years of it!

III

Of those student days in Emmitsburg we find little in the records. Occasionally Flanagan and his friends were free to visit nearby Baltimore, still a stricken town after the past year's disastrous fire that had burned over one hundred and forty acres of business streets, with a loss of one hundred and twenty-four millions of dollars.

Again, they went to Washington, where Theodore Roosevelt was still swinging his big stick.

But such excursions were rare. The discipline of study was confining, yet different in spirit from the bleakness of Summer Hill. In Ireland it had been a severe, utilitarian life. Here at St. Mary's he found a warmer and more aspiring world. Many wealthy youths came to Emmitsburg, including youths from Mexico.

With the same implacable energy that had baffled tyrants back in Sligo, Flanagan threw himself anew into his studies; his heart was already in his future at Dunwoodie. Such industry and single-mindedness appalled and depressed his fun-loving friends. They told him he was not playing the game. Indeed, it is one of the traditions at St. Mary's that every student must at some time in his career violate the rules and so qualify as a "mountaineer." This term came from the nature of the punishment: erring students had to climb the hillsides while memorizing a specified number of lines of poetry. It seemed clear that Eddie Flanagan might never achieve that historic distinction, so one night a delegation trooped into his room. He had been in Emmitsburg almost two years; when did he intend to qualify as a mountaineer?

"Nobody else has ever gone two years without doing something wrong," they protested. "Can't you please commit some small offense?"

To his shamed regret in later years, he never did find the time to become an Emmitsburg mountaineer. Not that his classmates thought of him as a prig; they knew he was a very serious fellow. But in after years, when he talked of his failure, we caught a note of nostalgic apology in his voice.

"Perhaps," he said, "I should have misbehaved a little!"

The bachelor-of-arts degree which the archbishop had required of him was conferred on Edward Joseph Flanagan in June 1906, when he had just turned twenty years of age. He was the youngest graduate in his class.

And then, while New York was seething with the murder of a millionaire on the roof of Madison Square Garden, Eddie came back to his sister's flat on East Twentieth Street. He paid little attention to the scandals and troubles going on in the world, except for such news as the earthquake and fire in San Francisco.

His mind was centered on the one thought: to become a priest, just as quickly as possible. At once he matriculated at St. Joseph's Seminary in Dunwoodie, confident that now he stood on the threshold of the last big hurdle before reaching his goal.

A Dunwoodie classmate who well remembers young Flanagan is the stalwart Monsignor Aloysius Dineen, pastor of the famous Church of the Holy Innocents, near the Metropolitan Opera House and just below Times Square. It was Dineen who followed Father Duffy as chaplain of New York's "Fighting 69th."

"In those days," declares Monsignor Dineen, "Flanagan was still a raw boy, although those years in Emmitsburg had begun to polish down the edges. He was not a longmouthed fellow, but a very thoughtful one. His eyes could look right through you and never even see you when he was busy in his dreams. And I can tell you this—no one in Dunwoodie during the brief time he was there would ever have voted Flanagan the one most likely to succeed. I think the majority view would have been that he would wind up as pastor of some little country parish, where the world would never hear of him. And how wrong the majority view would be—as usual!"

IV

In addition to his studies, Flanagan began working among the most neglected patients of New York hospitals.

In the early years of this century the word "tuberculosis" was just coming into use, replacing the old and frightening doom word, "consumption." Many patients did not know the more scientific term and so they did not regard it as the death sentence it was quite likely to be in those days before pneumothorax and other modern techniques.

Of consumption people stood in stark terror; that was why the free wards of hospitals, where tubercular patients were kept, had only a few daring guests on visitors' days. These wards were aisles of despair, where every wretched patient watched his own spittle: blood or merely phlegm? Pearls or rubies, as they said.

The first assignment given the new seminarian from Dunwoodie was to visit these tubercular wards. Soon after he entered St. Joseph's, back from the Hudson River and a few miles north of New York, a group of classmates volunteered to visit those pestilential places, and Eddie was one of them. But they all were doubtful as to what they should say to the patients and decided that each had better write out a little speech to be memorized.

"My speech," Flanagan told us, "was studied, formal, full of stilted phrases. But I didn't realize that. I very carefully memorized every word."

It was early autumn as he walked into the hospital. An apathetic attendant offered no obstacle to the long double rows of beds. There was constant coughing; faces were almost lifeless. He stopped by a wheezing ghost of a man. Every eye in the ward was on the seminarian, and in the extremity of his embarrassment Flanagan knew that whatever it was they might want from him, if anything at all, it could not possibly be his speech.

"You want to say something?" the sick man asked.

Flanagan made a helpless gesture with his great hands.

"I thought I did. But it's left me. Is there anything you would like to hear?"

From farther down the ward, above the gasping and coughing, one old man called:

"Tell us about outside."

An eager chorus backed up this plea. Hemmed in by white walls, windows on a court, they missed the world of people in health, the world they used to know.

Flanagan began to talk about the city as an immigrant beheld it: the Hudson, which was so different from the languid and yet remarkably glorious Shannon; about the ferryboats with their great crowds; ocean liners, too, and the sailboats. All over town he took them on a mental sight-seeing tour; every now and then someone applauded with hands so pale and thin that he could almost see light between the bones. Flanagan kept on for more than an hour. Next week he visited two wards instead of one, the second for women; from bed to bed he went, talking about the world outside.

Toward the bottom of the row, he heard an old woman's voice, thick with brogue:

"And what county would you be from?" she was asking archly.

Her own birthplace was a town not far from Roscommon. Flanagan had been there several times. But this woman, not having seen it for ten years, plied him with questions. Many of her own folks were still there but she never heard from them any more.

"I am not strong enough to write," she explained. "And if you can't answer 'em, people won't write to you after a while; you know that."

Flanagan produced a pad of paper and a pencil.

"Tell me what you want to say!"

An epistle to Paul, her brother. "I know it has been a long time, but I'm here in the hospital . . ."

Everybody in the ward was listening; they began screaming for his help for them too; before he knew it, Flanagan was public scrivener of the pearls-and-rubies ward. The problem of postage was soon acute; the sick people were penniless and so was their scribbling visitor. But Nellie Flanagan shared in her brother's work; she found the stamps. Years afterward, recalling these days as public letter writer, Father Flanagan said:

"If I had not become interested in anything else, there was work enough for me to have done all the rest of my life, just in visiting condemned, terminal cases in hospitals for the poor. Anyone who wants to go to work for God can start there, writing letters for the desperate and the helpless. And others can write letters *to* them. There is no more heart-rending hour than mail time in some of our hospitals. They lie there, helpless for the rest of their lives—and never get a letter. This world is full of careers for people who are willing to help. Every hospital, every asylum, every orphan home is a want ad for a position with the Lord, doing His work. And the pay lies in helping to bring to someone a little moment brighter than the rest."

Such were his thoughts, after having labored among the victims of tuberculosis. And then, with hideous suddenness, he found himself battling to save his own lungs.

V

His family, broken up for a while as the children grew up, was beginning to come together again, at least partly, in America. John and Nora Flanagan had been unable to stand the loneliness of Leabeg after their brood had flown away, so they sold all their holdings and possessions and followed across the Atlantic.

Now the parents were living in New York with Nellie, and there was worry among them about Eddie. Everyone in the Flanagan family knew that from infancy he had been a prey to weakening, devastating colds. No wonder that Nora Flanagan began to be anxious when she learned about Eddie visiting the tubercular wards, especially since she was sure he was working too hard. His studies at Dunwoodie were demanding enough; the extra mission in the hospital wards, she felt certain, would be too much for him. But Eddie tried to kiss and hug away her fears. He had convinced her, too—until Christmas Day in 1908. In that year of great financial panic the winter was hard and bitter.

On Christmas morning the students of St. Joseph's were taken from Dunwoodie into the city to attend Solemn High Mass at St. Patrick's Cathedral. It was a day of snow and sleet, yet the cathedral was thronged, as always on tremendous occasions. Because of the crowds, the students had to stand, jammed together in one corner, and Flanagan found himself backed up against an old-fashioned steam radiator, the hot pipes against his spine.

After the long service Flanagan, overheated from his siege with the radiator, stepped forth into a blizzard. Fighting the wind, wading through deep snow, he walked downtown to the house on East Twentieth Street. Over Nora's roast turkey he began to cough; his face felt flushed all the cold ride back to Dunwoodie, and in the morning chills coursed through his body and he was too weak to get out of bed.

Roommates bundled him up in overcoats and carried him to the college infirmary, where doctors were so alarmed that later that day John and Nora Flanagan were called. The chief physician told them their son had double pneumonia and a stiff fight ahead of

O'Neill, Nebraska, 1912. Father Flanagan's first parish: The priest with parishioners.

Refuge: This was the first hotel where the young priest gave shelter to the homeless harvesters.

The second hotel: Business was growing. Here they housed over a thousand a night.

Birthplace of Boys Town: The first home, at Twenty-fifth and Dodge streets, Omaha.

The first five boys.

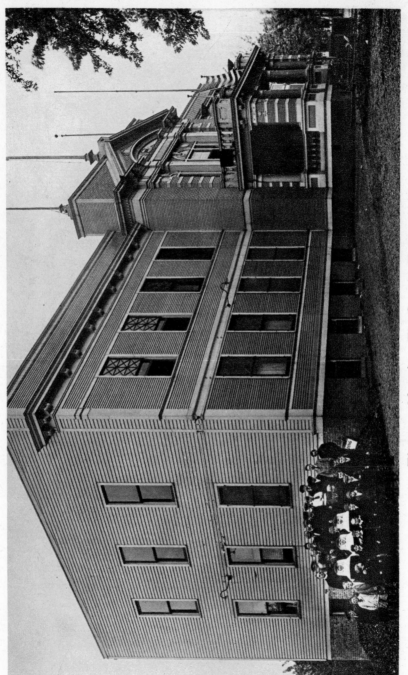

The second location: The German Home.

him. No penicillin! No sulfa drugs! The doctors said Flanagan had, maybe, a fifty-fifty chance. No more! A long convalescence, at best, with great danger.

The old couple understood. Should Eddie's lungs be affected, it might take years before he completely recovered, if the white plague, indeed, did not carry him off.

On that day after Christmas the chances seemed very slim that Eddie Flanagan would ever be a priest, and before long they were to become even slimmer.

CHAPTER FIVE

Disaster at Dunwoodie

After three months the doctors were satisfied Eddie would get well, but only if he gave up his studies for a year. Privately he rejected their judgment, turning instead to a heavy-set, bluff young priest who paid him bedside calls: Father Francis Duffy. In a future neither of them could then guess, Father Duffy was to win world renown as a heroic chaplain of World War I; his monument stands today in the coign of New York's busiest crossways.

The young Father Duffy listened to the rebellious sentiments of the sick student. He wanted to get out of bed and go back to his classes.

"But it might kill you, fellow! Do you think you have the right to risk the precious life God gave you?"

"God gave me a purpose, too, as well as a life."

"And what makes you so certain that the purpose is for you to be a priest?"

"Because," Flanagan chuckled mournfully, "I am not fit for anything else."

Father Duffy lowered his eyes; he had that way of asking for guidance, for light. Soon he left, the question unresolved between them. But not in Flanagan's mind. Never had he seen his own case more clearly. Here, and alone, as darkness gathered in the infirmary room, he forced himself to examine some of the questions Father Duffy had thrown at him. Why did priesthood mean so much to him? He knew it was more than habit or background. It was more than the influence of the house at Leabeg with its deep religious overtones. More than the piety of the home or the training at the side of his father. Or any desire to imitate his big brother, who had become a priest before him.

They were all factors, no doubt, yet not the reason. He would be a priest, all he had ever wanted to do, because that was his calling. Just as some men are born scientists or bricklayers or poets, so he was born to do God's work. That was why the Sligo slums had cut into his soul and the New York street boys tortured his memory even now.

In the late afternoon he closed his eyes and began softly to pray. An attendant, bringing medicine, noticed the tall young patient sitting erect against the pillow, eyes closed, lips moving, fingers at his beads.

II

The answer came on the next day, in the form of a young attendant who bounced into the sickroom with a stack of books, pencils, and paper. He dumped these supplies unceremoniously on the bed.

"You're Flanagan, aren't you? These books are for you. If you figure on getting out of studying over here, you're wrong. You're going to study in bed!"

Later, Father Duffy explained that the doctors would allow him to study two hours each day.

"With me to help you," the priest added with a wink.

Nor did Father Duffy ever fail to show up. Every afternoon the two worked together over the first-year theology course. These sessions, with Duffy's strong, breezy intellect, were of lifelong significance to Flanagan; daily contact with a brilliant mind and a truly charitable soul.

In the last weeks of the term Flanagan was strong enough to get out of bed and attend classes. The physician in charge of his case— stern-faced Dr. John Brady, who was also a teacher of dogmatic theology—bade him, however, never to overtire himself. He still had frequent spasms of coughing.

But his one aim was to pass the examinations, and as the time grew closer he began staying up after midnight as he had done years before in Sligo. Several times Father Duffy warned him of this excessive study. The hacking cough was obviously growing worse. But Flanagan, on fire with the desire to complete the year's work successfully, could not have halted.

He passed the examinations with high honors. Many of his teachers were astounded that the youth who had been out of class so long was still able to finish near the top of the list.

But the price had been high. A routine checkup at the infirmary had the doctors worried. His lungs were not in good shape. Danger of tuberculosis was imminent. The physicians held a council of war.

When they finally called Flanagan in, he knew by their grim expressions their decision was against him. Dr. Brady gave him the news with bluff sympathy. Because of his weakened health, it was not advisable for him to return to Dunwoodie next fall.

Flanagan looked from face to face, searching for one glint of hope. At last he demanded:

"And what must I do? Where would you suggest I go?"

"You need clear, dry air," Dr. Brady answered.

"You might want to take a trip out West," one of the others added.

Alone in his room, he tried to subdue the bitterness of his disappointment as he prayed for guidance. In the darkness, seeking a way, his thoughts turned to Patrick, his older brother, out in Omaha; the city that sat on the doorstep of the West. The older brother was forever writing enthusiastically of the clear, healthful air.

The next day young Flanagan sat down with his parents and sister and informed them of his disaster at Dunwoodie. And then he launched into his new plan. He was going out to Nebraska, where Brother Pat was.

"And I think it might be a good thing if all of us went out there together."

To the Flanagans, Omaha had always sounded like some frontier town in a wild-West melodrama, in spite of Father Patrick's disillusioning letters. To Mother, particularly, it seemed like an outpost of civilization.

"But it isn't at all," Eddie reassured her. "Why, it's very much

like Ireland in some ways. They say a good many Irish have gone
there, straight from the old land."

It took considerable argument. But in the end young Flanagan
won the others over to his point of view.

More Flanagans of Roscommon, Ireland, were on their way to
Omaha.

III

"Welcome to the front door of the West," Father Patrick had
written; to Omaha, perched on the western banks of the rolling
Missouri, almost exactly midway between the Atlantic and Pacific
coasts. In the life span of great cities, Omaha was scarcely more
than a child; but a sprawling, rambunctious youngster, growing fast.

The last years of the nineteenth century had seen Omaha grow
from a gangling village of only sixteen thousand in 1876 to nearly
one hundred thousand in 1905.

The Union Pacific had thrust its tracks through the city, and its
stockyards became a central collecting point for cattle from all over
the West, second only to Chicago. At Farnum and Sixteenth Street
—the heart of the city—cowhands and ranch owners with their
spurs and great hats strutted cheek by jowl with sedate businessmen. Not far from this central point Jonas Brandeis had opened his
"Fair Store" back in the 1880s. Later they moved to Douglas and
Sixteenth and called it the "Boston Store," as it is still known today.
Boston in the first decade of the century was still Paris to Omaha,
style setter for the ladies of the new West.

The church and parish of Father Patrick Flanagan was growing
in a section once farm land but now a rapidly developing suburb.
Ten miles outside of the town limits was a rolling section of farm
land which in those days was called the "Dodge Road Farm."
There were few houses in the region and only a narrow road twisting past. The farm spread over the crest of a high hill and Omaha
residents in summer months liked to drive out there in carts and
buggies; they would picnic at the top of the hill to admire the pano-
rama.

In those early 1900s there was none to guess what this rolling
farm land would one day become, least of all the Flanagans. None
could foresee then a magic city, with buildings, dormitories, classrooms, stadium and swimming pools and auditoriums, and other
structures which soar out of these fields—nor could they envision
the thousands of boys of all kinds and races who would crowd there
for refuge.

IV

Young Edward Flanagan found Omaha far different from the
cities back in Ireland. No narrow, crooked lanes or doddering houses
here; everything was young and new and a little brash; the streets
wide and straight. It was a brand-new, freshly painted world. And
there was an air of busy, hopeful excitement about the people. Pio-
neer spirit still throbbed within them; they were heading somewhere,
confidently.

It was also, as he soon discovered, a city of many creeds and
races. From founding days it had been a town of churches. As far
back as 1866, in spite of the small population, there had been
Catholic, Baptist, Lutheran, Methodist, Presbyterian, Episcopal,
Congregational, and other churches in Omaha, in addition to numerous religious and fraternal orders.

And again, in spite of—or perhaps because of—its mixture of
creeds, it had become a city of considerable tolerance. These builders, whatever their faith, knew that they had to work together. But
it was no Utopia. Here, as apparently everywhere, there were sections of abject poverty.

A gala time, that first dinner the Flanagans had together in
Omaha. Nellie and her mother were in the kitchen at Father Patrick
Flanagan's residence. Several of the other girls were there, and also
Michael, the very youngest of them all; he who was to be a singer
and to die at a tragically early age.

Tonight there was only gladness that they were together. Once
again Mother baked the bread and broiled the meat as she had done

all the years past at Leabeg. And it was white-bearded John Flanagan who said the grace before the meal.

Talk ran high at the dinner, most of it remembering. The time young Eddie had gone into Sir Nick's apple orchard. The big Christmas celebrations, when there were so many relatives in Leabeg house they did not know where to put them. How they would get the long table outside for the sheepshearers. And how much those men could eat.

They were all concerned, of course, with the plans of young Eddie. Inwardly the others feared that his idea of becoming a priest was now a highly precarious dream. But that night, at least, no one spoke of that.

A few days later Father P. A. had a talk with his younger brother. Taller and heavier than the younger man, Father P. A. was bluff and good-natured. A priest of deep sympathy and understanding, he had a way of seeming jovial and easygoing even when underneath his thoughts were most serious.

"Now you've banged yourself up this way," he began, "I wonder if you've learned your lesson about overdoing?"

"Patrick, do you mean—am I giving up?"

"The others say you ought to. A priest works night and day. Some think you haven't the strength——"

"I am going to find the strength—somehow."

"But to go on studying now—it might cost you your life."

Almost the same words Father Duffy had used.

"Then that is the way it must be."

Father P. A. gazed out of his office window to scattered homes of his parish. Young Flanagan went on: "But I don't really think I *will* die, you know. Not yet, anyway. I am sure our dear Lord is going to help me."

Certainty vibrated in his voice. The reality of God was the supreme fact in both their lives. Often in later years he was to make decisions and to take gambles which some would call courageous and others foolhardy. But to Flanagan neither was correct. Always he knew he was not alone. Whatever the trouble, the words at his lips were the same: "God will help us."

His older brother, in that moment in the little office, perceived the depth and confidence of this faith. An admiring smile relieved his lips:

"I suppose there's nothing for it, then, but to see what we can do."

Through Father P. A. he met many church leaders in Omaha, including Bishop Scannell who had traveled widely and studied at great schools.

"There is one place where you might go," the bishop said. "Where you could, at any rate, learn the most. That is, if your health——"

"Your Excellency—I am well now," Eddie assured the aged ecclesiastic. "The coughing is gone. I have gained weight. I am strong again. The doctors at Dunwoodie were mistaken about me. Where is this place?"

"Rome."

Flanagan had not expected that! Here in this hinterland of prairie and wheat fields the name of the Eternal City seemed unreal, like a far-off date in history.

The bishop went on: "There is one supreme qualification which sends a young man to Rome to complete his priestly studies. That is superior scholarship. Eddie, you have that qualification. You will be maintained there by the bishop of this diocese. That's me! So what have you to worry about?"

It was like the sounding of a sudden trumpet.

"If I could only go there!" Eddie said. "Of all places on earth!"

They talked about his past studies and previous preparations. All was in order. His high marks at Mount St. Mary's and during his year at St. Joseph's made his acceptance at any university almost a formality.

"It is up to you," the bishop declared. "Let me know!"

Once again there was a conclave of the family, and once again young Flanagan overrode all objections. His cough was entirely gone. He was over the effects of the pneumonia.

Late that summer Edward Flanagan, by now a seasoned traveler, returned to New York alone by train. A few days later he set sail.

CHAPTER SIX

Banished from Rome

To any young man preparing for the priesthood it was a rare opportunity to study in Rome, center of Christendom and home of the Church, with the whole pageant of history and many civilizations marked on its walls and stones and its ruins emerging out of centuries-old debris.

But for Flanagan the precious chance was also a desperate gamble.

About that hazard he had no private illusions. Physicians had admonished him, as had members of his own family. The climate of Rome was no health resort for anyone with weakened lungs: sudden shifts in temperature, enervating heat followed by chill nights, dampness which clung to the city, fever that lurked in its ruins.

But the traveler took comfort in the fact that by 1907 engineers were at work to lift Rome out of its ancient lethargy and transform it into a modern European capital. To some degree its principal streets had already been cleaned of their filth, drinking water partly purified, and tramcars clattered past sites of long-dead glories. Yet the job of ridding Rome of its dirt and disease moved slowly; there were still streets which reeked with rotting refuse and still days when water was unsafe. Prevalent also was the "Roman fever," which frequently struck down newcomers. Visitors blamed the often fatal illness on climate and food, but Romans said it was no more than a variety of typhoid such as might be picked up in any European city.

The Romans insisted, moreover, that the city was a healthful place where anyone could stay well, provided he lived as the Romans did. That meant eating heavy meals, getting plenty of sleep, avoiding overexertion.

But Flanagan felt he had no time to follow the leisurely pattern of the average Roman. His schedule would have taxed the strength of one much stronger than himself.

When Flanagan arrived in Rome, on October 4, 1907, he was enrolled necessarily at the Gregorian University.

The Gregorian, which included the school to which Flanagan came with such high hopes, was steeped in history. Just seven years after the Council of Trent had condemned the doctrines of Luther and Calvin, it had become a university under Pope Julius III, but as a simpler school it had been founded much earlier by St. Ignatius Loyola and St. Francis Borgia.

When Eddie Flanagan came to Rome it was known as the Gregorian Pontifical University and there were faculties and courses in theology, philosophy, and canon law. Since his day there have been added the faculties of missionology, sacred scripture, oriental studies, and history.

Even its location was different in those old days; the university was then on the Via dei Seminari, only a few steps from the famous Church of St. Ignatius, where the bodies of St. John Berchmans and St. Aloysius Gonzaga are buried. Often Flanagan worshiped in this church and meditated there upon the mysteries of the past, present, and future, having in mind, we feel certain, that Saints Berchmans and Gonzaga were distinguished above everything else as patrons of youth!

Today you will find the Gregorian University, as we did last year, on the Piazza Pilotta, at the rear of the grand congeries of buildings of the North American College by the Via dell' Umilita and in no way evocative of the puzzled Irish boy who came there to study in 1908. Since 1932, American students who formerly would have studied at the Propaganda University have gone instead to the Gregorian. But in the year that Father Flanagan died (1948) ground was broken on Janiculum Hill in Rome for the new three-million-dollar North American College.

The department of the university where Edward Flanagan dwelt and did most of his studying was called Collegio Capranica, often also referred to as the Almo Collegio Capranicense, and was established in 1457 by Cardinal Dominic Capranica.

In Flanagan's day, as now, the university was in charge of the Society of Jesus and virtually all of the professors were Jesuit fathers. This does not mean that Father Flanagan could be described as a Jesuit; he had never studied to join that austere order, nor any other; he merely happened to be instructed by teachers who were themselves Jesuit. These instructors came from all parts of the world, spoke in a babel of native tongues, and were helped out by some Roman priest teachers and a few lay professors.

The students, too, came from everywhere to study at Gregorian for the secular priesthood, that is, without joining the Jesuits, Dominicans, Franciscans, or any special orders. But members of many different religious orders and societies also studied there, of almost every nationality and country. In fact, there was no more cosmopolitan institution in the world of Catholicism; some priests of our acquaintance believe that Flanagan's association at Gregorian with young men of all races and colors helped to plant and strengthen in him the great dominant belief that was to be his in later life—that all people, of all nationalities, races, and colors, can work together for a good purpose. For he himself had sat in class and mingled daily with youths of many differences in social standing as well as race and language—all working and studying together "for God's greater honor and glory."

The day of the student in Rome began early, with breakfast at seven, following early morning Mass. Classes began at eight and continued on through morning and afternoon, with a brief time out for a lunch and a short siesta.

It was a round of textbooks, lectures, and research from original sources in the libraries and museums. Late afternoon would find him poring over some Latin record text in one of the great libraries.

Lecture assignments were heavy and there was almost no time for relaxation. Evenings were usually taken up with study and preparation for the next day's classes. At Capranica College, where he lived, midnight often found him still bent over his books. Flanagan felt he must work harder than the others because of time already lost.

Five days a week he attended lectures at the university, together with occasional classroom instruction, though not often; the lecture system was dominant. Now and then there would be university-wide discourses for the entire student body. All the lectures were in Latin and all examinations were conducted in Latin; it was the common language shared by all the students.

These lectures and classes were held on Monday, Tuesday, Wednesday, Friday, and Saturday, with five lectures of one hour's duration each as the minimum of the day's work. Classes began around the fourth of November, a month after Flanagan's arrival in Rome; he expected to take his year's examinations during the first week of the following July. But here Flanagan again lacked the gift of prophecy.

On Thursdays and Sundays it was the custom for students to visit famous shrines of Rome and historical sites of ancient glories and defeats. On these occasions Father Flanagan went out with new friends who were to last a lifetime. Among his schoolmates were Enrico Dante, a native of Italy, and John C. Vismara of Detroit. They made many sight-seeing trips together. Forty years later these two friends of Father Flanagan made a special journey together to visit Boys Town. One was now the Right Reverend Monsignor Dante of Rome, the other, Right Reverend Monsignor Vismara. Monsignor Dante was now Prefect of the Apostolic Ceremonies in Rome, and, as such, Master of Ceremonies for Pope Pius XII and also First Assistant Secretary of the Congregation of Rites; one of the great ritual scholars of the Church. Yet he had taught philosophy and dogmatic theology, having among his pupils Cardinal Spellman of New York.

The two old friends stood beside the bier of Father Flanagan in the Boys Town Chapel. They were remembering not only that scant, long-ago stay in Rome and the heartbreaking departure. Much clearer was the memory of Father Flanagan's return to Rome in March 1948. With Patrick J. Norton, Father Flanagan was a house guest of Monsignor Dante in Vatican City only a few days before the end in Berlin.

Flanagan and his classmates explored together the Roman Forum, the Pantheon, and the treasures of the Vatican. Occasionally, on fine October afternoons, they would saunter past the Colosseum, and tramp on out of the city, over the hexagonal stones of the Appian Way, to the Catacombs where early Christians sought refuge.

Most glorious of all to Eddie's eyes were the great churches of the Eternal City—St. Peter's and then the Basilicas of San Giovanni, with its twin peaks and obelisk, and the magnificent Santa Maria Maggiore with tower and domes. These were his favorites, and after them the golden mosaic of St. Paul Outside the Walls, with the figure of the great missionary, sword in hand, in the front garden.

Those were days long before Fascism, yet with their own special brand of wickedness, especially the shrill packs of beggars, called lazzaroni, who clung like human flies to the outer doors of the churches, pursuing the more prosperous with outstretched, scrofulous hands and shrieking for alms.

Though Flanagan had seen the shades of poverty and young crime in the alleys of Sligo, the lower east side of New York, and the stockyard streets of Omaha, here, in Rome, he saw their most hideous reality. Against the long stepway leading up to the church at the Piazza di Spagna he observed the brutishness of life as little ragamuffins lived it among flower booths there—gutter urchins like the melon eaters painted by Murillo, but without their idealized innocence. The Rome of Julius Caesar and of Nero, with all its silken and voluptuous wickedness, the city that had known the blows of Goth and Visigoth and Hun, the excesses of the Renaissance, seemed no more wicked than these days of poverty and misery which he could see. And though his soul was lifted up with the singing of the boy choirs in St. Peter's—a matter he was to remember long afterward—and though his spirit was touched with ecstasy by the Sistine Chapel, he still could not efface from his mind those foulsmelling youngsters and the tales of their monstrous misdoings. For years they beleaguered his conscience; boys were in his heart and he was never to get them out.

He had seen these children—literally baby bandits—do unspeakably wrong things. Many people considered them beyond all hope of reclamation.

"But, busy as I was," Father Flanagan told us, "I couldn't keep away from those kids. They taught me a profound lesson, for which I am grateful to this day—the lesson of *why* they are good, for all the evil they do, and *not* bad. The hopefulness I got from watching those beggar children made it possible for me to face the toughest customer we ever had in Boys Town."

And here Father Flanagan told us that simple tale which one of us has told already and which has too deep a meaning not to be told here again.

II

One winter night a long-distance phone call came to Boys Town.

"Father Flanagan? This is Sheriff Hosey—from Virginia. Got any room for another boy—immediately?"

"Where is he now?"

"In jail. He's a desperate character—robbed a bank, held up three stores with a revolver——"

"How old is he?"

"Eight and a half!"

The gaunt, blue-eyed priest stiffened at the telephone.

"He's what?"

"Don't let his age fool you. He's all I said he was and more. Will you take him off our hands?"

"If I can't manage an eight-and-one-half-year-old child by this time, I ought to quit," he said unguardedly. "Bring him out!"

Three days later, near the end of a cheerless afternoon, Sheriff Hosey and his red-faced wife set down their prisoner in Father Flanagan's office—an unnaturally pale boy with a bundle under his arm. He was no higher than the desk; frowzy hair of chocolate brown dangled over the pinched and freckled face—eyes shut beneath long dark lashes. From one side of his mouth a smoldering cigarette drooped at a theatrical angle.

"Don't mind the smoking," pleaded the sheriff. "We had to bribe him with cigarettes to behave himself."

Meanwhile the wife laid a long envelope on the desk.

"There's a complete report," she snapped. "And that's not the half of it. This good-for-nothing criminal is not worth helping—it's my personal opinion he ain't even human! Good-by and good luck —you're going to need it!"

Looking upon this patched wraith of childhood, Flanagan thought that never had he seen such a mixture of the comical and the utterly squalid and tragic. But he could not foresee that during the next year all Boys Town would be plagued with the same godless mixture of belly laugh and heartbreak.

Waving the newcomer to a chair, the priest turned on the desk lamp and began to read. It seemed that people had forgotten the boy's last name; he was just Eddie. Born in a slum near the docks, he had lost father and mother in a flu epidemic before he was four. In water-front flats he was shunted from one family to another, living like a hungry and desperate little animal.

Hardship sharpened his cunning and his will. It was literally true that at the age of eight he became the boss of a gang of boys, some nearly twice his age. He dominated them, as older toughs of the neighborhood taught him to do; he browbeat them into petty crimes which he planned in logical detail.

But about six months before the law caught up with Eddie his rule was challenged by a new member of the gang:

"You never do anything yourself. You're no leader."

"I'll show you," replied Eddie. "I'll do something you wouldn't dare . . . I'm going to rob a bank."

The bank was housed in the basement of an old-fashioned building. When most of the clerks were away at lunch Eddie lowered himself through a window, entered unseen, and crossed to an unattended slot of the cashier cage. So small that he had to chin himself up, he thrust in one grimy paw, seized a packet of green bills, and hid them in his jacket. Then, with complete sang-froid, he walked into the street, to divide two hundred dollars among his comrades. But the exploit was a flop; the bank concealed the theft, and there were no headlines.

"You're only cracking your jaw," the gang jeered. "You found that dough somewhere."

For several days Eddie vanished from his favorite street corner. Some vicious oldster had sold him a Colt revolver and stuffed his pockets with bullets; for two days Eddie stayed in the fields beyond town, practicing marksmanship.

This time the local front pages were full of him. Slouching into a restaurant at an empty hour, he aimed his gun at the terrified counterman while his other palm received a day's take from the cash register. Next he dragged a cabbage of bills from the pants pocket of a shivering tailor. His third call was on an old lady who kept a candy store.

"Put down that thing," this grandmother cried, "before you hurt yourself!"

She smacked the gun out of his hand and grabbed him by the hair. Like an insensate little demon, he began to struggle; he might have killed her, but her screams brought policemen. Now Eddie had wound up in Boys Town.

Putting aside the manuscript, Father Flanagan looked musingly at the villain of the piece. From this night on the past must be a closed book; the idea was to forget it and start over again.

But certain things were already clear. This was not a villain but a victim. Born under another roof, Eddie could have been another kind of boy, knowing the sweetness of home, birthday candles, Christmas parcels, mother's tender vigilance—yes, and the strong, wise counsel of a father's pride.

Something else showed in the report: Eddie had resourcefulness and a realistic brain; one must respect his intelligence and appeal to it.

"No matter what he says or does," Father Flanagan resolved, "I'll never give up until I've won him over."

In the dimmish light Eddie stood unmoving, head lowered, looking at the floor; it was hard to see much of that pale wrinkled face. But as the man watched, the child produced a small piece of white paper and a sack of Bull Durham. One-hand-cowboy fashion, he deliberately rolled his own cigarette and, having lighted it, thumbnail to match, he blew a plume of smoke billowing across the desk.

Then long eyelashes lifted for a flash, to see how the priest was taking the exhibition; Father Flanagan's first sight of those bright brown eyes.

"Eddie," began the leader of Boys Town, "you are welcome here. The whole place is run by the fellows, you know. Boy mayor. Boy city council. Boy chief of police."

"Where's the jail?" grunted Eddie in basso profundo.

"We haven't a jail. You are going to take a bath and then get supper. Tomorrow you start in school. You and I can become real friends—it's strictly up to you. I love you and someday I hope I can take you to my heart. I know you're a good boy!"

The reply came in a single shocking syllable.

About eleven o'clock next morning Father Flanagan, smiling rue-fully, was looking over the inventory of Eddie's bundle—a few odds and ends of shirts, unmatching socks, a fresh pair of drawers, and a white rabbit's foot—when the door to the office opened and the new pupil swaggered in. His hair had been cut and neatly combed and he was clean. With an air of great unconcern he tossed on the desk a note from one of the teachers:

DEAR FATHER FLANAGAN:

We have heard you say a thousand times that there is no such thing as a bad boy. Would you mind telling me what you call this one?

Back in that classroom the atmosphere was about as cheerful as Mother's Day in the death house. The teacher described how Eddie had sat quietly in his seat for about an hour; suddenly he began parading back and forth in the aisle, swearing like a longshoreman and throwing movable objects on the floor, finally pitching an ink-well, which landed accurately on a plaster bust of Cicero.

Replacing Eddie in his seat, Father Flanagan apologized:

"It was my fault . . . I never told him he mustn't throw ink-wells. The laws of Boys Town will, of course, be enforced with him, as with all the rest of us. But he has to learn them first. We must never forget that Eddie is a good boy."

"Like hell I am!" screamed Eddie.

The child seemed made of stone. He made no friends among boys or teachers, least of all with Father Flanagan, for whom he reserved his supreme insult, picked up God knows where—"a damned pray-ing Christian." Spare time he spent roaming about stealthily, looking for a chance to run away. Sullenly he stood aloof in gymnasium and on baseball and football fields: "Kid stuff!" Neither choir nor band could stir him; the farm bored him.

Given the slightest chance at freedom, he showed himself proudly unregenerate—upsetting a jigsaw puzzle laboriously put together, tearing a book apart with his bare hands, and, in the midst of class prayers, mewing like a cat.

And in all that first six months not once a laugh, nor a tear. Soon the one question in Boys Town was whether Father Flanagan had met his match at last.

"Does the little guy learn anything?" he asked the sisters.

"Somehow he is getting his A B Cs," they reported. "In fact, he's learning more than he lets on. But he's just eaten up with hate!"

One night an older boy reported that Eddie was groaning in his sleep. Walking into the dormitory, Father Flanagan stood beside the bed, touched the flushed face and felt the warm sweat of fever.

"Just a sick little boy," he thought penitently. "It is shameful and foolish of me to lose hope. How can a little boy be bad when he is so soon from God?"

Perhaps the Lord had been trying him out with Eddie, to see how deep was his faith.

"Well, I'm going to take all He wants to send—with the help of God, of course!" he added hastily.

There must be something in Eddie that could be worked out. By the ruddy name of Flanagan he would find it!

Through dark and gusty grounds the priest walked that October night, his grieving face set against the wind. It came to him then how real fathers must feel toward little sons. Sometimes they love so much that they spoil them. Eddie had been spoiled, all right, but not that way.

"I'll have to throw away the book of rules," grumbled Flanagan. "I'm going to try spoiling the little devil—with love!"

As he reached this peak of noble intention a blast blew off his hat and for a quarter of an hour he was on his knees, prowling among the bushes.

In the infirmary Eddie snarled at the doctors, but when they accused him of being afraid he swallowed the medicine without a grimace; he walked into the darkness of the X-ray chamber with the air of a condemned man unbroken as he marched to the chair.

Well again, he became more silent than ever. An apathy settled upon him just when the leader of the village was giving him more attention than he had ever given anyone else. Boys and teachers began to watch the new strategy as if it were a contest; a sporting proposition, and the home team was Father Flanagan.

Upon these weeks and months he looked back with a reminiscent shudder, especially at the scores of B-picture programs they sat through, all double features. It is still a medical wonder that Eddie did not get ulcers from hot dogs and hamburgers, nut and chocolate bars, peanut brittle, ice cream, Coca-Cola, Pepsi-Cola, and tonics of thirty rainbow colors. Inside his puny body there lay some cavernous area capable of infinite absorption.

Yet never once did Eddie say that anything was fun or sweet or refreshing; never a remark came unprompted; all answers briefly severe. In summer dawns, smelling of pines and wild clover, he would trudge stolidly down to the lake, but no grunt of excitement came when he landed a trout. After each private excursion he would leave Father Flanagan with the same overbearing smile.

Only once toward the end of that unhappy experiment did man and boy come closer together. That was at a street crossing in Omaha when Eddie was looking in the wrong direction and a truck tore around a corner; Father Flanagan yanked him out of harm's way. For one instant a light of gratitude flickered in the startled brown eyes, then the lashes fell again; he said nothing.

Stalemate! Even to the man of faith it began to seem that here was an inherent vileness beyond his reach. Hope had fallen to the lowest possible point when one soft spring morning Eddie boldly appeared in the office, announcing that he wanted to have it out with Father Flanagan. This time the brown eyes were glowing with indignation.

"You've been trying to get around me," he began, "but now I'm wise to you. If you was on the level, I might have been a sucker at that. I almost fell for your line. But last night I got to thinking it over, and I sees the joker in the whole thing——"

There was something terribly earnest and manful in Eddie now; this was not insolence but despair. With a stab of hope the priest noticed for the first time a quiver on the twisted lips.

"Father Flanagan, you're a phony!"

"You better prove that, Eddie—or shut up!"

"Okay! I just kicked a sister in the shins. Well? Now what do you say?"

"I still say you are a good boy."

"What did I tell you? You keep on saying that lie, and you *know* it's a lie, it *can't* be true—doesn't that prove you're a phony?"

Dear Father in heaven, this is honest logic! How can I answer it? How defend my faith in him—and in You? Because it's now or never with Eddie—God give me the grace to say the right thing.

Father Flanagan cleared his throat.

"Eddie, you're smart enough to know when a thing is really proved. What *is* a good boy? A good boy is an obedient boy. Right?"

"Yeah!"

"Does what his teachers tell him to do?"

"You bet!"

"Well, that's all you've ever done, Eddie. The only trouble with you is that you had the wrong teachers—wharf toughs and corner bums—but you have certainly obeyed them; you've done every last wrong and rotten thing they taught you to do. If you could only obey the good teachers here in the same way, you'd be just fine!"

Those simple words of unarguable truth were like an exorcism, driving out devils from the room and cleansing the air. At first the tiny human enigma looked dumfounded. Then came a glisten of sheer downright relief in the brown eyes, and he began to creep around the side of the sunlit desk. And with the very same relief Father Flanagan's soul was crying; he held out his arms and the child climbed into them and laid a tearful face against his heart.

That was a long time ago. For ten years Eddie remained in Boys Town, until, well near the top of his class, he left to join the United States Marines. On blood-smeared beaches he won three promotions.

"His chest," boasted Father Flanagan, "is covered with medals. Nothing strange about that, though; no wonder he has courage. But God be praised for something else; he has the love of the men in his outfit—brother to the whole bunch he is—an upstanding Christian character. And still the toughest kid I ever knew!"

III

The priest who could labor so valiantly for one little bank robber learned to understand boys like Eddie in the unclean streets of Rome —and yet, in those days, it looked more and more as if he would never be able to practice all that he was learning. The Roman winter was proving too much for him. Flanagan, attempting to take in all that he could, found himself in an unending race with time, and it was draining his strength. But he also believed he must complete his course, must reach, here in Rome, the goal of priesthood, or there would be no further chance for him.

Early in November the long siege began to close in; the most treacherous winter Rome had known in many a year. Cold rains and moldy dampness in the walls; freezing everywhere. The cough which had cleared up in the dry air of Omaha returned and the ankle he had twisted when he was a boy became swollen once more.

Trying to brush aside his worries over his physical condition, Flanagan kept at his studies with redoubled intensity. But soon there could be no more doubt of what the damp and poorly heated rooms and the bitter winter, plus the strain of his heavy schedule, were doing to his health. He was losing weight, while the cough grew steadily worse.

One of the professors warned him again, early in January, that he was heading for disaster.

"I have seen many like you, Flanagan," the Jesuit teacher began bluntly. "Slow down or else——"

Throughout January he grew weaker, until at last he was forced to go to the physicians at the university infirmary. With heavy heart he presented himself there; same time of year as before in Dunwoodie, and again the student for the priesthood at the infirmary. How he detested his own physical weakness!

"You have been giving yourself too much punishment," the doctor declared. "Now you are finished with such foolishness. I am not telling you that you must merely slow up a little, I am telling you you must give up your studies and go home."

"And if I won't give them up?" Flanagan asked.

"I cannot order you to leave. But I can assure you, if you remain here in Rome, you will soon be a dead man."

IV

So again, and still not a priest, on January 27, 1908, Flanagan began the long journey across the Atlantic and over half a continent —back to Omaha.

And still lacking the gift of prophecy, he did not, could not, foresee in his depression—a despair so deep that he had begun to suspect he was never intended for the priesthood—how one day, because of his faith and because of his zeal, those Italian urchins would find shelter in a kind of home that he alone had dreamed up. There would be Boys Town in Prenestina, a suburb of Rome, in Santamariella, and in Palermo. On the lonely voyage he could contemplate only the past, littered with dead hopes, and the barren present, as day by day he sailed closer to American shores.

The family were at the Omaha station. There was forced gaiety, and no reproaches. They all wanted him to feel safe and welcome; not one even looked as if in mind was the banality of all banalities: "I told you so."

When they finally discussed it, he said that whatever the future held, he could never be content to be an invalid parasite.

"I'll have to go to work, at least. As soon as possible," he told the older brother. "You couldn't expect me to sit around and do nothing at all."

Father P. A. scowled.

"Eddie, that is just what you've got to do, if you want to live. So it's orders."

Spring now, the white frost gone from the stubble in the fields, and the warmth and the clear air like a tonic. At the home of his parents, just outside the town, the returned voyager obeyed his brother and the doctors; he loafed endlessly, stretched out in a backyard hammock, swaying in the sun, reading a little sometimes or dozing off. He had given up everything—except dreaming.

Indeed, these days of prolonged rest brought him to the humble contemplation of his past overzealousness. He realized at last that he could not design the pattern set for him to follow. Even so, his faith was unshaken; there were still for him a pattern and a purpose and someday he would see them clearly. Never was he completely despondent; never did he feel his soul to be stagnant, although the waters of life did seem to be still.

As the summer wore on, his health again began visibly to improve; he gained back his weight and once more there was color in his face. Early in the fall the family physician, Dr. A. W. Riley, was brought in for another examination. As he put the stethoscope back in the bag he faced his young patient with an encouraging wink:

"Eddie, my fine lad, I think you are really getting well this time. If you take care of yourself, and make up your mind to live a normal life, get a job and not try to study your brains out——"

The convalescent stood up indignantly. What was this sawbones talking about? Didn't he know he was going to be a priest? That was all he had ever lived for.

"When can I start studying for the priesthood?" he asked sternly.

The physician shook his head.

"I told you you were stronger. Strong enough, say, to hold down a job doing some light kind of work. But not to carry on any heavy schedule such as is required in the study you speak of."

There was authority in the voice. He did not seem to know that his words were, to Flanagan, a sentence of doom.

"There are plenty of easy jobs," the physician hurried on in a genial tone. "Take something with little physical work connected, that allows you to keep regular hours. Something interesting, that you *like* doing."

His voice trailed off. The physician could not, of course, sense the irony in his own words. When he was gone the twenty-two-year-old Flanagan sat a long time. The decision he came to was simple and wise: he would have patience and faith, and meanwhile seek to know the will of God and perform it!

Only a few days later he came home with news: he had a position.

"I've always been rather good at figures, you know," he reminded them. "Particularly at handling financial matters. Not that I'm going to be a financier exactly, but I'm on the way. They've agreed to take me on as an accountant in the bookkeeping department over at Cudahy's."

Cudahy's, the great meat-packing company in Omaha, had hired the boy who had once taken care of the sheep and cattle in Roscommon and was now going to be in the business of adding up the totals of cattle and lamb brought in for slaughter.

CHAPTER SEVEN

For Beef and for Boys

The new bookkeeper in the accounting department at Cudahy's was regarded as a bird of strange plumage. He had flitted from Ireland to New York and to Rome, for one thing; to his fellow clerks he seemed like Marco Polo. Almost from the first day he came into the office he found himself a cause of gossip and speculation; they all knew he had wanted to be a priest and failed.

In the prosaic, routine lives of most of the accountants Ed Flanagan was a kind of double symbol—adventure and frustration. Some smiled, some felt sorry for him, but he seemed not to belong to any of them; still set apart, although he kept on good terms with them all. He fitted his ways easily into the rigid, accurate pattern of his job, but always, in his pocket, he carried his missal. A saying began to go around the office that Flanagan couldn't get his additions right until he had said his prayers.

One evening Flanagan was walking home from the plant with a husky young clerk called Hank, who had started out as a handler in the bull pens and had won promotion finally to the accounting office.

"Can't get it," Hank was complaining. "Fellow like you, going around all the time with a prayer book. Still hoping to be a priest someday?"

To no one had Flanagan spoken of his faith in the future since he had taken the bookkeeper's job. But now he answered:

"Yes—I have faith that I shall still be a priest someday, Hank. But that's my secret and yours. Okay?"

Hank kept the secret, and the conversation aroused new strength in Flanagan. He had put into words something that had been deep in consciousness—his continuing faith that someday, in spite of all, he *would* be a priest. His family and friends had completely written off his original plans.

Flanagan even began to tell himself that this bookkeeper's job might have some special part in the pattern, even though he could not yet comprehend it. That was when he resolved to make himself as proficient as any bookkeeper in the firm and learn all he could about business methods. He had a ringside opportunity to study not merely the mechanical processes of accounting but the modern operation of a great financial corporation dealing in millions. Cudahy's, like other big packing firms, was expanding rapidly, merging with other companies, and many of the transactions were intricate. Flanagan studied the techniques with indefatigible curiosity. Someday all this banking and financial skill could come in handy, and for a far different purpose than packing meat. Most certainly he did not guess that with only a few borrowed dollars he was one day to start his home for boys—a home which under expert and inspired financial management was to grow and expand, becoming itself an enterprise of millions of dollars!

There would be no money profits in this great building program he was to direct, but the job could never have been carried through without someone at the helm with a firm grounding of business skill and training. In fact, quite often some of the latter-day plans of Father Flanagan would seem too ambitious to those of less financial experience. But Father Flanagan, recalling Cudahy's again, would tell them not to worry, always adding: "If they could do it for beef—we can do it for boys!"

Slowly, with steady hours and lack of strain, he really regained his health. So much so that early in the spring of 1909 he resolved once more to reconsider his plans.

II

In that year there was a sense throughout the world of growth and achievement and the opening up of vast new avenues of progress. On the sweltering twenty-fifth of July, as many old-timers can still remember, Louis Blériot crossed the English Channel, from Calais to Dover, thirty-one miles in thirty-seven minutes—and not on the water but in the sky.

In New York City the three rivers and the southern water front of Manhattan glowed with illumination and skyrockets as for four noisy months the island celebrated one hundred years of steamships in the Hudson-Fulton jubilee. And in far-off Seattle there was a world's fair, called the Alaska-Yukon-Pacific Exposition. All the world was thinking of man's demonstrated capacity to triumph over obstacles in nature, in his fellow man and in himself.

So it was natural for Edward Joseph Flanagan—thus far only a packing-house clerk, a rejected candidate for holy orders, and a weak-lunged prospect for tuberculosis if he were not inordinately careful—to demand anew the right to conquer his own obstacles and to try again for the dream of his soul.

He looked stalwart now, tall and sturdy, and he was utterly convinced that he had subjugated his rebellious lungs; had completely subdued all the illness of his body. But this time he would leave nothing to chance, nor would he worry his loved ones. Alone, without informing his family of his intention, he paid a call on Dr. Riley. The examination lasted long; not content with this, the doctor insisted on consultations with other physicians.

"You have made a most remarkable recovery," Eddie was finally told. "You seem well enough to take on any job. Only, to be absolutely safe, it should be in a clear, dry climate. Mountain air would be best."

The rejoicing Flanagan once more, after almost two years of work in the packing plant, called a family conference. Of course, if he was strong enough, he should return to his studies. Money? The whole family would help out.

The suggestion came from Father P. A.—why not a seminary in the Alps? Back in Rome, Flanagan had known students who had previously studied at the University of Innsbruck in the Austrian Tyrol. The idea of going to this famous center of learning, high in the Alps, sounded most reasonable, since mountain air was a blessing to weakened lungs.

Writing letters, filing applications, long weeks while the letters crossed the ocean. It was almost summer before the University of Innsbruck accepted Edward Flanagan as a student in its Department of Theology.

Once again a rupture in his family life as a month later Edward Joseph Flanagan recrossed the Atlantic.

CHAPTER EIGHT

One with the Apostles

Father Flanagan fell in love with the Tyrol—its snowy peaks, its heady air, its sports, its student taverns . . .

String music in the corner, and the loud banter of students hugging the bar of a centuries-old taproom. Some young men in bare-kneed, green-jacket Tyrolean costume, others garbed in seminary black; these future priests listened while more worldly young men teased the barmaid, whose golden hair was wound up in braids.

"Elsa, is it true you are going to elope with a fiddler?"

"Tell us his name," another wailed. "We'll tear him apart!"

"You'll all have long beards," she said, "before I'll marry anyone. Especially any of you!"

They raised their steins then, in diurnal, ritualistic toast to Elsa; traditionally, each student had his own stein, with his name lettered in gilt, and when not in use it would hang on a peg in the wall.

In a corner of the sawdust floor Flanagan had a favorite table, which he shared with three other theological students. Here they often sat, deep in discussions and paying small attention to the frivolity of those crowded around the bar, except when the students lifted their steins. Flanagan and his friends, a serious four, nevertheless stood up and hoisted mugs in the daily toast. Then they would sit down again and plunge anew into the debate over errors in the Hegelian theories.

From first to last Flanagan reveled in his three years in the Tyrol. Never had he felt so strong and so sure of his health; his whole being tingled with the glories of the storybook town of Innsbruck, cupped among jagged and soaring snow-capped peaks, its romantic past lingering on in timeworn streets, lined with ancient houses and shops.

Forty years afterward Father Flanagan would turn to us, nostalgic fervor seething in his voice, and demand: "Are any other such vistas to be found anywhere else in the world? Innsbruck! It is an unforgettable unreality."

And he would recall to us the broad, Middle Ages area of Maria-Theresienstrasse, lined with the tall fronts and pointed roofs of business houses; the orange-painted streetcar on a single track hurtling along like an overgrown toy, and behind the memorial shaft at the end of the street, rising, prodigious and pure, with unmelting snows, three great Alpine heights—Sattelspitzen, Seegrubenspitzen, and Hafelekai. And Flanagan loved the old clock tower in Friedrichstrasse, and the house called the Golden Dache, with its roof tiles of gilded copper. He learned that the famous dwelling was put up in 1425 by a certain Friederich, who gave the street its name; he was Count of the Tyrol and was known as the one "with the empty pockets." There have been a lot of counts since then, Father reminded us, who could have taken the words to themselves.

There is a saying in the Tyrol that a man can live closest to God on a mountain peak. People of this area, largely Catholic, have always been deeply religious. Faith here, as Flanagan soon found, was, as in Ireland, part of daily life. There were shrines in the fields, and many tales of religious miracles were told and many Stations of the Cross were built along the mountain trails.

But Innsbruck was also a university town, renowned as a center of learning. Students in most cases were serious young men like Flanagan preparing for priesthood, medicine, or law. But they still had the high spirits of youth which blended with the gaiety and song of the yodeling Tyroleans themselves.

Here, the bookkeeper from Omaha discovered, the student—at least, one like himself, in second-year theology—was almost entirely on his own. He lived in a dormitory of what was called Canisianum Convictus, or, as the townspeople called it, Theologisches Konvikt. By any name, it was a boarding home for poor students.

Through special privilege, granted to him, there was no strict regime of hours of classes to be attended. A student did have to register his name on a bulletin board occasionally but beyond that was free to study as he pleased. He took his examinations when he felt he was ready. For the first time Flanagan could study without feeling himself under pressure.

Often he would spend hours with some companion strolling through the arcades beneath the frescoed buildings and winding up, for an hour of prayer, in the Franciscan church, with its world-famous cenotaph of Maximilian and its Silver Chapel, named for the silver Madonna on the altar. In this church also were the tombs of Archduke Ferdinand of the Tyrol and his non-royal wife, Philippine, the story of whose marriage is one of the romantic legends of those high mountain passes.

It was a world rich in legend and tradition, but it was also, for Flanagan, primarily a world of work. Most of that work and study he did at his quarters in Canisius House. The dormitory had been assigned to him by the rector of the seminary, Father Michael Hoffman, S.J., a priest who had not only the gift of inspiring love for learning but of increasing it in those already prepared.

There were great frugality and absence of worldly luxury in this Jesuit institution. The room which Flanagan shared with another student was like the cell of a medieval monk, furnished only with two straight-back chairs, a bureau for clothes, and beds with straw mattresses, and an oil lamp.

At the start in the austere retreat, diet was a problem for Flanagan. The Tyrolean cooks followed Germanic recipes, and the food was heavy and greasy. It took a little arguing to convince the authorities that this American boy had to have special dishes, but they finally gave in. He was determined at all costs to be careful. Not only about food and study, but he had fully learned by now the need for relaxation.

Much of his free time was spent in hiking with an alpenstock, the long staff of the Tyrol, climbing along mountain roads. Often they hiked and worked, discussing religious and philosophical questions around which examinations would center. For half an hour or so they would rest weary young bones in some herdsman's hut. In those sheepmen's high chalets hospitality was invariably kind, and an earthen crock of cheese, or potsherd of *schmierkäse,* unfailing. There, for the edification of strong mountain farmers and housewives, Flanagan sang many an Irish air and danced them many a jig. For he was young and full of the joy of youth, new strength, and well-being, and loved to lift his *basso cantante* in the sorrowful ballad about Where the River Shannon Flows.

On the way back down, trying to outstrip the twilight into town, the students would talk of many matters: pictures one had seen in the Alten Pinakothek in Munich, or a new type of bicycle, or the danger of war to come. And again, on the way, they would ask him to sing Irish tunes. Once having heard them, they disputed among themselves whether, perhaps, Renan, in resurrecting the glories and patriotism of the Irish bards of the sixth century, had not caught the vision of his Life of Christ—and betrayed it!

The shadows would deepen around them, and there would come a deep, murmuring sound of the wind in the trees, a soughing of troubled branches, and the light, growing dimmer, would in its last glow fondle the solemn peaks in all their majesty and mystery and power. All around the descending young men there would be a gloaming and a sadness as if they were in the midst of the Ragnarök; the twilight of the Gods and the doomsday of the world.

So they would return for dinner quite often feeling full of *Weltschmerz*. But after a supper of cold pigs' feet and hot black beans they would feel a rekindling within soul and body.

II

On more than one vacation journey Flanagan would wear the native *Schützenfest* costume, green velvet pants, short leather jacket, and pointed hat with the cocked feather and turned-down brim. With great amusement in after years he showed us old snapshots of himself thus arrayed.

In addition to theology, Flanagan learned the mysteries of yodeling, in the Tyrol, where it is a high art. This falsetto facility was later to cause consternation among the family back in Omaha.

There was one night the choirmaster of Innsbruck said to him:

"Our people sing because music is a kind of healing. Singing can

The Mothers' Guild: Making blankets.

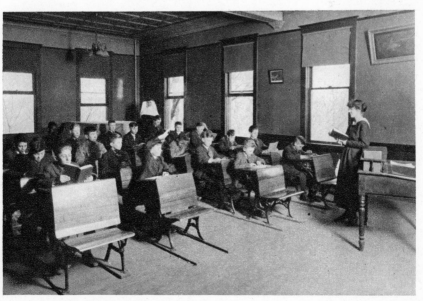

The first school: A classroom in the German Home.

A new city starts: The farm that became Boys Town.

Growing up: The city begins to take shape.

keep you well. Say you are angry and wrought up inside—that may make you sick. Well, you sing and you keep well. You forget about grudges."

That teacher's philosophy of singing was to play a curious role in Flanagan's future; at a very dark hour the world-famous Boys Town choir was born of nostalgic memories.

Serious almost beyond credence as the Innsbruck students undoubtedly were about their work, they nevertheless found time for theatricals. On one notable occasion they staged an American minstrel show. Flanagan, in blackface, played Mr. Bones; one of the few times in history that Mr. Bones yodeled—and with an Irish brogue.

At Oberammergau, where he witnessed the Passion Play with a classmate named Frank Abts, later a distinguished physician of Cincinnati, he also met Anton Lang. Already Lang had achieved renown for his portrayal of the Christus. Flanagan, Abts, and other students had dinner with the actor at his home. On the wall was a large black wood crucifix. Flanagan bought it from Anton Lang; many years later we were to see it hanging in the chapel of the home he built for boys.

A great deal went forward or backward in the world during the three years that Edward Joseph Flanagan spent in the mountains studying for holy orders. For one thing, Andrew Carnegie, the steel master of Pittsburgh, made a gift of ten million dollars for world peace. In those innocent days ten millions was still an almost inconceivable sum of money and the simple-minded believed that with such wealth, anything, including peace, could be procured. The millionaire's foundation was regarded as an act of finality; there would be no wars; good will to the world had come at last, in the year 1910, four years before Sarajevo.

True, in that same year revolutionists dynamited a newspaper office in Los Angeles, killing twenty-one innocent men and women. True, also, in the next year war with modern weapons broke out between Turkey and Italy. And true, again, a man flew in the air all the way from New York to Pasadena in the first transcontinental flight, and army officers began to think what soldiers might do in a flying machine.

Only another year later there was greater war in the Balkans, with Turkey, Montenegro, Bulgaria, Serbia, and Greece involved. And only a few weeks before the greatest day in Flanagan's life the liner *Titanic,* on her maiden voyage, struck an iceberg and sank to the bottom.

The need for Christian charity and the love and fear of God had never been greater in the world than on that summer's day in the Alps when Flanagan lay face down before the altar and offered his life to the service of the Prince of Peace.

III

Even in his darkest hours he had never really doubted the day would come when he was to be anointed, the sacred oil poured on his hands, as he became a priest of Almighty God.

In the shadowy aisles of St. Ignatius Church at Innsbruck the ordination procession began on the morning of July 26, 1912.

He was a long way from home and family and friends. Others who lived closer by had their families to witness this uplifting moment. But crossing oceans and continents was no simple overnight matter then as it is now. The Flanagan clan were thousands of miles distant, back in Omaha, and not wealthy. For his ordination ceremony Flanagan was alone. Alone at the most solemn and holy moment of his life. In his full conviction, the Church was the Kingdom of Christ and he was now to be a part of its ordained priesthood, deriving its powers from Christ and communicating to him, from this day on, to be bestowed on the faithful within reach of his voice, the benefits of redemption.

To Flanagan the priesthood represented Christ and continued His mission. In this solemn hour he, Edward Joseph Flanagan, of Roscommon and Omaha, was being commissioned to forgive sin as Christ forgave sin and to sanctify men in His name. In Flanagan's creed it was Jesus Himself who had been first to confer the priesthood by laying His hands on His apostles. But that ceremony had not ended with the death of the apostles, no more than was the Church to come to an end with their death. Ever since, the priesthood had been continued by this very sacrament of holy orders. So Flanagan believed with all his might and strength and soul and mind.

First the procession: Bishop Elder, with golden miter and tall crozier, and the ten young candidates marching from the sacristy into the sanctuary. Like his nine companions, Flanagan was wearing the alb, maniple, and stole, and, like the others, he carried in his hands a chasuble, the vestment worn by every priest while celebrating Mass.

Then the bishop began the celebration, but after the reading of the Epistle he turned and looked young Flanagan straight in the eye. This was the time when the bishop—breaking the traditional paten of the sacrifice—must sit on a faldstool at the altar and ask questions about the worthiness of Edward Joseph Flanagan and these nine others, all of whom wanted to be made priests.

The notary reads the ten names aloud, while the young candidates range themselves before Bishop Elder in a wide half-moon. An ancient question concerning their worthiness is asked by the bishop, and the archdeacon, answering, and conceding the frailty of human nature, vouches for them as ready to undertake the burden of priesthood. His Excellency seizes upon the word, to address the watching clergy and people. Burden? Yes! Have the ten thought carefully upon that? Let no one underestimate the weight of the burden that is being assumed here.

Two by two the ten kneel before the bishop. Without a prayer he lays both hands on Flanagan's head and the heads of his companions. All the other priests near by come forward and do the same. The bishop and the priests raise their right hands while the prelate prays. Now each candidate's stole is rearranged upon his breast in the form of a cross by the bishop, and over the shoulder of each is laid the chasuble. It is time for the bishop to remove the miter from his head and to stand up, while all the others kneel. Having prayed, he kneels with them, all facing the altar, their voices joining the choir in the singing of "Veni, Creator Spiritus." During the solemn singing, with Flanagan's mighty baritone ringing out, Bishop Elder is seated once more. He draws on his episcopal ring, dons his gloves, and an apron and towel are placed in his lap; the candidates, one by one, approach nearer to him, while he dips his right thumb in the oil of catechumens. With the oily thumb he draws two lines in the form of the cross on the hands and finally anoints the whole of both palms of them all. Linen cloths are bound around their hands, while Bishop Elder, purifying his thumb of oil with a piece of bread, gives to Flanagan, and to them all, separately, a chalice, holding wine and water, and a paten on which lies the host—they are receiving power to celebrate the Mass.

And as the Ordination Mass continues, Flanagan comes to Bishop Elder with a lighted candle in his hand. So come all the others with their symbolic offering of fire and warmth and light. They repeat the Credo; they kneel again and with the bishop's hands again laid on their heads, they receive the Holy Ghost.

It was then, with his joined hands held between the viselike palms of Bishop Elder, that Flanagan made his promises of reverence and obedience and, with a kiss on the right cheek, knelt for benediction and the final blessing. That was when Father Flanagan felt the Holy Spirit entering into his body and mind and soul. At last Edward Joseph Flanagan of Leabeg and Omaha was a priest.

He was one, now, with the apostles in spiritual descent, nor could he ever be deprived of his heritage, because, like baptism, this ordination sacrament would imprint an indelible character upon his soul.

Next morning Father Flanagan said his first Mass. Then he began to pack. He was going home to Omaha, after three years of separation—going home, with his collar buttoned in the back.

CHAPTER NINE

In the Hinterland

"Father Flanagan! Father Flanagan!"

Voices he would have known anywhere: Nellie and another sister, Susie, who had made the trip from Omaha to be his welcoming committee at the dock.

They stayed with their cousins, the Larkins, to whom he owed much help, for a few days. At the church where the Larkins often went—St. Anne's on East Twelfth Street—Flanagan said his first Mass in America. Later he held his first benediction service at Grace Institute, located a few miles out of New York on the banks of the Hudson, where one of his cousins, Sister Celestine, was now a teacher. Then he and Nellie and Susie were on the train, bound for Omaha.

Father Edward, they called him, in the intimacy of the family, just as they called the older brother Father P. A. It was three years since he had seen them all—and this time it was a triumphant return to Omaha. No need for forced gaiety this time as they welcomed him. Still another great day for him was when, on his first Sunday home, he said Mass in the Holy Angels Church in North Omaha, where Father P. A. was pastor.

Naturally he and Father P. A. talked again about the future. Father Flanagan would, of course, become attached to the diocese of Omaha. But Father P. A. warned his brother to have patience, whatever the assignment might be. The bishop would certainly want him to gain practical experience as assistant to the pastor of some obscure parish church. A week after his arrival in Omaha, Father Flanagan was ordered to a town called O'Neill, two hundred miles northwest of Omaha.

II

His first parish, as curate, had a raucous and unruly history.

It had been founded in the middle of the last century by an Irish rebel and adventurer, one John O'Neill, as a settlement of a restless and excitable group who called themselves the "Irish Colonization Society."

In earlier days it had been a typically lawless frontier town, barrooms, gambling halls, and quick money. Justice was often a question of who managed to draw first. Brawls, thieving, and gunplay had been a major part of the social activities of the community.

But by the time Father Flanagan arrived, in 1912, the frontier town was vanished and O'Neill had long taken on the quiet respectability of a farming and cattle-raising area. Many eminent figures in Nebraska and national life came from O'Neill.

Pastor of St. Patrick's Church was Father Michael Cassidy, later Monsignor, a white-haired priest, devout and silent, who spent a large part of each day in prayer and meditation. At mealtimes, Father Flanagan often recalled, their conversations consisted mainly of a greeting and a few words about the state of the weather.

But although it was difficult to adjust to these silent meals, Father Flanagan appreciated his superior's spiritual concentration.

"I learned from him," Father Flanagan said, "the meaning of meditation in the life of a priest."

There was a great deal of work for the tall young curate among cattle raisers whose homes were scattered over the most undeveloped section of the state. Parish calls, sick calls, administering the Last Sacrament, straightening out family quarrels, kept the new curate on the go eighteen hours every day. Several mission chapels had been established in outlying regions, and it was the job of the assistant pastor to visit these missions to celebrate Mass. He would make his rounds in an open buggy, sometimes traveling thirty miles a day. In winter months the snows piled up two or three feet deep, but these trips still had to be made. Sometimes his legs and arms would be nearly frozen.

They were good people, the parishioners. Their spiritual needs were simple. A new baby must be baptized, a grandfather buried, a boy and girl married. They grew fond of the young assistant pastor who never failed to keep his rounds, whatever the weather. His arrival at one of the missions was a great occasion, particularly in the long blizzards when they were virtually cut off from the outside world. Yet he could not feel that this out-of-the-world loneliness of long drives was new or foreign to him. While there was nothing austere or withdrawn in Father Flanagan—above all things he loved his fellow man—yet there was in his nature an old need to be a recluse, if not a hermit. All his life he had known periods of silence and solitude; in the shepherd fields of Leabeg, in a hospital room, in the high mountains, and now in the wintry hinterland. Somehow he felt attuned to the snowy and desolate winter through which he had to drive.

When he was back at O'Neill he used what little spare time there was for study. It was natural that he should be thinking of the future, of ways of being of more service, even though he realized he was learning the first great lesson of priesthood: self-denial.

Father Cassidy sensed his desire for wider opportunities.

"Perhaps," the older priest said one day, after Flanagan had been there six months, "perhaps this is too lonely a spot for you."

"Not really, Father," the young priest protested quickly. "I've many friends here. And I have been learning——"

"It is the nature of youth to want more action," the older priest insisted calmly. "The time may have come for you to have wider scope. You have done your work well here. Perhaps now you will gain greater opportunity."

Father Flanagan did not know what was in the mind of the older priest. But a few days later orders were received from the Bishop of Omaha. He was being transferred to that city, to become assistant pastor at St. Patrick's Church.

He rode on the rattling train across the cornfields of Nebraska, heading back to Omaha—which means going upstream, going against the tide. It was as if Heaven kept drawing him back to this city, as if some special job awaited him there.

CHAPTER TEN

The Hotel for Lost Men

Heat and drought, searing the Middle West in the summer of 1913, burned up the wheat and corn. The havoc wrought by withering winds brought to the young curate of St. Patrick's a chance to help an army of lost men. And through that army, although he could not know it then, he was to find the start of his life's mission.

Father Flanagan had worked hard the whole blistering summer, in routine duties as assistant to the Rev. John T. Smith. It was Father Smith who years before, as pastor back in O'Neill, had captained the drive to wipe out vice and lawlessness in that frontier town which Flanagan had found too peaceful.

As Father Smith's assistant, Father Flanagan came nearer than ever to the sick and poor, the confused and afraid. Already there were many in want in the Omaha of that day. The city was a place of shifting population. As hundreds poured in each month, seeking jobs with the railroads, in the stockyards or the meat-packing plants, there was always a pool of the unemployed, many with families, in hungry need.

Watching out for such "floating families" became one of his self-imposed assignments; he found them food and jobs. Helping them was his "extra" task, similar to his visiting in the hospital wards, years before, in New York. This extra work was simple enough; the great burden came with the drought.

There were then in the Middle Western states thousands of itinerant harvesters. Tough, strong, hard-working men, they followed the crops, starting out usually in Kansas and working their way north, state by state, timing their movements to the harvests. They traveled in groups of forty or fifty. Their pay for harvesting the crops of

America's "breadbasket" was good. As a rule, by the time they reached Nebraska they had earned enough to see them through winter; during the cold months they usually idled in Omaha, waiting for spring.

But in that blighted summer of 1913, when the workers started out in Kansas, they found no crops to harvest. They kept moving north, as they had in past years, but everywhere it was the same bitter story. Only in isolated patches were there crops to be harvested; work for only a few.

By early autumn haggard refugees were drifting into Omaha. They came in small, disconsolate groups. Having had no work since the preceding year, they were penniless. Yet when they tried to get jobs in the city they learned that the poor harvests had also depressed business conditions; jobs were scarcer than ever.

Making the rounds of his parish, Father Flanagan saw these chapfallen men standing on the corners, faces full of hopelessness and fear. They had been workers, never beggars. Now they were asking, not for money, but for food and warm clothing.

From his tiny salary—it was twenty-five dollars a month—Father Flanagan could do little, but he was able, through the parish, to distribute some food. Soon, however, the number of jobless harvesters following him to the rectory so increased that he realized the parish was being drained. Some new plan of help had to be found.

Near the rectory was a small grocery shop, and the storekeeper was a friend of Father Flanagan. The two discussed the problem.

"We can't let men starve," the groceryman volunteered.

"At least," agreed Flanagan, "we should give them some coffee— and a little bones and meat for their mulligan stew."

The priest agreed to pay for part of the supplies from his salary; the storekeeper matched him and both promised to pester friends for help. They worked out a careful rationing program, by which, when a jobless man showed up at the rectory, he was given a "food order" which he could exchange at the grocer's for coffee, milk, canned meat, and vegetables.

Since the number of food orders they could hand out was limited, it was soon clear that they could not begin to meet the demands. Hungry men were clamoring at the rectory door. And meanwhile

Father Flanagan had learned that food was only part of the problem. Many were without shelter, too, sleeping on newspapers in empty lots, others in coal bunkers beside the freight yards. The city authorities seemed helpless to cope with the problems, and winter coming nearer every day.

One night at the rectory he discussed the situation with an Omaha businessman who had already helped him in a charitable collection drive for the St. Vincent de Paul Society. This friend asked: "Could I see for myself how these men live, Father?"

That autumn night the air was as cold and damp as a dog's nose as they headed for the yards and coal bunkers. Gradually they began to make out the figures of the men, a few standing, but most huddled on the ground or on old planks or in the coal piles, all using newspapers for blankets. There were scores of such men, every one willing to work, with a history of steady employment—but they were unable to find jobs and they were broke and no one was doing anything about it.

"Can't welfare people in the city help?" the businessman demanded.

"The city helps the women and children. But about the only real help these fellows get is from those food orders we've been giving out. And they don't go very far."

"Then what can we do?"

"We can pray and God will show us," answered Flanagan confidently.

All that long night, as he lay awake, he was turning over in his thoughts ways of arousing the public will to help. At last he saw the glimmering of an idea; a fantastic notion, he realized, for a simple priest, but he felt strangely impelled to try.

Father Flanagan was thinking about starting a hotel.

II

Naturally he went first to his pastor. What might Father Smith think of the idea of starting a free hotel? Father Smith shook his curate's hand and called upon the bishop. His Excellency pointed out that church funds were limited and the diocese was already carrying a heavy burden in the care of orphans, sick, and needy. They could not neglect these cases, nor could they stretch their funds to support new scores of unemployed men.

"But if you wish to go ahead anyway," Flanagan was told, "you have our blessing and every moral aid possible. Beyond that, you are on your own. Financial aid from us is out of the question."

Far from being discouraged, Flanagan walked out in warm elation. He had been given authority to go ahead! That was victory. All he had to do now was to find the money.

"I was," he admitted to us, "a very rash and enthusiastic young man. I'd never thought much about money before, you know. Now I was to find out it could be mighty important."

That night he called together some of his friends of the St. Vincent de Paul Society, all rash and enthusiastic young men like himself. And all were supporting families on small salaries; none could raise more than a few dollars.

Father Flanagan began to add up figures.

"I could count possibly on a total of five to ten dollars a month from you men," he said. "Probably I could raise a little more from members of my own family. Hardly enough to operate a hotel. Unless we could find some place for about nothing a month!"

"It would have to be a miracle, Father."

"Right!"

So, beginning the next morning, he walked the streets of Omaha.

Even in those days of blighted trade as well as farms, when buildings were for rent anywhere in the city, the prices were beyond what Flanagan could afford. The grocer was doubtful: "A fine idea, Father, but how can you rent a hotel when you have only a few dollars for capital?"

"Faith is a kind of capital too," Flanagan barked at his friend.

And, in fact, it was only a day or two later that he found what he had been seeking. It did not look very much like a miracle. It was an ancient, dilapidated, two-story brick building, at the corner of Eleventh and Mason streets. Once, in days of its glory, it had been known as the Burlington Hotel; the name was still painted, in fading white letters, on the red brick wall. But no one had lived in it for years; the glass windows were broken, the doors boarded up.

As he gazed upon the abandoned hotel, Father Flanagan's heart pounded with excitement. For him it was like the discovery of a rare gem. The worse the place appeared, the more likely were his chances of obtaining it for his purpose.

Through a real-estate agent he found the owner, who led Father Flanagan on a personal inspection tour of the interior. The condition inside was even worse than he had anticipated. As owner and prospect walked through cobwebs and dust, Father saw how the doors were forsaking their hinges and plaster falling from the walls. On the second floor he looked up through a gaping hole in the roof and beheld the lazy, fleecy clouds in the skies over Omaha.

"It does need a little fixing up," the owner admitted.

But the price the optimistic owner was asking was only a few dollars a month. Father Flanagan already had raised, and had in the pocket of his black trousers, enough to pay the first month's rent.

Even so, he was already a good enough businessman not to appear too anxious.

"I certainly wouldn't consider taking the place," he announced blandly, "unless you will fix up that hole in the roof. I couldn't bring in poor men out of the rain and snow—and put them where the snow and rain would pour in on them all over again."

The owner apologized about the hole. It had not been repaired only because the place had been unoccupied for so long. If Father Flanagan rented the place, the owner would have that hole patched up.

On this agreement the two shook hands. Young Father Flanagan had himself a hotel.

III

Excited at the achievement, friends in the St. Vincent de Paul Society raised a few more dollars for the general fund. They declared themselves ready to help in any way possible, but as all were holding down full-time jobs, the task of getting the hotel into operation fell squarely on Father Flanagan's shoulders. So once again he turned to an old reliable.

His sister Nellie came over to take a look at Father Edward's new venture.

"But it's falling apart, Father Edward," she demurred. "Are you going to let those men live in a place that is falling apart? And could it ever be fixed?"

"We're going to fix it all up," he told her. "Just don't ask me how, right now. But I have an idea!"

That night he returned to the freight yards and coal bunkers and stopped finally at a communal bonfire.

"I'm thinking of starting a hotel," he confided bluntly. "Not an ordinary hotel. A place for you men!"

They looked at him stonily.

"Don't you know we haven't money, Father?"

He described the Burlington Hotel. Wouldn't some of them help to fix it up? It would be a place of free shelter. By this time there were a hundred men crowding around him, shouting their willingness to pitch in:

"We've got men who can do anything you need, Father. Plumbers, carpenters, they've been everything——"

"But," cut in the priest, "the plaster's falling off some of the walls. *All* of the walls!"

They had a plasterer too. Also a fellow who had started out to be a cabinetmaker.

Close to winter now, there was no time to be lost. The next day the men met Father Flanagan at the "Hotel de Gink," as he already called it. It was undoubtedly one of history's oddest jobs of interior decoration, performed by a group of penniless but self-respecting men, grizzled crop pickers with half-forgotten skills out of the back yards of their past, working under the direction of a parish priest to turn a ramshackle building into a refuge.

Next step was the job of obtaining materials. Father Flanagan set out on a tour of stores and factories, telling the tale of what they were all doing and managing to beg, buy, and borrow such items as paint, brushes, plaster.

Carpenters also had a job to do reconstructing furniture; from junkyards and refuse piles they hauled treasure-trove, and as word of the hotel project began to spread in the city, lumberyards sent them gifts of boards and planks.

Out of odd pieces and spare lengths the crop-picker carpenters began to refashion tables and chairs and beds and even lamps and desks, in their improvised workshop opened on the first floor. Not that their packing-case pieces were triumphs of artistry, but they were built strong enough to take punishment.

Within ten days the Burlington's walls and ceilings had been re-plastered, floors and trim repainted and revarnished, and furnishings spread about. The hotel for the harvesters was a reality.

Meanwhile Father Flanagan had been begging for food, calling successfully on grocers, dairymen, and bakeries. One grocer promised cans of beans regularly; the next offered a weekly bushel of potatoes. Bakeries delivered unsold loaves; so with the dairymen and their un-sold milk. Small sums of cash, too, came in from friends and relatives, while Omaha housewives began to send in clothes, bedding, blankets, and even idle beds ferreted out of attic jumbles.

In its rebirth in emergency, the long-silent, broken-down Burlington Hotel had now become a scene of bustle and excitement. The night the doors were opened Father Flanagan computed their expenses thus far. The total was just a few cents under one hundred and fifty dollars! Those costs had all been fully covered already by gifts from friends. There were even a few dollars left over, after paying all the bills, to apply to the second month's rent.

The hotel for lost men was in business!

CHAPTER ELEVEN

Behind the Front Desk

Yet there was no immediate scramble for accommodations. They came in but slowly, even suspiciously, those crop pickers from the coal bunks and the freight yards. The first night there was only the original group of volunteer workmen plus a few more who straggled in, cold and hungry but still not quite sure they cared to accept priestly hospitality.

Father Flanagan was in the lobby, first on one foot, then on the other, to welcome them in and show them to springless beds, stale bread, and milk; the kitchen was not yet in operation. Meager enough, what he could offer—but warm, roofed, and with kindliness around—better far than the coal bunkers!

They kept on coming the next day, showing up in blear-eyed groups of three or four. They would stand outside the hotel a few minutes, peering in uncertainly until they spotted someone they knew and then they would enter.

In the first week fifty-seven "guests" were registered. Soon, as more beds were built or donated, the figure rose to more than a hundred. All had to share in the chores of this new kind of inn, and did so congenially.

It was natural for Flanagan to remember Leabeg, to recall the big family with its chores as well as its abundance; each lad knowing what was his task, each with a part to play in keeping the household operating smoothly. Only here now in Omaha the chores were performed by crop pickers, many of whom were already white-haired.

Each man had to do some of the sweeping or dusting, bedmaking or window-washing. There had to be cooks and dishwashers and cleaning men, and others to prepare menus, do the marketing, or cajole food donations. Several acted as "interviewers" of new men applying for admittance.

Of course there were some troublemakers. Only a few days after the opening Father Flanagan was crossing the lobby when he heard a commotion on the second floor and ran up to find one of the harvesters pummeling another with a wet mop, while five or six onlookers were trying to climb into the combat. But a yell of outrage from the priest brought silence and repose.

"Well, now—what is it about?"

"Well, now, Father——"

The man with the wet mop had been wiping up the room and had been wearing at the same time a reasonably white handkerchief around his head. The other had come and started shouting: "Look at the old lady mopping!"

The "old lady" had forthwith lifted the mop and aimed at his tormentor's skull. Now, as they crowded around Flanagan, attacker, attacked, and smug onlookers, he demanded to know if they had forgotten where they were living now.

"This is no place for brawling. Would you fight like this in your mother's home?"

"Sure!"

"Well, not here!"

In general, things ran smoothly. Meanwhile Flanagan suggested that they set up a tailor shop where some old garments, sent in, could be repaired. The sewing was done by a "guest" who, before joining the crop pickers, had been a tailor. Promised a small salary by Father Flanagan, he opened up shop on the ground floor, with a new sign done in school crayons: "Have your clothes restyled at Joe's!"

II

One morning Father Flanagan beheld three Omaha matrons coming through the front door; they were from rich families and they wanted to help. That was the start of the hotel's "Ladies' Aid," in which social leaders of all faiths were to take part. They helped not only in getting donations but in brightening up the rooms, working in the kitchen and doing the marketing. Father Flanagan was delighted; he was still carrying on his regular parish duties, and the hotel was merely an "outside activity" for extra hours.

Before long several of the men—the day and night clerks in the front office, among others—were put to work on a full-time basis and paid for their services. On the ground floor an "employment agency" was also operated by one of the harvesters behind an improvised packing-box desk. This agency quickly became an Omaha community effort; people all over town were on the lookout for jobs and reporting them to the Burlington.

As long as the guests were without funds they could stay at the hotel for nothing, and when they had earned some money, and could pay for board and lodging, the rates at the Flanagan hotel were ten cents a night for a bed and five cents a meal.

"Permanent guests" numbered about seventy-five. There were always transients, too; frequently the Burlington housed more than one hundred men a night, so crowded that some had to sleep on cots in the lobby. But it was a matter of pride with Father Flanagan that not one was ever turned away.

In the evenings Father Flanagan would sit with the men in the lobby and discuss world and national problems with them as if they were all elder statesmen. It was thus that Father Flanagan became involved in the story of a grim-faced man they called Chuck.

III

Chuck was a lanky young man, with thin face and intense, piercing eyes. He would drape his gawky frame over one of the chairs and listen silently. When, rarely, he would speak, it was to throw out some bitter comment.

The young priest began to ask the others about Chuck. Their answer was a shrug. "He's sour on the world," they told him. "Anything you say, he is sure to be against it, even if it's good."

One evening Father Flanagan contrived to get Chuck off to himself, but when he began asking personal questions, Chuck whirled on him angrily.

"What do you want to know about me for?" he demanded. "What do you care about me? The church don't care about people like me, only for what we can give them. They're just like all rich people. All they think about is money."

Something frightening gleamed in his eyes. Society, Chuck had decided, was his mortal enemy; he had feelings of being persecuted. So he had become a political radical: down with the government, down with religion, "down with everything except me and men like me."

Father Flanagan demanded: "But if all we think about is money, why do you suppose I'm running this hotel? You can hardly imagine I make any profit here now?"

Chuck pondered a moment.

"The church ain't running this place," he said finally. "You're running it, and I ain't saying anything against you personally. It's the system——"

"But I'm part of the church—part of the system," the priest persisted. "And you must admit that some of those rich people you talk against are helping us out right here with food *and* money. Without that help I doubt if we could keep on."

At some cost in self-mastery Father Flanagan steadily refused to grow wroth at the man's venom, being curious to discover the reasons behind it. What special injustice did this man believe he had suffered at the hands of society, so that he set himself apart from the others?

Chuck had once been a member of a church, but he had long since given that up: "It's a lot of kneeling and praying—and for what? Do you think He ever listens to you? Maybe you do, but I've never seen any evidence myself."

Gradually more of the man's background came out. He was married and had a young child in another city not many miles distant.

"I had to leave them there," Chuck said. "I didn't have any money and couldn't get work. Then I wind up here—broke—with these crop pickers."

"And that's what you want most in life—a job and money?"

"I want to be with my wife and baby."

"If I could find you a job, would you take it?"

"Just offer me one!"

So it was as simple as that. Once again the young priest went job-hunting personally, and found one in a packing plant in South Omaha. That was the beginning of the road back for the radical. A metamorphosis began almost with his first day of work, a slow changing. Soon he had a flat of his own, wife and baby installed there with him. Together they returned to the Protestant church he had derided so bitterly. He became a solvent and devout man.

"And what was the significance of an ordinary incident like that of Chuck?" Father Flanagan one night demanded of us. "It was that he wanted love. He knew what love was. He had given it and had received it. He was still capable of it. But he had lost it—and no one around him seemed to understand that. It was not enough to give Chuck his wife and baby back again, nor to feed them all. You had to love him and them while you were doing it. Otherwise he was also capable of blowing up the City Hall! Paranoia is easily induced in a man if you treat him like a cipher—a unit of humanity, a machine entity. But love brings grace abounding and can change the characters of men, transforming them from evil to good. It's very simple and hard to understand in this overcomplicated world! Love may seem but a sentimental weapon but in the end it will prevail over every ism."

By winter's end the hotel had become a smooth-running organization. The jobless harvesters had learned their housekeeping duties so well that members of the "Ladies' Aid" began complaining that there was nothing left for them to do.

But as spring approached, the men wanted to go back to their own work. Another summer, and, please God, another harvest. By June most of them had gone; the reborn Burlington Hotel again was a hushed and deserted place. For Flanagan it was a breathing spell, a chance to add up totals. Financially, they had been successful. Support of Omaha citizens had enabled them to operate on a pay-as-you-go basis. They even wound up with a small surplus. Meanwhile they had given food and shelter to hungry and homeless men. They could have helped many more if space and facilities had not been limited. Father Flanagan was convinced now of the need for a permanent center, offering shelter not just to harvesters but to any man. This expanded concept would require greater space.

He decided he would have to find himself a new—and much larger—hotel.

IV

The new hotel he found had been known as Livesy Flats. It was a red-bricked, four-story building with a basement, a rambling place, roomy enough for hundreds.

Rent was low, and the building, located on Thirteenth Street in downtown Omaha, was in far better condition than their first hotel had been. Repairs were made by the few men who had stayed on at the Burlington. They pitched in and within a few weeks had the new Workingmen's Hotel, as it was to be called, ready for their "winter clientele."

This year crops had been good and returning men were not in distress, but many hunted out the new hotel because they wanted to stay "with the Father." But, beholding the improvements, some of the old-timers became worried.

"When word gets around," they warned him, "you'll be overrun with all sorts. Not workers like us. The dregs'll be coming in. Tramps! Drunks! Dopeys! You'll be running into trouble."

Father Flanagan sighed. Maybe he should welcome the tramps and the drunks and the dopeys! Anyway, he wanted advice. How would they suggest he handle these "dregs," as they called them. There were immediate suggestions. Pack a gun! And a billy! Hire guards! The men seemed most concerned for Flanagan's safety. All insisted that the worst types should be segregated in a separate part of the hotel.

"It all sounds sensible, you know," Father told them. "What would you say to fixing up the basement as a sort of dormitory where we put the troublemakers?"

The men agreed: "Put them out of harm's way. Down in the lower regions."

From then on the hotel's basement dormitory was always known as the "Lower Regions." Here, as predicted, during the winter months of 1914 the leftovers of humanity, drunks and dope fiends, thieves and murderers, came to find food and shelter, and a bed on which to rest, in Father Flanagan's hotel. Many were errant law-breakers, notoriously bad citizens, gangsters and bullies. The priest's cheap lodginghouse for vagrants was more generous than the doss houses they had known, where men sprawled in squalor and listened to each other groan and curse; better because it was cleaner and gentler and run for compassion rather than cash. The devils that often occupy the hearts of such derelicts were scornful of the holy challenge of charity.

"Go ahead, Flanagan!" they seemed to say. "Cast us out if you can. Exorcise us! We stay with these hopeless creatures and alienate them from God. What can you do about us, Father Flanagan?"

CHAPTER TWELVE

A Priest Among the Dregs

Not much, as he would soon learn to his sorrow. It was a procession of the furtive and the obstinate. To Father Flanagan's Workingmen's Hotel—soon known as a welfare center for the whole city—came men from every back alley of life. They fitted no common pattern. Some were merely down on their luck. Others were professional tramps like grizzled old Harry who hid the whisky bottle in his brown derby and lived to tell the tale to runaway Stubby in the boxcar. A few had the mark of crime in their penitentiary walk and eyes—hunted men, "on the lam," "taking a powder."

No questions were asked. The men could tell as little or as much as they wanted about themselves. If they had money, they paid the small tariff. Otherwise bed and meals were "on the house."

By mid-October they were housing and feeding nearly five hundred every night.

There was plenty of difficulty, but Father Flanagan quickly acquired a sixth sense about troublemakers, and these were promptly assigned space in the "Lower Regions."

Special precautions had to be taken with the basement gentry, because of the ever-present danger of a flare-up of violence. All who slept in the cellar quarters must be in bed by ten.

"We never knew," Father told us, "when some one of those poor men might go berserk. Many of them had followed atrociously evil ways."

One night Father was alone behind the desk in the lobby. A man about thirty years old came through the door. His clothes were frayed but looked as if once they had been part of an expensive wardrobe. With great dignity, the stranger asked if he might stay the night.

"I regret," he added, betraying a European accent, "that I have no money to pay."

"I will show you where you sleep." The priest smiled. "You understand we don't have private rooms."

They had been operating for many months now and had seen every kind of man. But this new addition to their lists was most mysterious. He seemed completely co-operative, but about himself or his background he revealed not a word.

Everyone liked the mysterious stranger. He was intelligent and witty and soon proved himself a skilled mechanic and a hard worker. But because he was so tight-lipped he was also the center of rumors in this lost man's hotel where any story *might* be true.

In spite of gossip, the unknown so won Father Flanagan's confidence that the priest offered him the job of night clerk. His only worry was that so young a man might not be seasoned enough to handle late drunks and ruffians, whom he would have to deal with alone. But the gentle-appearing mystery man proved equal to any kind of trouble. If some drunk started a fracas, he put a stop to it as if by incantation. Drunks spoiling for fights were handled as if they were children: coaxed or slapped down, with equal facility.

One night, when they were alone together, the clerk said: "I suppose, Father, you've wondered about me. Well, don't let it prejudice you against me, but I am of noble blood; I am a Hungarian count!"

II

The Count told his story simply. He who mingled so agreeably with the tattered spirits clustering around him here had been born on a large estate and had grown up with every advantage of wealth and education. He had come to America to complete his studies.

"Then—trouble started in Europe. I don't know what happened to any of my people. Only, I couldn't reach them. My money was running out. As a foreigner, I had trouble getting work. Besides, I had no experience whatever in business or practical affairs."

When his cash was used up, the Count had taken to the road. He had paid his way by doing odd jobs at farmhouses; had soon learned how to ride freights and to mingle with criminals and confidence men, who pleaded with him to join with them in flimflam schemes. In a town some miles from Omaha he had heard about the hotel of Father Flanagan and had promptly tramped his way here.

Having told the story to Father Flanagan, the night clerk was able to tell it over again, next day, to the day clerk. Soon the tale of the noble night man spread among the down-and-outers, who heard it with zealous glee. They were being served by the nobility. And the nobility could fall just as low as they. Hooray for the Count of Goulash! That "moniker" stuck to the nameless wanderer and was celebrated among thousands of drifters throughout the Midwest. But it was less a spoof and more a mark of affection; the "Count," whether phony or real, had inbred courtesy, gentleness, and a friendly instinct for his fellow man. For the rest of his life Father Flanagan held him in gratitude.

And indeed, on several occasions the Count saved the priest from bodily harm, and perhaps even from death.

Danger was constant in their lives because they were dealing not only with unfortunate men but also with the riffraff of mendicant outlaws. Sometimes a man who seemed most peaceful would start a rumpus in the twinkling of an eye. One night Father Flanagan was standing near the door when a hulking man staggered toward him. With huge hands he grabbed the priest, lifted him up bodily, and hurled him halfway across the lobby. At lightning speed, then, the drunk followed after his fallen victim. But even more quickly the Count leaped over the counter and threw himself upon the attacker.

It was over in a few minutes. Aided by others in the lobby, the Count subdued the giant and lugged him to the Lower Regions, where he fell instantly into sodden sleep. The next morning he remembered nothing of his murderous onslaught.

Harry, the boxcar counselor of runaway Stubby, held a resentment against Father Flanagan for taking away his liquor. He did not know—as Father and the Count knew full well—that liquor seeping into the Lower Regions was like gasoline leaking into a furnace. It could touch off disaster.

Some were psychopathological cases, men who resented Father

Flanagan and held him responsible for all their troubles. The hatred of these bitter, sick-minded men often ran deep. Frequently the Count warned Father Flanagan that he was too careless, walked too freely among such men at all hours. At first the priest discounted these fears.

He had no suspicions, certainly, on the night he received a telephone call asking him to hasten to an address on the other side of town, where a woman lay close to death. Neither of the priests of her own parish were at the rectory and the time was desperately short; a dying woman was crying for extreme unction, the last sacrament of her faith. Father Flanagan promised the unknown caller he would come at once.

The Count had been listening grimly. He knew the neighborhood to which the priest was called, one of the toughest in the city.

"Maybe you had better let me come along with you, just for protection?" the Count suggested.

"But it is a sick call," Father Flanagan protested. "I'm just a poor priest. Who would be likely to do me harm?"

Nevertheless he gave in finally to the urgent entreaties of the Count. The house at which they arrived proved to be a dingy building, apparently a rooming house. At a desk in the lower hallway a wizened little man sat with registry book and a tray of keys. He informed Father Flanagan that the sick woman was on the third floor and that he would have to go up without his friend.

The priest turned toward the Count, only to see the latter already halfway up the stairs. Flushed and infuriated, the clerk pounded the desk and screeched for him to come back.

The rule that the priest should go up alone to see the sick woman was not unusual. But the apoplectic anger of the little man, in what should have been, to him, a matter of routine, was suspicious. Father Flanagan started up the stairs after the Count, who by now was lost in the upper shadows. But as the priest neared the first landing the Count reappeared.

"Go back, Father!" the Hungarian cried out. "This is a plot against you!"

"But I don't understand. How can they hope——"

"This isn't any rooming house, Father. All the rooms are empty except one. In that room—I saw their faces—are men who used to be at our hotel. It's a trap! They plan to frame you, to disgrace you, blackmail——"

The frame-up, conceived by men who, for their own imagined grievances, bore grudges against Father Flanagan, had been carefully planned. He might easily have found himself in what could have appeared to be a highly equivocal situation had it not been for the quick action and warning of his friend.

The great number of men who stayed at his hotel—and there were times when they were packed in like sardines, now over a thousand a night—admired him. In the evenings, just as at the Burlington, they would sit in the lobby and talk. One fact about them all stood out: religion was missing from their lives. While most of them professed some vague belief in God, when questioned, none of them went to their church or gave any thought to questions of faith.

They were willing to help him in running the hotel, to pay when they had funds. But when he mentioned religion or God, they shied away.

"We're too old for that, Father," they would say. "It's too late for us."

There were a few exceptions, men who at his urging went back to their churches. But in most instances the men would just smile.

"I've done too many things wrong, Father," one of them explained to him. "I couldn't change my habits, anyway. Not after all these years."

But they did not lack courage. As the war in Europe continued, scores of mendicants and beggars who came to the hotel volunteered for services with the British or French. Many of these down-and-outers proved themselves heroes in combat. Some died in battle.

Their war record was only additional proof of what Flanagan had seen in their day-to-day lives. There was good in them, often latent and unsuspected, hidden by the hard shell they had built around themselves. They could respond to the call of battle—but not to the altar. Why? As for reaching them with the regenerative word of God, he had found that what they said was true—they felt it was too late.

Occasionally a half-grown boy would show up, and such young-sters always presented a special problem; Father Flanagan shud-dered at the harm that could be done to them by mere association with some of the older men. That was why, on the top floor, away from the other dormitories, he set aside a few special rooms where young guests could stay.

It is a literal fact that Boys Town had its genesis in those upper rooms.

III

One evening a youth strolled into the lobby. He looked no more than fifteen years old, but wore his hat pushed back on his head, his cigarette at a corner dangle, and in his swagger it was obvious he was playing the role of a "tough" who knew all the answers.

"Hear you got a place where you put guys up," he began affably. "If you got a room left, I'd just as soon stay a couple of days."

But he gasped at the priest's reply: "Come along—dear!"

Father Flanagan and the boy ate together that night at a table off by themselves. The boy stiffly refused to tell his name or his home town.

"That's my business, ain't it?" he said. "I don't have to tell any-body my name unless I feel like it."

Father let him talk on, but he listened intently to small clues, regional references, local idiom, until at last he began to feel sure he had placed him. Casually he mentioned a town in western Nebraska. Caught off guard, the youth said: "Sure, I know that place. It's only a few miles from where——"

He stopped, realizing he had almost disclosed his secret. There was an embarrassed hiatus in the conversation. Father Flanagan pretended not to notice, but after the boy had gone to bed the priest sent a wire to the chief of police of the town he had mentioned, giving a description and asking if they were looking for any run-away boy who looked like that.

In the morning the Count called the rectory. The answer had come. The boy had run away from his home; his widowed mother was half crazy with fear, the police reported. Would he return the boy?

The Count also had further news to relate: the boy was gone!

Ah, Plato, how right you were when you said that, of all wild things, a boy is the most difficult to manage!

Apparently, during the night, the nameless young loafer had grown suspicious. Perhaps he had reflected upon the slip he had made in talking at dinner and decided the priest was more clever than he had realized. At any rate, before the others were awake he had sneaked off.

Father Flanagan felt sure he had not had time yet to leave town. And, being still a boy, he would want something to eat before he started out. The place to look first was in the Omaha restaurants. On this quest Flanagan started out alone. Up and down the main streets of the city he searched, peering into every open hash house. At last, in a one-arm lunchroom, he saw the boy seated alone. The police chief's wire had given the boy's name, so Father Flanagan suddenly loomed beside him:

"Hello, Bob."

Bob looked up. His lips twisted and he turned pale. "What are you trying to do—put me in jail or something, now that you've found me?"

"I not only found you, Bob. I've found out all about you."

"And you're going to make sure I suffer for my sins!"

"No. Not I. You suffer *in* your sins—has no one ever told you that simple fact? Just as you are rewarded *in* doing good. But I do know what your sins are doing to your mother. It's a terrible thing, Bobby, to make her suffer for your sins, to worry her until she's half sick with fear——"

But Bob shook his head fiercely as the priest sat beside him.

"She wouldn't ever be worried over me. She doesn't care that much. She just works——"

"Works, Bobby? And what for? Isn't it to take care of you, because you haven't any father?"

The boy's manner softened a little.

"Well, maybe she does work to take care of us both, sure. But she's never home. I don't get to see her hardly at all. What difference does it make what I do? And this way she won't have to take care of me."

Such was his logic, and, of course, his bitterness. Flanagan found it easy enough to piece the simple picture together.

Without question, he told himself, this lad needed love and direction. He had not been objective enough to appreciate how much his mother was already doing for him. All he knew was that he was miserably lonesome; he felt rejected, unwanted, a burden. Running away was his idea of a grown-up and courageous solution.

Father Flanagan earnestly began to talk about what his running away had meant to his mother. To some degree, at least, he could see his words were reaching home. Here was no hard, unbreakable shell, such as the men he dealt with had built around themselves. The shallow arrogance of the boy began to vanish as the priest talked.

"I caused Mom sorrow?" Bob demanded at last, close to tears. "But wasn't it better to do that, anyhow—I was only trying to help her——"

"To help—by breaking her heart? No, Bobby. You're old enough to undertake *your* part in helping her. And you didn't do that, you know. You ran away from your own responsibilities. Yet you don't look like a coward, Bobby—dear!"

There was no need for a policeman to take Bobby home. Father Flanagan put him on the train that night. Several years later he received a letter. Bob had gone to high school. He and his mother were living happily in their new home. In another week he would be graduating and getting a job. And he was writing to thank Father Flanagan for sending him back home before it was too late.

In the lobby at his hotel Father sometimes would watch the men when a boy came in, seeking shelter. Always they would follow the youth with intent, searching eyes. And always the expression was the same—a mingling of pity and fear.

"Father," one would say, "look at that boy. I used to look like that, forty years back. That kid could almost be me!"

CHAPTER THIRTEEN

A Priest and a Little Boy

It was as if, in the stray youths, the weary old guests recaptured a symbol of the chance they had missed to make their own lives worth while; a lost opportunity. Already Father Flanagan knew in detail the histories of many of his guests; long evenings by the stove in the lobby he had listened to autobiography in mass production. After the narrators had trudged off to their bunks, he had made notes. Now he sat down to make an odd kind of tabulation, a survey of this background information, to find, if he could, in the accounts of how bums became bums, any common dominant factor.

There were a myriad complications, yet, strikingly, in story after story, the starting point was often the same—the disruption of a home.

"Everything was fine," a story would go. "Only my pop drank, see? When he got drunk he was mean. Guess it was a good enough home, but I was too young to appreciate it. Me and another kid took off. I got caught and put in a state reform school as a runaway. When I got out . . ."

Another would tell how, after his father died, he and his mother tried to carry on. But the task had been too much for her strength, with a big family to support: "I lived with a couple of aunts of mine for a while but I didn't get on with 'em. So one day I lit out . . ."

Again and again, as he reviewed the cases of these broken-down old tramps, Flanagan traced the theme of the broken home. Clearly to be perceived in his brief jottings is:

"John S. ———. Ex-convict. Mother ran off with sailor. Father couldn't support him properly. Arrested for thefts from fifteen years on."

"Richard J. ——. Orphaned at ten, lived with uncle on farm. Didn't get along and was sent to orphan's home. Ran away."

"Henry H. ——. Parents poor. Both drank a lot. Left to his own devices most of time. Father deserted home. Ran away when sixteen."

While details varied, essentials remained. The great majority of these hapless men had started out as boys crawling away from homes that had been unstable or broken, homes where religion and God had no place, homes lacking in love.

II

One night Father Flanagan was alone in the lobby when there came walking toward him from the big front door a small boy about nine years old.

His face was smeared with grease and dust; red sweater torn; no coat, no hat; the child was visibly shivering.

"Are you the man in the black suit?" the boy asked.

"Well—I'm one of them, I guess," Flanagan admitted.

"I've got to talk to the man in the black suit!"

"And what do you want to ask me—dear?"

"Can I stay here?"

How often he was to hear that same plea in later years. The priest knelt down beside the child.

"Why do you want to stay in this place?"

"Don't you take in people for nothing?"

"Yes—but not boys. A boy like you must have a home."

"No, sir," the boy insisted. "I ain't got any."

His name was Paul. His mother had been caring for him until a few weeks before, when she died. Since then he had been staying here and there; for the last few nights he had been sleeping out of doors, and for twenty-four hours he had had nothing to eat.

"Well," the priest said, "we'll have to wash our faces and get ourselves clean now, won't we? Before we have something to eat, I mean."

After Paul had scrubbed up, they went into the dining room, where late workers extemporized a banquet. When Paul declared he was "full up," he was taken upstairs to bed. In the darkness the boy said good night: "Father, the bed is warm, and I like the eats swell."

Greatly disturbed, Father Flanagan considered the problem of Paul. What did one do? Paul's plight sooner or later would have come to the welfare authorities. Action would have been taken. Paul would have gone to a state asylum. In this case Father Flanagan was able to place the boy with a childless couple.

But in checking on Paul's story the priest discovered that the boy had not a single living relative within hundreds of miles. The tragedy was that the case was no isolated instance; there were many others like it, in every town. And the child was not always an actual orphan. The boy whose parents, through lack of interest and love, left him to shift for himself on the streets was orphaned too.

Daily, in the papers, Father Flanagan was reading lurid stories of boys being "picked up" by police for delinquencies of all kinds; "young thugs" being shipped off to reform school. He remembered samples of predelinquent youth on the streets of New York, knowing now that the situation was little different even in small farming centers of the Middle West. Already he had seen rural slums from which came some of the most murderous of gangsters.

Slowly, in the days which followed the encounter with their nine-year-old guest, a new idea was beginning to take firm hold in his thoughts.

For more than three years he had been working with lost men. His hope had been to help them rehabilitate themselves, but, excepting for only a handful, he had failed. He had been no more than an innkeeper, providing food and shelter; that was all the vagrants had asked, or would take. They simply no longer cared. They said it was too late.

But it was not too late for the boys, not if someone were willing to take trouble about them and for them. He had been working on the wrong side of the ledger, where the entries were already filled in and the sums almost ready to be added up. Reconstruction of a man—salvaging of a soul—was like any other repair job on earth. It had to begin on time, before decay had eaten too deep, before the clay had hardened into some unrevisable shape.

It had to begin when the man was still a boy.

CHAPTER FOURTEEN

A Priest in Court

In the back row of juvenile court in Omaha Father Flanagan watched in silence as a parade of prisoners filed in for trial.

Occasionally he had visited courtrooms, to study procedure and methods, but never before had he seen a procession of culprits to equal this.

These "criminals" were all children.

Police and guards brought them in. They sat in the prisoner's box awaiting their turn. One by one they were brought out to stand before the robed judge as the facts at issue were unfolded in legal terminology. On completion of the presenting of evidence, the glum-faced judge would hand down his verdict.

Among those in the parade of young criminals was a boy named Johnny. He was twelve years old. He had red hair and freckles and his lips twisted in a self-conscious grin as he stood before the bench.

Up to the stand, to testify against the boy, stepped a store detective. One of his duties, he explained, was to keep a close lookout for shoplifters. On the morning of the crime he had been making his rounds on the first floor when he had noticed this defendant walking up the center aisle. Something furtive in the behavior of the prisoner instantly attracted his attention.

Keeping back out of sight, he had followed the accused, had watched him stop at a counter where sweaters were on sale. Glancing around to make sure no one was looking, the boy had slipped two sweaters under his overcoat and then hurried on, mingling with the crowds of shoppers.

The detective then described how he had followed this same defendant to the back of the store, where baseball bats and gloves were on display in the sporting-goods department. The boy had picked up one of the gloves, slipped that also under his coat, and hurried toward the door.

It was outside the store that the detective had collared the culprit and placed him under arrest.

Listening to the detective's description of the case, one might almost have imagined he was talking about some major public enemy rather than a child.

Moreover, it appeared that Johnny had been in trouble before. He had a long list of delinquencies to his discredit, although thus far he had always gotten off without any serious punishment.

There must be no leniency this time, the assistant district attorney pleaded. The accused did not deny the crime. The evidence had been found on his person. The sentence should be as severe as the court could impose.

The prosecutor, of course, was only doing his job. Yet, to the listening priest, his words sounded as if he were demanding the extreme penalty for some hardened criminal. How was the judge taking it? He knew of some of the judges of this court. They were good men, but they could act only under the limitations of the laws and of the physical facilities available in the state.

In this instance the judge declared he had no course open to him except to send Johnny to reform school for an indefinite term.

The self-conscious grin was gone from Johnny's face as he heard the sentence and he was led out. Another boy was brought in and another detective took the stand to testify.

To Father Flanagan the most incredible fact was the way in which the delinquents were tried, as if they were adult offenders. Elsewhere, he knew, different, more understanding methods were being tried. Yet he was skeptical, even of these modern experiments.

In fact, a remarkable prescience on the whole subject of juvenile delinquency was displayed by Father Flanagan in the year before we entered the war. He had made many inquiries by mail and was aware of various struggling projects to deal with the problem, from Junior Republics and Boys' Brigades to the juvenile-court work of Judge Ben Lindsey, then of Denver. New paths were being hacked out by sincere idealists like Floyd Starr, who was getting ready to establish his Commonwealth for Boys at Albion, Michigan.

In those early days he started, and for all the rest of his life Father Flanagan continued to keep himself abreast of modern inquiry into the field of children and their relation to crime.

At many a later confab with psychologists and criminologists of all degrees and variations he held his own. He was at the opposite pole from many of these advocates of the theory of determinism in the psychological sphere; the hypothesis of cause and effect in the realm of psychology. Pundits would seek to instruct him about mental mechanisms, the diseases of the nervous system, the theories of William A. White on the genesis of emotions, especially love, hate, and guilt—and he would reply that none of those things mattered, of themselves. When they tried to amaze him by their penological radicalism, he would assure them there was nothing new about unlocked doors and open gates; they should have a look at Boys Town. On the other hand, he would add, something more than open doors is needed: more, even, than an open mind. There must also be the open heart. The scientists shied away from such metaphysics.

He was, of course, a student of J. L. Gillin's *Criminology and Penology* and the great work on the same subject by F. E. Haynes. With respect and hope he followed the laboratory work of Dr. Arnold Gesell, director of the Clinic of Child Development, School of Medicine, Yale University, and his associate, Dr. Frances Ilg; also, later, the attempts of Ernest Ligon at Union College to blend modern psychological diagnosis with the remedial counsels of the Sermon on the Mount.

He had studied the case histories of delinquent boys who became cashier killers and auto bandits, all as reported in the work of Healy and Bronner: *Delinquents and Criminals, Their Making and Unmaking*. And he studied Clifford R. Shaw's true scientific account of the career of *The Jack Roller* and his *The Natural History of a Delinquent Career*. He knew the theories of the new criminology, as expounded by Dr. Max S. Schlapp, professor of neuropathology at New York Post Graduate Medical School and Director of the New York Children's Court Clinic, and having studied his work, Father utterly rejected the glorification of chemical causation of abnormal behavior in which all the crime and sorrow of the world became one vast glandular disturbance.

Father Flanagan had also informed himself in detail on the deliberations of the National Conference of Criminal Law and Criminology, held at Northwestern University, Chicago, in June 1909, when the American Institute of Criminal Law and Criminology was organized. A part of its work was to arrange for the translation of important treatises from foreign languages into English, and Father had kept track of those translations; he studied with particular alertness *The Individualization of Punishment* by Raymond Saleilles, of the University of Paris, and *Crime and Its Repression* by Gustav Aschafenburg, professor of psychiatry in the Cologne Academy of Practical Medicine. All represented, he knew, serious efforts to come to grips with the problem, but none seemed to grasp the possibility that God could serve any useful function in the process.

Unquestionably Father felt nearest to the noted priest-sociologist, Father Eligius Weir, chaplain of the Illinois State Prison, whose book, *Criminology,* was published by the Institute for the Scientific Study of Crime. To this notable work Father contributed an introduction; the volume was dedicated to the "parents and educators of American Youth."

Both Father Flanagan and Father Weir were steeped in personal experience with crime and degradation. In defiance of scholars and scientists, they agreed that the first basic cause of crime was lack of religious instruction. They were at one, as well, on contributing causes: lack of wholesome home and proper parental guidance; lack of scholastic training, physical and mental disease and handicaps, the exaltation of crime in popular media of expression, the influence of organized criminals and racketeers, and the unjust distribution of wealth in the world.

"I preach and teach," said Father Flanagan, "that kindness, love, and religion remove incentive for crime. Father Weir's experience bears out that theory."

Bright new theories were in the air, but Father Flanagan could see clearly the innate defect in many of them.

"I know," he said, "what happens to youth if God is not a part of daily life."

His fears were to be justified, for the offenses of the young kept on rising until, in the year of his death, boys and girls accounted for 16.1 per cent of all arrests in the United States. Before he died he was to know a time when every eighty-eight seconds four major crimes were happening somewhere in the United States: bank robbery, burglary, armed holdup, murder. Every twenty-two seconds, minute in and minute out, all the twenty-four hours of all the three hundred and sixty-five days, a major crime is still being committed in this land of freedom.

From the outset Father Flanagan felt certain there was no crime problem that could be considered apart from a children's problem. If you wanted to save the man, you had to begin with the boy. And even when one came to understand that much, there was to be found nowhere a scientific panacea; there is no cure-all for crime, except the love of God in the heart of man. His hope lay rather in strengthening agencies already earnestly and valiantly at work and creating a synthesis of their efforts, working prayerfully under God.

In years to come he was to find an ally in J. Edgar Hoover, director of the Federal Bureau of Investigation. Both men knew that law enforcement, however vigorous, without Christian vision, was not enough. Crime cannot be ended in the United States, or even greatly reduced, merely by superior marksmanship of policemen, by superior cunning of detectives, or by raising the standard of integrity and ability in prosecuting officers. Law enforcement can cut down the weeds but it cannot remove the roots. It is not merely a sociological problem; it is a moral and religious problem.

Meanwhile, as Father Flanagan would wryly point out, the cost to taxpayers of maintaining the criminal army is fifteen billion dollars a year. That, considered by authorities a reasonable estimate, is 400 per cent more than we spend for education. Until the war, it exceeded all our taxes. It lays a tax of one hundred and twenty dollars a year on every man, woman, and child in the United States.

As a mere matter of dollars and cents, Father Flanagan felt that Americans should be more interested in the crime problem than in any other domestic question. Yet at the beginning of his work he was to discover that the average citizen is cynically indifferent. We all are likely to think the cost of crime does not reach us personally. We imagine we do not pay any part of the underworld's bill. Of course we are very much mistaken. Because of the cost of police and courts and prisons, and of racketeering in business and industry, every American citizen is taxed to keep the criminal army going. There is a crime levy on every meal we eat, on the hats and coats and shoes we wear, on our rent, laundry, moving-picture tickets— on almost everything.

Clearly, if we could cut that cost only in half, we could pay a large portion of our war debt without further expense of any kind. Only a strange public apathy to this tragic disease of democracy prevents us from greatly reducing our annual crime bill, reckoned not only in billions of dollars but also in human misery and death.

If all the criminals in the United States were to be assembled in one place, we would have a city of the lawless almost the size of New York. We are, Father insisted, confronted with a social plague. As such, it needs to be approached not only scientifically but religiously. We cannot deal with it merely as physicians have dealt with yellow fever, typhoid, smallpox. To eliminate the crime plague, social workers and law-enforcement officers must work hand in hand with religious leaders.

Furthermore, he was already aware of the secret alliance in virtually every town and city of the underworld and politics, generally complicated with domination over the police by the local political ring. One of Flanagan's deepest resentments was against an apparently responsible and more estimable class—lawyers for the defense. Close to the combination of government, politics, and crime, ironically, there stood the sinister figure called the criminal lawyer, often more properly to be called the lawyer criminal. Father Flanagan knew there were some honest men who specialized in the defense of criminals, and some undoubtedly practiced legal ethics, but Judas was always turning up. Furthermore, the indifference of reputable lawyers to the admitted evils in their own profession was hard to understand. Two statements on this problem greatly impressed him, one by the American Bar Association, which said:

"We know that we do have some in our ranks whose activities

are a continuing menace to decent society and that the Bar as a whole has been strangely apathetic concerning them, to say the least."

Thomas J. Courtney, state's attorney in Chicago, put it even more vividly when he said:

"Imagine a community stricken with a great epidemic—typhoid, influenza, black plague, cholera, or infantile paralysis. Suppose, in the midst of the life-and-death battle, some of the physicians exploited the situation by helping to spread the disease for their own financial advantage. Then, to keep this simile, picture the rest of those physicians, engaged in the conflict, apathetically countenancing the dastardly actions of their fellows. But see what actually does exist in the legal profession! And little or nothing is being done about it."

Public opinion itself, Father Flanagan maintained, was a major problem, difficult to understand. Why were people indifferent to the heart-rending results of these conditions? Why were they blind to the grisly dangers of the future? Why did they side sentimentally with criminals and make front-page heroes of the worst types of men and women? Many have asked that question.

Some years ago a magazine editor began to wonder why crime statistics of England were so much lower than the American figures. He sent Frazier Hunt, journalist, to London to find out. First, Hunt learned that the Federal Bureau of Investigation and even some local American police departments were undeniably the technical superiors of famous New Scotland Yard. American detectives were better trained, and, on the I.Q. tests, more intelligent. Our methods were more advanced. As for equipment, we left the English far behind. For example, at that time New Scotland Yard had on file half a million indexed fingerprints; now they have two million. In our own Federal Bureau of Investigation we have on file more than a hundred million indexed fingerprints. By turning a few gimmicks and gadgets an operator can find any particular one of the one hundred million within three minutes. So Hunt's report only increased the mystery. Why, with our superiority, did we have so much more crime than England?

The supreme difference lay in public attitude. The masses of

English people had the will to stamp out crime; the public was solidly behind law enforcement. In any street row, spectators were for the bobby and not against him. In the courts, justice was stern and swift. Jurors acted like jurors and not like spectators at a Class-B Hollywood tear-jerker. They voted their verdict with a sense of responsibility in the administration of justice. No long-drawn-out appeals, either. After fair trial and swift appeal action, if a man were found guilty, he had to take his medicine.

Would anyone argue that such conditions are to be found in our country? No. Our critics from abroad still indict us as a lawless people. We advertise cars that will go eighty or even ninety miles an hour, even though it is against the law to go more than fifty miles an hour in every state in the union. When we get caught for speeding and the officer gives us a ticket, then we look for a kindly friend who "knows somebody downtown." In other words, we try to "fix" it. Small as these indications may be, they seemed to Father Flanagan symptomatic of a national attitude. When America passed a law, citizens immediately began to figure out how to evade it.

Father Flanagan was especially incensed because of the corruption of youth by movies, radio, magazines, and newspapers.

"I realize," he told the authors of this book, "it is the fashionable, intellectual attitude to laugh at such charges. But talk to children behind prison bars and you will change your mind. They will tell you where they got their ideas. The great majority in radio, movies, and publications, of course, are beyond criticism, they are so fine. But there is a 10 per cent that does not care, and that 10 per cent does a great mischief in this country. Give our children heroes, not villains, to imitate."

In this he was right; all too often our children develop admiration for criminals of the worst type, an admiration that occasionally amounts to hero worship.

In a New York theater a newsreel was shown of Dillinger, notorious Midwestern gangster of some years ago. The police who were chasing Dillinger were hissed, Dillinger applauded. That episode startled Homer Cummings, then Attorney General of the United States. How could he induce youngsters not to admire gangsters? He must give them a hero. For what heroes did our boys and girls have? English boys and girls admired their bobbies, were proud of Scotland Yard. Canadian boys and girls cheered with passionate loyalty the Northwest Mounted Police—reliable, dashing fellows who always got their man.

But American children were playing Dillinger and Al Capone. How to change that? That was when an apotheosis of government detectives was determined upon—the exaltation of the federal sleuth. Government offered the American boy a new hero and called him the G-man. Not long afterward Hollywood stopped making pictures of Scarface; stars stopped playing gangsters and became G-men. The accent changed.

Ninety per cent of the newspapers were behind the plan, behind the police, as the standing army of the law-abiding. The remaining 10 per cent Flanagan called the "don't-give-a-cuss-word press."

In editorial columns all newspapers, of course, stood behind law enforcement and child protection. The field for improvement lay in the news columns of the careless 10 per cent. Let us revert for a moment to the criminal lawyer. One way for newspapers to help the community was to show the lawyer criminal to the public in his true colors instead of reporting him as a star performer in a courtroom. Why glorify the career of a man who used his knowledge of the law to give daily guidance to professional criminals, keeping them safely out of jail? Why exalt men who make their success by bribery, corruption, intimidation, by foul and scandalous devices to free crooks they know perfectly well are guilty? Why describe a man as a brilliant trial lawyer when he is nothing but a crook working for crooks? Why dramatize as skillful performances snide little courtroom tricks? Why not instead throw the spotlight on the victims of crimes, the citizens, justice, security? Newspapermen knew skulduggery when they saw it. They could make their readers see it if they would, and they could help by exalting the courage of witnesses who dared to tell the truth in open court in spite of their fear of gang reprisals.

Flanagan was to live to see an immense increase in social consciousness in the working press. The scoop at any cost became no longer the first principle of decent publications. Editors today count the cost to society of a scoop even in the face of competitive pressure. More and more newspapers are refraining from publishing news that warns the criminal and helps him to escape.

Most important, Father Flanagan argued, was that copy editors must take into account the power of the words they printed. Too many respectable papers were reckless in the vocabulary of headlines. A gang of criminals kills a couple of honest citizens and gets away with a pay roll. In the headlines the next morning Father would read:

"Daring Holdup Nets Fortune in Three Minutes."

That word "daring" was the cause of Father Flanagan's agitation. Wonderful word, "daring," with a magic sound in the ear of youth. What boy didn't think it wonderful to be daring? Here we find an honorable word, an adjective of heroism, one of the finest bestowals from the dictionary, laid like bay leaves and laurel on the brows of murderers. "Daring Holdup Nets Fortune in Three Minutes." What a thought for the youth hesitating on the line between a life of usefulness and a life of crime. Three minutes with a machine gun and if you are daring enough to get away with it—you're set for life.

What in Father Flanagan's eyes was the greatest mess of all, a mess clamoring for a cleanup, was the scandal of county jails. In spite of great advances, it still is a scandal. Out of the three thousand county jails in the United States, a few years ago, sixteen hundred had been condemned as unusable—and were still being used. Their sanitary inadequacies were a menace to community health. They were firetraps and their overcrowding was a spectacle to turn the stomach of Lucifer himself. The effect upon young first offenders, thrown into the horrible intimacy of these overcrowded lazarettos, was incalculable in its final effect on society. Yet there they still stood!

Early in his studies Father Flanagan had also learned about the rackets and evils of the parole system, as frequently practiced. Even worse, he saw the horrors that often attended the mercifully planned scheme of probation. Years afterward he was to find himself at one on this matter, as on most matters, with J. Edgar Hoover. Speaking of probation, Mr. Hoover once said:

"If parole is a scandal, probation is sometimes a horror beyond the conception of decent citizens. What happens when a youth hampered by lack of parental guidance indulges in his first infraction? He receives the benefit of that most necessary and laudatory system known as probation. It is right that he should have probation. It is a crime for any child upon his first offense to be incarcerated without a chance to reform, always excepting the very rare anti-social degenerate. But under our maladministered system we find very often the probation officer is ignorant, that he sometimes is himself a criminal, or that he is merely a political panderer willing to debauch the most sacred of tasks—that of the protection of our youth—merely to keep a job. And so in this modern pilgrim's progress toward the inevitable slough of despond, we find our child criminal sunk deeper and deeper, first through poorly administered probation, then into reform schools, which are not reform schools but crucibles where boil the worst instincts of humanity and where innocence vanishes and insolence takes its place. We find him educated step by step, not in law obedience but in law avoidance. We find him traveling from the reform school to the reformatory, from the reformatory to the prison, with rarely a thought toward his true reformation but always with the association of the vicious, the foul-minded, and the dangerous older criminals. At last he himself becomes a professor of crime and he, like others, carries on his recruiting in an ever-widening circle which at last has brought us to the degenerating position where each year in America twelve thousand human beings die by murder."

Having learned about such matters, it was soon apparent to Father Flanagan that the great and challenging task was that of crime prevention. And the only really effective prevention would be that which heads off criminal careers by saving children.

It sounded simple—but Flanagan knew it was a tall order. For clearly even the much-vaunted new juvenile courts were already a failure. Many years were to pass before scientists would agree with Father Flanagan in this radical conclusion, but the time did come when they had to do so. Meanwhile, for years Americans lived in a fool's paradise, proceeding on the mistaken theory that boys were like bottles. All one needed to do was to pour into the bottles a certain amount of information and the job was done. From then on the bottles would take care of themselves—boys would make their own way from life in school or college into the realm of adult responsibility.

Once upon a time, in Father Flanagan's view, that theory was reasonably true, when civilization itself was younger and simpler, as on the farm at Leabeg. A boy went to school and learned the multiplication table. When he was out of school he went into a small shop or factory or an office and made use of the multiplication table. Or he went back to the farm. There was no violent change.

Today no child is able to prepare himself adequately for the mental and emotional whirlpool of adult life. The growing youth finds himself faced by an overwhelming enigma. There he stands and there it stands—the riddle of what to do with his life. Even when well trained, a shortage of opportunity may confront him. Either he must become a ward of the state or else he is on his own. In either case he is likely to find himself not far from the door of the underworld. That is why most arrests in this country are of prisoners at the age of nineteen, more at that age than at any other.

But to get at crime prevention Father Flanagan knew that he would have to go behind the age of nineteen. In fact, the more one explored this problem, the further backward one went to the very day the child was born, and even earlier. There was a large and dangerous volume of potential crime always present below the ages affected by unemployment. The minor offenses of children were not inconsequential. They were instead the greatest menace of all in the crime war. Criminal careers began in childhood.

So Father Flanagan, even as a young, maturing priest, analyzed a national problem.

To him the offenses of juvenile criminals presented a problem not of guilt and punishment but of diagnosis and therapy. He would have to find out why children committed such crimes before he could hope to prevent them. Here of itself was a forbidding study with many factors. Was it an individual problem or a community one? Every survey showed, for example, neighborhood variations in crime. Where there was more child crime, there was more adult crime. Obviously, too, differences in background would correspond to variations in crime statistics. In any city there would be more crime not only in slum areas but in business and industrial areas than in suburbs. However, it would be wrong to suppose that with the elimination of slums, crime would disappear. Some of the worst criminals in recent history came not from the city slums but from fairly prosperous farms—Dillinger, Floyd, Nelson, Bates, Kelly were all farm boys. Some came from rural slums, but not all.

Of course juvenile criminals who later become adult criminals were in many cases the result of neighborhood slum conditions, whether the neighborhood was urban or rural. Yet Father Flanagan was eventually to study one case where two young brothers were put to death for murder and people blamed the city slums, where they were born, only to learn that there went to the electric chair with them their boss partner, who guided and directed their many crimes, and who did not come from the slums at all but was an honor graduate of the Massachusetts Institute of Technology.

In crowded city areas, in spite of playgrounds and recreational activities, boys always tended to form into gangs. But Father Flanagan did not believe that gangs were bad in themselves. Gathering into play groups is a normal phenomenon in childhood; what was needed was to take dead-end kids and turn them into ballplayers, football players, athletes, and good citizens.

In discussing this idea, former President Herbert Hoover, staunch supporter of the Boys Club movement, once pointed out to us that the average cost to care for such a boy is forty dollars. That forty dollars would take a boy off the street. Give him his chance to play and some direction in character discipline and you have a fair chance of turning out a good citizen. But if you keep that forty dollars in your pocket, and don't give the boy his chance, within a few years the taxpayers may be called upon to pay ten thousand dollars to burn him in the electric chair. With that thesis Father Flanagan profoundly agreed.

The dangerous lack in juvenile life today, in Father Flanagan's view, was the absence of authority and kindly supervision of religious influence. Fifty years ago all children went to Sunday school. They had to go. The church was then a powerful influence in crime prevention. The influence of the church had waned and needed to be brought back. As Father Flanagan put it: "We need to send our children back to church, back to God. And churchmen need to get a better understanding of this problem."

The public school was not and could not be a substitute for religious influence. Proud we may be of our pedagogical advancement, but schools do not give pupils the greatest essential of all education, which is training of character. They train brains but not spirits, and that is the greatest crime of the state. The backward child has special classes, but "backward" means only that he is slow at his lessons. But here, so Father Flanagan felt, we come nearer to an important opportunity. While we cannot develop any cut-and-dried mechanical process, because the problem lies too deep in individual intangibles, we can use the public schools to discover the child who is headed for crime and try to change his pattern, or, at least, its directions.

This ideal of Father Flanagan, which is already finding many forms of practical expression, opens up other doors. Always near at hand is the problem of ignorance of parents about child training. When parents lose control over their children, trouble lies ahead. Every worker in this field today agrees with Father Flanagan that 75 per cent of the problem children have problem parents. They, too, must be dealt with; adult education and re-education must be a part of any enlightened crime-prevention program. Essentially, however, it remains the child's problem: "When we learn to look forward with the child, instead of backward with the adult criminal, we will have made great strides in the prevention of crime."

In those days authorities and social-welfare engineers sincerely believed they were doing exactly that. Good citizens took pride in the new, liberal, and tolerant institution known as the juvenile court. They believed such courts were the answer to prayers for enlightened handling of juvenile offenders. Back in 1900, when the first juvenile courts were established in Chicago and Denver, it did seem as if the final answer to the problem had been found. A boy steals some plumbing fixtures from the back of a truck. Enlightened society steps in and says he must not be treated as a criminal. Instead there will be a special place for this boy—the juvenile court. He will be brought before a sympathetic judge, in chambers. There will be an informal hearing without a courtroom atmosphere. His parents will be there, and his priest, rabbi, or pastor of his church. No policeman in sight. Kindly adults will try to work out a sensible solution. If necessary, they will take the child out of a wrong environment. In later years psychiatrists also came into the picture. What more could society do?

Having established these enlightened courts, the public was lulled into a sense of false security. But not Father Flanagan, nor realists like him. Eventually came a bombshell. Professor Sheldon Glueck of Harvard University Law School and his equally eminent wife, Dr. Eleanor T. Glueck, undertook a study of one thousand cases of juvenile delinquents. The Gluecks did not start out with any idea of criticizing the juvenile courts. They believed in them and still do. They co-operated closely with the famous judge, Frederick P. Cabot of Boston, who was one of the financial sponsors of this elaborate scientific survey.

The results of the Glueck study were astonishing.

What happened to the boys who had come through the beneficent processes of the juvenile courts during a five-year post-treatment period? Appalling to relate, 88 per cent of these boys continued their delinquency during that test period. Those who were caught at it—and there were many who were not caught—were arrested on the average of 3.6 times each. Their offenses were not merely misdemeanors; seven tenths of the repeaters committed serious crimes. Out of one thousand boys studied by the Gluecks, 905 continued to commit crimes while under the guidance of the juvenile courts.

What is one to understand from this revelation? We have first to agree with obstinate Father Flanagan that in spite of all the efforts by sympathetic judges, psychiatrists, clinics, and community groups working earnestly and intelligently, the treatment had very little effect. An overwhelming majority of these boys were recidivists, "returnees," growing up after favorable attention into habitual criminals.

Was some ingredient missing? Could it be love?

The practical findings of a priest were simple, indeed, and undoubtedly sounded naïve. Yet they are the findings of most servants of the Lord. Father wholeheartedly concurred in the conclusions of Father Hugh Calkins who, in *Two Worlds,* argued that fathers needed to be taught the science of fatherhood through a real course in home training. All the womanly kindness and tenderness mothers impart cannot compensate for lack of manly toughness fathers can impart. The well-balanced child is a smooth blend of tender and tough. Tough and unyielding in character; tender and thoughtful in temperament. From earliest childhood there must be a constant interplay of these two. Women remember that; men neglect it tragically. What children need most emotionally is affectionate interest from both parents; interest in everything that concerns them. They must feel they are wanted by both parents. Not "Go to your father for this or to your mother for that." Women tend to spoil children with too much coddling. Men tend to be too hard with them. Blend those two opposite tendencies: the child benefits. A father must be half boy and half boss; must play with his kids and still keep their respect. You many fancy him clumsy in the nursery, but the baby needs and wants his heavy voice and rugged touch. Moral muscles must not be weakened by too much babying. So father counterbalances mother always. Dad clowns with them, builds blocks with them, plays horse with them. When they need adult guidance, he plans their strategy. And it is small use quoting God's Fourth Commandment at children. Unless you give them something to respect and love, they will not obey you. "Natural affection" for parents exists only in books. Children learn to love and respect only those parents who work hard to win respect and love.

In that fact lay the greatest opportunity in social service. Others, too, could win love, if they would only give it. That was why he was to plead throughout his long experience for a new consecration in social service: the vow to bestow love its basic imperative.

II

Father Flanagan, as he left the courtroom, indignantly condemned the antiquated methods he had just watched. They were like witch trials!

Beyond argument, the boys had committed acts of wrong. But beyond argument also, none was a hardened criminal. Any one of them, all of them, the priest felt certain, could have been reached with patience and loving understanding.

He became a frequent visitor to the courtroom. The hotel was running smoothly, and with the permission of his pastor, he could afford "time off" for this new study. It was a period of learning; through this "classwork," as he liked to call it, Father Flanagan became friendly with the judges. Often they would call him into their chambers to talk over cases which came before them.

He saw that these men, working under difficult limitations, were anxious to find honest solutions to problems of the children.

"Yet why is it," he demanded of one of the juvenile-court judges, "that you send all of these poor boys—older and younger alike, and orphans too—to the same so-called reformatory?"

"Because, Father, there is no other place to send them. Their homes are no good. We have to send them somewhere."

The simple arithmetic of the situation appalled him. The combination of public apathy, of overcrowded court dockets and equally overcrowded state institutions, run largely by political hangers-on, left the boys with hardly a chance.

Hungry to get to the roots of this problem, he branched out in his investigations, writing more letters to officials of every state, collecting data on homeless and delinquent children, on how their cases were handled in reformatories, state industrial schools, orphanages, and other institutions of discipline and correction.

Father Flanagan let no opportunity pass to study every movement designed to help the wayward boy. In after years many of these same organizations invited him to visit with them and explain his techniques. Thus, as one after another came to his notice, he studied intensively with leaders in the all-too-lonely field. Eventually he knew the plans and methods of the Boys Clubs and Big Brother Movements; the Children's Village at Dobbs Ferry on the Hudson, an enterprise that has flourished for the last ninety years, and the previously mentioned George Junior Republics which have been in existence more than sixty years. Among the less expansive undertakings along the same lines there was the conspicuous example of the summer camp for delinquent boys at Lake Greenwood in Franklin County, Ohio. The camp co-operates with the Domestic Relations Court in Columbus.

For many nights his "homework," after he had completed his other duties, consisted of studying these reports, interpreting cold figures and bluntly detailed facts of case histories.

In all of these plans, and in many others, Father Flanagan found something to admire and commend. But there were still two things wrong with nearly every one of them: they left out loving tenderness, and they left out God.

In his mind those living and dynamic realities transcended all blueprints for organizational combinations. Father Flanagan was not opposed to psychiatry, or welfare engineering; he fought for boys and for God. He used to say with simple solemnity:

"To save children from crime is to end crime. If we do not save our children from crime, we shall lose our civilization. That is the final and greatest challenge of this problem."

That was why he often came to the Omaha courtroom. That was why he was studying, inquiring, corresponding. Somehow he meant to get into this fight. The way was not clear, but he was still certain that the pattern was there and that presently he was going to find it.

III

He had already had a slight taste of working with boys in trouble. In the parish he had been asked to take a hand in cases of "problem boys," many of whom were habitual truants. Often he found that the truancy was caused by some underlying trouble: favoritism, fancied or real, for some other child, lack of interest or attention in the home itself. Once a home problem was solved, the truancy was usually cured.

He had seen also the boys who came into his hotel. Runaways. Young lads like that Bob, seeking an answer in flight to a problem which seemed to them too difficult to solve in any other way. Bob was doing all right now. But what would have happened to Bob if, instead of going home, he had been sent to some institution as a runaway?

Officials in the Omaha juvenile courts, in their talks with the priest, soon began to recognize that he had exciting ideas and information about the problems of boys. One morning, after the court session was ended, the judge called him to the bench.

"Did you observe those two boys found sleeping in the alley last night?" the judge asked.

"Oh yes," Father Flanagan answered. "But they've got a home——"

"Yes, they've got a home," the judge hurried on. "But the father drinks and the mother isn't strong enough to control them herself. Not bad boys. But they need looking after. I'd rather not send them away. I was just wondering . . ."

He paused, regarding the priest with an affable smile.

"I wonder if I could parole them into your care, Father?"

Though he had no place to take them, he agreed. He talked with the two youngsters, aged twelve and fourteen, and arranged to have a meeting with them one night a week. Since he did not want them to come to the hotel and meet hobos, he arranged a rendezvous under a street lamp in front of the building of the Northwestern Bell Telephone Company.

There was nothing stuffy about these curbstone meetings. The boys gave him a report on their activities, their work in school, their play, their progress and profits in selling newspapers.

If they were in any kind of trouble, he made sure that they told him about that. But he made absolutely no move to check up on their stories. They were on their honor to tell him everything.

"You're both good boys now," he told them. "I know I can count on you."

Occasionally, in the pool of the lamplight on the darkened street, he would talk to them about religion. Their father and their mother did not attend church. The boys had some vague idea that God was some unsympathetic governor in the sky who might someday smite them down.

"God punishes you," the younger boy informed him at one of their meetings. "That's what He does. He punishes you when you're bad."

"You mustn't be afraid of God," the priest said quickly. "He's a loving Father—don't you think He understands how a boy gets into trouble sometimes?"

They were Baptists, nominally. Within a few weeks he had the two youngsters attending Baptist Sunday school regularly, as a part of their new program.

"You must be true to God," he told them. "You must let God have a part in your lives."

The father still drank heavily, and the mother was still sickly and unable to give them proper care. But the two boys were not in trouble any more. They were sleeping in their room at home instead of wandering around, as they had been, in the middle of the night.

In at least partial measure, under the Flanagan direction, the boys were able to follow normal lives. And the judges, seeing the good results of the experiment, went further.

Other youths were soon added to his list of "parolees." There still being no other available place, he had to meet them all on street corners. But his techniques of understanding, of trust, were just as effective with the new charges.

Presently juvenile-court officials were astounded at the record. Father Flanagan's "protégés" were making good, not showing up again as "repeaters" in court. What kind of magic was he using?

IV

It was hard for some of these practical men of the law to accept the priestly statement that his was the magic of love and understanding.

On warm nights he would walk with his charges through an Omaha park. They would throw themselves on the grass, and talk, and he steadily continued his practice of always taking them at their word. Never did he attempt to frighten them with reprisals that might lie ahead if they again did wrong. All of them knew that he had to make reports about them to the court. They knew it was up to them.

Once they were certain he was their friend, the boys rallied around him. One night, as they were winding up a park-bench meeting, one of the youngsters said: "Father, you keep telling us you know we'll make good. How do you know?"

The priest considered a moment.

"There really is only one answer to that," he said finally. "I know because I am sure you are learning to follow God's path."

And the fact—incredible as it seemed to some outraged professional social workers of the community—was that Father Flanagan's little band of parolees *were* following that path. The sessions under the street lamp were paying off.

Most of his parolees, it was true, had been waifs, whose "crimes" had been of minor character. But his next step was to bring him into a far different, more serious juvenile problem.

There was a "crime wave" current in the Omaha of that day. The entire city was aroused over outbreaks of store looting, housebreaking, and senseless, unprovoked attacks on pedestrians. Behind the outbreak was a gang of youths from South Omaha.

According to the police, it was a typical, tough, street-corner gang, of shifting membership. Often some member would be shipped off to reform school, to return a year or so later with added glamour because he had "done a stretch."

The street on which members of this gang congregated had become well known. Because of the vile language and outrageous acts of the youths, decent people avoided the street as they would a plague district.

Parents in the neighborhood, living in fear that their own children might come under the influence of the gang of hoodlums or become victims in one of the vicious street fights, were demanding that the gang be broken up. The terror had to be stopped. The ringleaders, the parents insisted, had to be put away where they could no longer contaminate the other children of the neighborhood.

Under pressure of this rising public clamor, the police "cracked down." Special squads assigned to the case collected evidence against the ringleaders—enough evidence to send them to the reformatory until they were twenty-one.

Father Flanagan was in the court the morning the police brought in the seven leaders of the gang. He was fully aware of the public attitude. These were "really bad boys"! At the hands of the law they deserved no mercy.

There was scattered booing and the judge had to rap for order as the young terrorists were brought in. They stood in a line in the prisoner's box. The priest leaned forward to scan their faces, and sat back, astonished.

Not one in this group of "gangsters" could have been more than fifteen years old.

The papers had pictured them as arrogant young criminals, defiant of all authority. But there was no arrogance on their faces now. They were seven frightened boys.

The long indictments of their crimes were read aloud. None of them denied any of the thefts, vandalism, beatings. The youths were, according to the reports, antisocial and incorrigible.

But they were palpably afraid now, and to Father Flanagan that was a most important and significant fact. Had they been hardened in their ways, this moment would have been a kind of headline triumph. They would have stood here still defiant, determined to prove themselves above any rules of society.

That fear was the clue he sought; they were still only boys; they could still be reached.

The judge told the prisoners to stand up. As he started to pronounce the sentences, Father Flanagan also stood up. The judge hesitated, glanced over at the priest, then asked: "Is there something you want to say about this case?"

"Yes," came the voice, like the crack of a rifle. "Yes, your honor. I would like to ask that these boys be paroled to my care."

There was a buzz of hostile comment in the courtroom, and the judge pounded for order as he called the priest to the bench. While the judge was well aware of the success Father Flanagan had won with his parolees, he also knew that they had all been comparatively minor cases.

"Do you realize," he asked, "what you would be taking on with these boys? Have you seen the records of what they've done?"

"I know the records," Flanagan answered. "And I know also, from what I've read and seen myself, the conditions under which they live. The temptations, the lack of supervision——"

"And you believe you could do something with boys such as these?"

The seven "incorrigibles" were standing close by. For the judge, the decision was not easy. An angry and frightened public opinion was demanding that the boys be punished. Political interests in the city would have no desire to outrage the community by letting the culprits go free. Yet the judge was a fair man and he had seen the skill this priest had with boys. At last he said:

"Father, I am going to give you the chance you ask. I hope you will be able to cure these boys. I am going to parole them in your charge."

His Honor turned to the prisoners.

"Now you are getting a chance," he told them. "I don't know if it will do you any good or not. Father Flanagan thinks he can help you. I hope that you'll remember that had it not been for him, all of you by now would be on your way to reform school."

Most stunned of all in that courtroom were the boys themselves. They looked at each other and then at the priest with bewilderment. Until this moment they had been confidently expecting prison bars.

If Father Flanagan was aware of how startled they were, he gave no hint of it. He walked over and asked them to follow him.

Numbly, silently, they obeyed. Every eye in the courtroom was watching as Father Flanagan herded his new charges from the prisoner's box and followed them, Indian file, down the center aisle of the court and out to the street.

CHAPTER FIFTEEN

The Vision of Father Flanagan

On the steps of the courthouse Father Flanagan excavated from his pocket a paper bag of chocolates. In grave and decorous silence he passed candy from one young brigand to another, until all were solemnly chewing. The incorrigibles looked dazed, but their spirits were rising; as they set off, across town, they began to chatter.

"Was I scared of that judge!" muttered one.

"Geeze, yeah," another said. "The way them prune-faces——"

"Boys," cut in Father Flanagan, "let's cut out any more talk about this morning's prune-faces. We're forgetting all unpleasantness."

One boy protested: "How can we forget? We got to go to that courthouse, and report regular, ain't we?"

"You'll make your reports to me—I'll take care of any formalities with the courts," the priest answered. "Our only concern is what happens next and from here on out: the future!"

They kept on walking. Presently another parolee summoned up the courage to ask: "Father, what are you going to do to me?"

"I don't know yet," was the candid answer. "But I'll bet you'd make a pretty good first baseman."

"Sure, only what's playing baseball got to do with it? That ain't no punishment, Father."

"There is no punishment," he roared. "Try to get it straight— realize what I'm saying to you—you're beginning again!"

Ahead of them was an empty lot. The priest halted the little group and examined the region with a critical eye.

"I think this place might do," he said. "We can sit down here and talk."

"Sure."

It was plain what was in his mind; they were sure of that. They were going to get a lecture now. The priest was going to start his sermon. But they soon saw their mistake; in their conference with Father Flanagan no mention was made of sin; the topic continued to be baseball.

They were delighted that the severe-faced priest knew as much as they did about game and players, the standing of the clubs and the batting averages. They agreed that victory lay in real hurlers and sluggers but most of all in teamwork.

"There aren't any houses right around this open field," Father Flanagan remarked. "It just might be that we could use this field; I could talk with the proprietor. This place is a part of your chance to start over. We've got to make the most of it; prove, working here together, that we can make good. We could make a good baseball diamond right here."

By now they were sure he was their friend, so they listened attentively as he raised a warning finger:

"If we work along as a team, there's nothing to keep us from succeeding, right here on this vacant lot."

"Here's where we ought to put home plate," one boy screamed in excitement.

"Sure. Get a rock or something. That would be the pitcher's box right out there——"

They were all talking at once; for the moment they forgot why they were here, forgot that they were supposed to be criminals. They were laying out a ball field.

"When do we start, Father?"

The question was a poser. He still had his regular parish duties. He still had his hotel to manage. He had other parolees he had to meet at least once a week. And these seven additional "incorrigibles," he knew, would need closer watching than all the others put together.

"You will all have to go on living at your homes," he told them, "but we'll meet together three evenings a week. Right here, after supper."

Summer coming on; evenings getting longer; plenty of time for baseball in these twilight sessions. But what would they be doing the rest of the time? Father Flanagan prayed and turned this problem over to his Father in heaven.

In their first game they had one catcher's mitt, one fielder's glove, one bat, and one secondhand ball, all begged by Father Flanagan. But that was enough for their practice game. Neighborhood boys watched and were allowed to join in. And as the seven grew rapidly into two teams, Flanagan accumulated more gloves, balls, and bats, and masks. The story of the new team, at once unofficially dubbed the "Flanagans," spread, and challenges came from sand-lot teams all over town.

Well aware that they were still on parole, the boys wondered if they dared accept the challenges.

"Why not?" Father Flanagan protested. "You *are* incorrigible— pessimists! Don't you think maybe you're good enough to beat them?"

He was at the games to cheer them on. When they scored a run, he yelled louder than anybody else; if they lost, he was utterly dejected. After each game he would talk with them, not about baseball but about their daily activities. For some he had found summer jobs. And, at his behest, all seven were attending their churches.

None of them, however, behaved like angels. Again and again they got into fights; they had a lot to learn about self-control. But there were no more violations of the law. Occasionally they were involved in some minor crisis; but the uncontradictable fact is that not one of those seven "hopeless cases" ever got into trouble again with the police, then or for the rest of their lives.

II

More and more youngsters were paroled into his care. In spite of parish duties—Mass, confession, pastoral visits, and all the activities of societies and sodalities in the church—he never refused a request from the bench. What troubled him most was that it was all so haphazard. There was no equipment, no systematic way of caring for them. The park bench remained the meeting place.

But even this adventitious park-bench rehabilitation program had shown him what could be done; beyond doubt his original idea was correct: no boy was so bad, so far gone in ways of evil, that he could not be helped. The most vital parts of any rehabilitation program lay in bringing love to the boy and the boy to the church.

Late one night he came to a conviction about it. He was alone in his office at the Workingmen's Hotel, with time to reflect. It was clear to him now that the rehabilitation of young lads was nobody's part-time job; such work called for the consecration of a man's whole life. A new idea began to bloom in his thoughts like the instantaneous growing of the Hindu conjurer's mango tree.

He would have to give up this hotel. That was it. The care of jobless men would have to be carried on by other agencies. Father Flanagan had another job to do—a lifetime job. He would not close the hotel at once. Already it was early fall; the harvesters would be counting on a winter home. It would have to be kept in operation at least until spring, when others could take over. By April his new enterprise would be ready.

How will you do all this? asked Father Flanagan politely of Father Flanagan.

He was still living on the slight income of a parish priest. He had no wealth of his own, and no idea where he could turn for the money he would need. But his faith held; he would get the money for the exciting new project springing even higher like that magic bush in his dreaming mind.

Certain only that God would somehow see him through whatever difficulties he would face, Father Flanagan that night reached the great decision of his life.

From his new vision he knew he could never retreat: the founding of a new kind of home for the homeless, the unwanted, the misdirected boy.

Book Two

CHAPTER SIXTEEN

Given in Secret

Behind the great desk in his archiepiscopal residence, Archbishop Jeremiah Harty regarded with tolerant smile this young priest of great faith.

The archbishop wished he could help. To the seneschal dignity of a cathedral executive he added the kindliness of a good shepherd. All Omaha knew of his gentleness and goodness of heart, as well as expertness of management in a burgeoning diocese.

Tragic stories of children, of their neglect and abuse, came across the archbishop's desk with saddening regularity. He could well understand the need for such a home as was now being proposed, nay, urged upon him with rich Irish eloquence.

But the diocese was already maintaining one orphanage and helping to support others. Funds were limited, dollars earmarked for recurrent obligations, and no money to spare for new ventures.

"You understand," His Excellency added gently, "you would have to look only and entirely to your own resources?"

Flanagan nodded grimly. He could hardly expect the bishop to risk sorely needed funds on a vague vision of a curate. In fact, it was reassuring that Archbishop Harty was impressed at all; before the interview was over, Flanagan had authority to proceed on his own.

All he needed now was cash.

He was jubilant, even though he did not minimize the difficulties. No longer was he a neophyte in the heartbreaking business of scrounging for charity funds. Keeping his hotel in operation month after month had been a stern apprenticeship.

Now it was going to be harder. People could readily understand the need to help homeless old men who had nowhere else to turn.

But boys—hoodlums loose on the streets—delinquent kids in trouble with the law? Were there not orphanages and state industrial schools and reformatories?

Older now in experience than in years, he foresaw many pitfalls. The job, he realized in all humility, called for abnegation of even elementary comforts. He would have to give up everything. In the self-deprivation he was now facing there would be no time, even, for reading (and there were hundreds, thousands of books he still wanted to read), nor for the most innocent pleasures. He must renounce the maximum, adjure far more than was required of the average parish priest. This would be a work demanding complete consecration. But he had no fear.

Around the dinner table with the family at Father P. A.'s rectory he broke the news. Starting a home for youngsters was quite an unexpected proposal, and they all had their reservations.

"You've been working with these boys, sure," his mother conceded. "But now you'd be taking them into the family. You've never brought up a family."

He smiled.

"But I lived in a big home, Mother—dear," he reminded her. "And in a big family, too, with the best of teachers running it—you! I know how it goes, how each must do his part. The kind of home I grew up in is the kind these boys ought to have."

"Yes, but back there you had all of us to help. It was the women who did the cooking and sewing. Who'll do it now for your houseful of boys?"

"Well, now," he said, "I hope you and Nellie have your needles handy, just in case. The archbishop said I might have a few Sisters to help out when I get underway, and the dear Lord will guide us too, we may be sure."

He would not be swerved, they knew, once he had set his course. Within an hour he had them all convinced. Father P. A. summed up the general attitude:

"If he wants to do it, he probably will, you know. And there's little for us to do but pitch in and give him our help."

But others in Omaha were not so ready to join in.

Father Flanagan teaching school in the early days at Overlook.

The World's Greatest Entertainers.

Anyone who loved boys loved Father Flanagan. Will Rogers, Babe Ruth, and Lou Gehrig were typical of the visitors who stopped by.

Father Flanagan at the time the home began to build on a solid foundation.

Father Flanagan and Henry Monsky, one of the earliest Boys Town supporters.

Father Flanagan with his mother, receiving the First Citizen Award from the American Legion.

II

There were citizens who insisted that the problem of boys without homes, or boys in trouble because of bad home backgrounds, should be handled entirely by the state.

"It's a matter for the police and the courts," one declared. "Your job, Father, is to spread the word of God. Okay—spread it! But this problem of juvenile crime, that's a practical matter."

"And bringing the word of God to unfortunate boys—doesn't that have practical value in their lives?"

"We've got institutions; let them handle the problem."

"And forget about what happens?"

"If anything were wrong in these places," the critic insisted, "the public would find out about it soon enough."

But the public had not found out. To this day it does not know. Many in Omaha seemed unwilling to believe that there were homeless boys, sleeping in alleyways or riding freight cars, boys without food or proper clothes, without love or care, wandering city streets.

"We give decent boys every advantage we can," one father told him. "These others you speak of, Father, are just the bad apples. Let the law take care of 'em. That's why we pay taxes."

They were not coldhearted. Their apathy grew from their unwillingness to believe in the actuality of the poverty and neglect he described, the viciousness he pictured in the reform schools. And they would not come with him and see for themselves. Such things couldn't happen in a country like ours. In coming years he was to meet that attitude again and again.

But others of influence in the city did understand and were ready to help: Catholics, Protestants, and Jews, men and women, many of them young like the group that had helped Father Flanagan's hotel.

Riding on a streetcar with one of these friends one day, he talked of his plans.

"They are all so unsettled," he admitted. "First, I must find a building. It has to be in a neighborhood where there won't be too many temptations for the boys. And it has to be at a very low rent."

The streetcar stopped and several passengers got on, among them a pretty, dark-haired woman. Father Flanagan's companion waved to her.

"That's Catherine Shields," he said. "Say—she's in the real-estate business!"

They walked over to where she sat, and the friend explained the problem, upon which Miss Shields exclaimed: "I think I know just the house. It's right near here. In fact—we'll have to get off this minute. Conductor! Stop the car!"

At the juncture of Dodge and Twenty-fifth streets they stopped in front of a two-story red brick dwelling in the gingerbread Rutherford B. Hayes style; back from the street, withdrawn and silent, it was a rococo remnant out of an opulent past. Their footsteps echoed on elegant hardwood floors as they wandered through the dust of high old rooms. And all the while Father Flanagan was shaping his dream into place. Here would be the dining hall and down there a game room and yonder the general living room. The small room on the side would be a chapel for morning Mass and evening Benediction. There would be space upstairs to sleep twenty, maybe twenty-five.

Miss Shields had one more point to mention. The ninety dollars' rent was payable in advance!

Father Flanagan divulged the fact that he hadn't quite that sum on hand at the moment. But he kept to himself the fact that in his ecclesiastical pants pockets he had less than ninety cents.

"You could wait a day or so?"

The ninety dollars for that first month's rent were borrowed from a friend.

III

Of all the stories which have grown up around Boys Town, none has created more speculation than the legendary origin of the ninety dollars.

From whom did Father Flanagan borrow it? There are some who say it was from a pawnbroker. Others aver it was lent him by his friend, the late Henry Monsky, who was one day to head B'nai B'rith. Still others believe it was a Protestant layman, who later became an officer in the Grand Lodge of Free and Accepted Masons.

Father Flanagan never revealed the name. When we talked with him, in his study at Boys Town, we entreated him to disclose the identity of this "ninety-dollar man of mystery," but he shook his head: "You'll never find out from me."

Why all the mystery? The answer was characteristic:

"People tell all these different stories, you see. Now it is one man, next someone else. So they all share a little glory, you know. And why should I spoil that now by telling which one it really was?"

So we just don't know! Father carried the secret with him into the next world.

IV

Miss Shields, the real-estate agent, asked no questions about the lender when her customer walked in and placed on her desk ninety dollars in bills and a handful of silver. All she asked was when he would take over occupancy; then she filled out a receipt for the first month's rent and wished him good fortune.

He did not know, as he paid her the money, where the next ninety was coming from. He knew only that this was the start.

Boys Town was about to begin.

CHAPTER SEVENTEEN

Castoff

At the start there were five boys. None came from the "crime wave" ball team, because they all had homes and Flanagan insisted they must stay there. Of the beginning five, three were homeless orphans paroled to Flanagan a few days before and two had been assigned to his care by the juvenile court on that very morning of December 12, 1917.

He brought the first two over from the court in the morning and hustled together the other three later in the afternoon. At the door of the new home to greet the arrivals were all the members of his staff—two nuns and a novice of the School Sisters of Notre Dame, "lent" to the home by Archbishop Harty.

In the entrance hall the first two boys who arrived looked around with incredulous eyes, and the older one remarked: "We're sure gonna be living in a swell dump!"

Swell it did seem to their unaccustomed eyes. Alas, it was, in fact, no gleaming mansion. The founder had only a few weeks to gather the furnishings. He and his brothers, sisters, and friends had launched an intensive door-to-door campaign begging for old furniture.

The result was a weird conglomeration of attic castoffs. Nothing matched anything else. The chairs around the dining-room table represented a half dozen ages and designs in furniture making, from a broken-down Duncan Phyfe forgery to a Macy basement special. The meager supply of chinaware, the knives and forks and spoons, formed a rag bag, a junk box of kitchen equipment. So, too, on the second floor; a chaotic jumble of beds, cots, blankets, and spreads brought into orderly usefulness in the dormitories.

The archbishop came and dedicated the chapel, on the first floor; above the altar there was hanging the crucifix bought from Anton Lang of the Passion Play at Oberammergau.

Such was the start of Father Flanagan's Home for Boys—a hastily furnished potpourri of secondhand things. His five first boarders reacted well for boys eight to ten years old. Once they had met the Sisters and deposited their few belongings on their beds, they set out to explore, from cellar to attic. By dinnertime they were over much of their strangeness, so that the Sisters had to yank two of them apart; hostilities had started over who was to have the bed by the window.

During the meal they plied Father Flanagan with questions. Were other boys coming in? Would they be going to school? Would they have time for play outside? He was frank with them:

"I don't know everything yet, you see. But there'll be school, sure. And there'll be time for play, too. Outside, if it's good weather. But you've got to stay out of the street now."

Not that any of these first five boys had committed crimes. Their worst offense lay in having no homes. The two who had been turned over to him by the juvenile court that morning were brothers. Many years later, during the second World War, one of these brothers wrote back to Father Flanagan from the Southwest Pacific:

"That morning in December of 1917 is indelibly stamped into my brain. I can never forget how, after the juvenile authorities had relinquished my brother and I and we were in your custody, you presented me with a bag of chocolates and I felt pretty good about it even then.

"When we got to your home on Twenty-fifth and Dodge and you had introduced us to Sister Rose, who then showed us our room, I remember how you had to rush away without even so much as a bite to eat.

"Every time I eat spaghetti I think of the Italian kid. Remember his mother used to bring us a quart of spaghetti every Sunday which was looked upon as a great delicacy to us in those days? As far as that goes, it would be quite delicious right now."

Father talked to them as if they were grownups:

"We've all got a lot of things to do—and to learn. We've got to get a school started here. And we've got somehow to get new clothes for you all, too."

His tone always revealed a slight touch of panic and bewilderment as he took stock of his tasks. Many a skeptic, listening to him, would take him for an impractical fellow—only to find he was up against an invincible man who prayed to God all day long!

Very soon he was reminded anew by his empty pockets how short he was of funds, how he was existing on a day-to-day basis. The gifts came in slowly, hardly enough to pay for the food they needed. And the amount of food they needed increased daily as more and more boys were sent into the home by admiring judges who, however, had no way to appropriate cash for the job they cheered him for doing.

There was, too, a vast difference between running a hotel for tramps and a home for boys. He was no longer an innkeeper for weary men; he was father and mother now for a houseful of exuberant boys—he was head of a home!

Soon Father Flanagan was torn between two great efforts. One was the job of sending out begging letters; the other to organize the program of work and play.

A few nights after the home opened he woke up to hear one of the boys crying. He got up and stalked into the room to find the boy sitting up in bed. He had an earache. Now that was something new to Father Flanagan. What ought he to do? Call in a doctor?

"When I used to have an earache," another boy volunteered in a matter-of-fact tone, "my mother always used to hoist me up and carry me around and sing."

The priest in his nightgown pondered the problem dolefully. Then he lifted up the boy and began to pace up and down the room, humming a tune softly, from old memories of his mother and her "lulla-lullay" in Roscommon. In a little while the child was asleep, and Flanagan felt immensely proud of the therapeutic qualities of his voice.

II

His five young charges did their best to help, although often they were more nuisance than assistance. One had dreams of being a juggler and wanted to see how many plates he could stack in one hand. After a downfall of china, his juggling lessons were restricted to pie plates, after hours.

Before the end of the first week, before Father Flanagan had got fairly under way, there were fifteen in the home. Every bed and cot was occupied and he must get more right away—and that took time.

In this crisis, fortunately, word came from Archbishop Harty that he was now satisfied the new work was so important that he was relieving Father of all pastoral duties. The message came none too soon.

"It seems to me that every time I turn around," he told Sister Rose with a lugubrious shake of the head, "there is another poor boy arriving from juvenile court. Even I never realized until now there were so terribly many homeless boys."

By Christmas Eve, less than two weeks after he had opened the doors, there were twenty-five boys in the home. The entire second floor of the house was given over to cots and beds.

III

Already they represented a variety of race and religion—Catholic, Protestant, and Jew, brown, white, yellow. From the first there was no segregation of any kind. Color or race never made any difference to Father Flanagan, and the sole religious requirement was that each boy attend services regularly in the church of his own faith. Run by a Catholic priest, and with the aid of Catholic nuns, the home began as, and has ever since remained, a non-sectarian shelter for the homeless.

But with all his good intentions, Father Flanagan's boys did not become angels overnight.

Perhaps things had gone along too evenly during the first week. In the second week, as the home began to become crowded, the headache of running a houseful of squirming, shouting boys began to be manifest.

It might start at dark with a scream from the second floor—a cry so loud and piercing that Father Flanagan and the Sisters would leap from their beds to see what was wrong. They never knew what they were going to find, a fight in the middle of the night or a new boy scared by a nightmare.

At dawn it might begin with an early riser, playing fireman. One tore the sheet from his bed, tied it to the bedpost, and threw the other end out of the window. By the time Father Flanagan had arrived, the culprit had climbed out the window and started down his "fire escape." Halfway down he got scared and screamed. Hardly had he rescued the boy when there was another commotion on the main floor. Five boys, helping to clean the living room, had got into an argument and in the melee smashed the best living-room chair. Meanwhile the front doorbell was ringing. Two more boys from juvenile court.

Like so many other things in this world, the beginning was the hardest. The warmth in Flanagan's heart did not chill, even though —while trying to get organized—a lot of time was needed to keep the little darlings from tearing down the place.

"Jimmy stole my sweater."

"The other boys are picking on me."

"Father, two of the boys have taken my best and only frying pan and are using it for a drum out in the back yard."

Sometimes, for an hour or so, he would steal away to the house where his parents and brothers and sisters were living. And as they listened to his doleful stories, he found himself laughing as he talked:

"They're wonderful, you know. And it's going to be much better when we get it all straightened out. But sometimes the things they do—it's hard to understand why they do them, you know."

His mother would smile at her son.

"And what did you expect, Father Edward?" she would say. "When *you* were a boy, you would do some queer things yourself."

He could not remember anything comparable in his own boyhood. But he would start back, reminding himself over and over that patience was one of the great lessons of life, only to learn from the Sisters what had happened while he was gone.

Perhaps that was the day Tommy and Len had fought with scissors. Or when several of the boys had borrowed one of the few table-cloths to play ghost in the basement. Someone—identity unknown—

having left the tap open, the bathtub had overflowed and the water was dripping down from the kitchen ceiling.

Fresh excitement upstairs. Young voices calling down to him, "Father! Quick!"

In quavering excitement, they told him it was about Danny, the little fat boy. What about him? Danny had vanished!

That was tough! The reason Danny was in the home was because he had run away repeatedly. Brought up by a sickly mother and a father who bullied him, the boy had become nervous and easily upset. Away from his family, even in these few days, he had seemed to improve.

The search began. It covered the entire house, upstairs and down, the grounds and blocks around. Danny's clothes were still there and his few other belongings. But no sign of Danny.

In the shadows of the hall on the second floor there was a closet. As he walked past this, Father Flanagan thought he heard a noise. It sounded like stifled laughter. He turned quickly and opened the closet door.

There was Danny, seated on the floor, laughing uproariously. With a sigh, Father Flanagan left Danny to the admonishments of the Sisters and went down to his office where bills for the week's food were piled up.

IV

Christmas was only a day away when he and the Sisters took counsel together on what they could serve for the holiday dinner.

"We have hardly enough left for just an ordinary meal," Sister Rose lamented. "Unless that lady sends over some more spaghetti, like she did last week, I don't know——"

The doorbell interrupted. This time it was not a new boy, but a delivery man with a barrel, all bound around with a red Christmas ribbon from which dangled a card. Hope revived; someone had sent them a kilderkin of Christmas joy. Out into the kitchen they rolled it, and knocked off the top. What was inside? Sauerkraut!

That Christmas party was unique. No gifts! No tree! But the boys strung up some homemade decorations, and they all sang carols. In the morning, Mass in the tiny chapel; while boys of Protestant background went outside to worship in their own faith.

And later, Christmas dinner: for twenty-five famished boys, plates piled high with the main course—sauerkraut.

"I wish it were something else, boys—dear," Father Flanagan said from the head of the table. "But it isn't, so we'll be grateful for what we have. And may Almighty God look down mercifully this day and every day on all homeless wanderers!"

They all plunged into the sauerkraut and for a while there was silence. Then a boy who had finished held up his plate: "Father—can I have some more turkey? One plate lasts awful quick!"

There was a small giggle somewhere and then yells of laughter. Contentedly Father Flanagan started in on his own second helping of sauerkraut, no longer any panic in his bosom. The warmth around the table was his answer. Praise God for the resilience and elasticity and native humor of the forsaken lads! They could take it!

He closed his eyes and let the organ music from the Apocalypse of St. John the Divine roll through his whole being:

> And God shall wipe away all tears from
> their eyes:
> And death shall be no more,
> Nor mourning, nor crying, nor sorrow shall
> be any more,
> For the former things are passed away.

He forgot the bills and other harassments. The job could be done. Things were all right. They would all come through with colors flying—the boys and their home.

CHAPTER EIGHTEEN

Carlo

Nevertheless it continued to be a winter of ordeal, a time of trial and skimping, with tomorrow's needs and the next month's rent always looming like dark shadows just ahead.

For one thing, he found himself a center of controversy. Some critics in Omaha were demanding to know what good this penny-poor priest could hope to accomplish. How could he help wayward youth in an overcrowded hodge-podge like this home, where often they hardly had enough bread to put on the table? He, who criticized state institutions, should know that the inmates always had plenty of good, plain food to eat—and roast chicken on Christmas Day.

It was at this time, when he tried valiantly to win over his critics, that Father Flanagan acquired a ripe distrust of official dispensers of alms. They did not have to tell him—he knew what hunger meant to growing lads: every one of them with a wolf in his belly, every one a ravenous appetite with a skin pulled over it. But that was not all, he reminded his critics. Every one had also a pitiful loneliness and wanted affection.

Others, particularly judges and attachés of juvenile courts, came to his defense. They were sure Father Flanagan had something to give his boys beyond price or calculation: love and care, patience and understanding; these were riches. Most of the judges were convinced the effort was worth while, but some professional social workers found it hard to grasp. Poverty in their notebook had always been written down as the prime cause of delinquency. And now this priest was insisting that poverty, while it played a part, was not the major cause—in fact, his boys were living in poverty with him and learning from it. In a home run on a shoestring and a prayer, he was proving his point.

And he offered cold facts to back his words. Boys who had seemed to be incorrigible candidates for reform school seemed to change completely under such guidance, to become like new individuals. That was why the judges continued to send him as many cases as he could handle. Now boys were beginning to come from other sources, too: institutions and private homes.

Every available space was being used; army cots had been set up in rooms on the lower floor, and, even so, he could not possibly take in all who were applying. They could squeeze in just so many and stretch the stew just so far. Now he was forced to pick and choose, on the basis of which boys were in most desperate need.

By the end of January there were more than fifty children in the home. They had to be fed and clothed, cared for when sick, schooled and given proper recreation. Handling their problems would normally have required a full-time staff.

The gifts which kept them going were not enough to allow for any such staff. There were still only Father Flanagan himself, the two Sisters, and the novice. Often Sister Nellie and Mother would take home baskets of the boy's clothes, for washing and mending and sewing on buttons.

"It's all right, Father Edward," Nellie would say when he protested it was too much for them to take on. "You told us to get out our needles. Besides, we're used to running a big family. Why, it's like old times back at Leabeg."

The problem of schooling was intricate. Because of broken homes and disrupted lives, the education of many of the boys had been haphazard or entirely neglected. The need of sound education in reconstruction was obvious. Since his overcrowded home was not yet equipped to take on the burden, Father Flanagan called on the Omaha public-school commissioners and explained his problem. He wished his boys to go to the same schools as other Omaha boys.

"They are not bad, you must understand," he assured the officials. "They're just homeless and neglected. They're making good at our home. But they have to have schooling and they're entitled to it."

It sounded a little preposterous to the officials; many of the boys, they knew, had been in trouble with the law. But the priest guaranteed their conduct and somewhat shakily they finally agreed to take the chance.

For a few dollars he was able to hire a horse and wagon, and in this conveyance his boys were hauled back and forth. In the afternoons they had a back-lot program of supervised sports, a long cry from the field house and gymnasiums and playing fields of Boys Town today.

Nor was he ever quite free of "breakers of the peace." They had their disorders and fights and violations of rules. Even so, in Father Flanagan's Home For Boys, from the earliest stage, physical punishment was forbidden. A whipping, even a slapping, he regarded as admission of failure by the adult—an attempt to enforce obedience through fear of pain. That could never be enough to build a character.

Chief disciplinary measure was the taking away of "privileges" and the imposition of extra study or work. Perhaps it would be an extra hour in the kitchen while others were out playing. Or a boy might have to give up a prized dessert, or a hike on a Saturday or Sunday afternoon.

Gradually, through the winter, the home was becoming an organized unit, even though its existence continued on a precarious basis, always close to financial disaster. But donations did increase as they went from crisis to crisis.

Other kinds of gifts came in, too: from a farmer and his wife, a sack of potatoes; an old lady up the street would knock at the door early in the morning with a tray of hot biscuits. Old clothes, old shoes, even extra brooms, a carpet sweeper—and a most welcome checkerboard.

Eventually the boys learned to play a large part in keeping the house clean, the rooms in order. Responsibility for helping with the "homework" has ever since been part of the system. Every boy today does housework in his apartment, not only making his bed and keeping his locker in order, but also handling some extra "charge" of cleaning or dusting.

Before the winter was over, the work of the home with such ideas began to gain wider recognition, particularly among women. Letters poured in from housewives and mothers encouraging Father Flanagan, often with a small check.

But the opposition also grew. There were—and are still—many who considered themselves hardheaded and practical and who stubbornly argued that the reform schools were the right idea; the one way to deal with bad boys was with a strap, and down with these newfangled Flanagan notions.

At meetings Father Flanagan attended to solicit help he encountered many of these "practical" opponents.

"How can you ever hope to teach young criminals respect for law and order by mollycoddling them with a lot of nonsense about love and understanding?"

Patiently he would try to explain that they were not criminals, but children. They did need love; they needed release from fear.

"Most boys want to do what's right," he would protest. "They want to be praised and admired. But sometimes they don't know the right way to win praise, and they do wrong things. You have to show them, by training and example, what is the right way."

Occasionally his words would have effect. More often, those who found his theories revolutionary remained unconvinced. After all, he still had comparatively little to show. He realized that this Dodge Street home was only a chrysalis; the work was in an undeveloped and transitory stage. The idea that society, and especially parents themselves, bore primary responsibility for delinquency among children was a bitter pill to swallow. It was more comfortable to believe that no one was responsible but the child himself—that some were just born with the devil in their hearts.

But at the home an outsider would have found it difficult to distinguish between those who supposedly had evil within them and those who had merely been orphaned.

They were just boys. And like any group of boys in the world, they wanted a dog.

All knew, of course, that the home had little money. No one ever asked outright if Father Flanagan would buy a puppy. But now and again there would be broad hints around the dinner table, until at last he talked it over with the Sisters. Back at Leabeg, Father remembered, they had always had a dog. It was a natural addition to any boy's life, as inevitable as ham and eggs. And a dog could be part of training, too, because it would give them something to care for and love.

"If we do get them a puppy," he told the Sisters, "it ought to be a mighty good one, you know."

II

The name of the dog was Carlo, and he has long since become one of the highly embroidered legends of Boys Town.

It began, as many of the stories in Father Flanagan's life seem to begin, with a coincidence. One day he ran into a friend on the street and happened to mention that he was looking for a puppy for his boys.

"Maybe I can help," the friend exclaimed. "I've got a collie that has just had pups. If you want to come out to my place, take your pick."

That night Father told the boys about the collie; he was to be their own, strictly, to care for and bring up by themselves. He started out the next afternoon; it was bitter cold, with flurries of snow; the streetcar ride was long and far, beyond the boundaries on the western side of Omaha. But it was on his way back that his troubles began.

He had selected the puppy that seemed to have the prettiest coat and the most cocksure expression. With the gentle and innocent creature warmly snuggled under his coat, he paid his fare on the home-going streetcar and sat down quietly in a rear seat. They had gone only a short distance when the motorman had to clang his bell. To the puppy, that seemed to be an alarm signal. He poked his head out of Father's coat and emitted a series of shrill, hysterical yells.

The conductor strode down the aisle. There were only a few passengers on board. It was perfectly obvious who was carrying the dog.

"Father," the conductor asked mournfully, "do you have a dog under your coat?"

"I'm taking it back to those poor boys in my home," Father admitted with jovial friendliness. "They are waiting for me now."

The conductor shook his head.

"You can't bring a dog on an Omaha streetcar. It's against the company's rules."

"But, man, won't you think of those poor boys—expecting us——"

The conductor was adamantine.

"It's still against the law," he said. "Municipal ordinance—no dogs on no streetcars!"

Father Flanagan arose from his seat with as much dignity as a man can muster when he has a wriggling canine concealed in his coat. The motorman stopped his car in the middle of the block, then charged on, leaving the unwelcome passenger in the darkening, wind-swept street. It was only a short distance back to his friend's home and the shivering priest was tempted to return the dog. Yet how could he do that when the boys were waiting for their puppy? No, he must go through with it. He had no money for a cab, so there was nothing else to do but walk: a long, cold, dismal six miles. As he started off, the early winter night closed around him, and, as if in one stride, the darkness came.

It seemed an endless time before he saw at last the lights of home. Once inside the door, he was too numb and tired to speak. But who noticed that? Screaming boys crowded around him as from inside his coat, like a magician producing a rabbit, he lifted out the six-weeks-old collie puppy. For no remembered reason, they named him then and there. Carlo became one of them, a part of their lives and inseparable from their history.

If one of the smaller children wandered into the street, it was Carlo who followed and stood barking until one of the nuns hastened out. After a while Carlo learned to take his duties so seriously that he would tug at the seat of a wanderer's trousers and yank him back to the sidewalk.

Carlo lived many years and was the friend of hundreds of boys. When at a ripe old age he died, none could bear the thought of being altogether parted from him. At their behest Carlo was stuffed and mounted by a taxidermist and placed on a stand in the front hall of the first "Main Building" erected on the present site of Boys Town. For a long time he remained there, a joy to the sentimentalists, a reproach to the squeamish.

Mounted and silent, he remained their friend. No boy ever passed in or out of that front hall without giving the stuffed Carlo a kindly pat on the head. It became a tradition to do that—a good-luck gesture, especially around examination time.

But the day of even a mounted dog must finally reach its end. Carlo's coat of fur became worn and torn by the constant patting of hundreds of boys. It was at last mercifully decided that Carlo's service had reached its close. One night the stuffed animal disappeared from its stand and was never seen again. No one was encouraged to ask any questions. Only in memory Carlo lives now, one of the legends of Boys Town beginnings.

III

By the spring of 1918, while the first American armies were crossing the Atlantic, the Germans were readying their last frightening push to the Channel and the whole country resounded with Woodrow Wilson's call to "force—force without stint, force to the utmost," Father Flanagan's home for future free citizens of the Republic was beginning to prosper a little, its financial condition at least precariously stabilized.

A small group of friends made regular donations. Moreover, whenever possible, parents or relatives of the boys were asked to pay a little. At no time has payment ever been required for admission. Most of the boys have no one who can take even a small share of the burden. But occasionally there were some boys who had parent, uncle, or aunt who could pay a few dollars monthly—and did so. That system, a wholesome one, continues to this day.

By spring Flanagan had also managed to beg some fielder's gloves, balls, and bats. On the lawn outside of the home the boys held "practice sessions," and whenever possible, Father Flanagan would shepherd them to the public park where they would divide into teams for regular games.

They had also launched their "music department." At first this consisted only of singing, but later they branched out, obtaining through benevolent sources a battered trumpet and a secondhand drum. Arrival of these instruments was a major event; everyone wanted to try them out, but unfortunately not one boy or adult in the home knew anything about either instrument. They proceeded entirely by trial and error, and Father Flanagan, although half deafened by the results, urged them to keep on trying.

"We're going to have a band of our own!" he rejoiced, somewhat prematurely. Now, as never before, he believed in his dream. The Workingmen's Hotel was closed up and all his time belonged to the home, which badly needed more space. Daily he was forced to refuse cases sad enough to crack the heart. A bigger house was imperative.

So he went back again to house-hunting, although he could afford little more rent than they paid for the Dodge Street home and they needed a great deal more room.

In late spring a friend called to say he had heard of a building on the other side of town which could be rented at a suspiciously low sum. Father Flanagan hastened to inspect the bargain, which was situated on South Thirteenth Street, not far from the stockyards. It was certainly a spacious structure: only two stories high, it was half a block long, with a large porch and an imposing entrance; ten times the size of the house on Dodge Street. And ground all around it.

One fast look and Father Flanagan told the agent this was exactly what he wanted.

"I'll take it!" he exclaimed. "I'll take it here on the spot."

Everything about it seemed wonderful, even providential, until as they started up the steps of the porch a stone whizzed past and smashed against the side of the building. The priest drew back, startled.

"What was that for?" he gasped. "Why should anyone throw a stone at me?"

The agent reassured him.

"Not at you, Father. But I neglected to mention how some people feel about this place."

This, it seemed, was the building that had been known for years as the German-American Home, where people of German descent had gathered for meetings and songs. They weren't meeting here any more, because America was at war with Germany. Father Flanagan smiled grimly. He would still rent—as a home for his boys— the most despised place in the city of Omaha.

CHAPTER NINETEEN

A Priest in New Quarters

In June, they moved in.

The odium clinging to the German-American Home was actually turned to their advantage. In the midst of war hysteria, no one else would have taken the place as a gift. But no one criticized its use as a haven for children; many approved and sent donations.

As they carted their belongings over to the new home at cockcrow, the priest carried in his pocket a strange list, not an inventory of material belongings but of youngsters, homeless boys whom he had recently been forced to turn away because there was no room. These would be the first cases considered for the new home. Thirty were accepted in the first week. The population of the home jumped in that brief time to more than a hundred.

Overnight enlargement of the family brought new problems. Handling a hundred active boys was no simple assignment. They had to have a larger staff.

But the added problems were an encouragement now; see how they were growing. The changes were visible in the boys themselves.

Here was a boy who a year before had stolen money from a neighbor's purse. Another had been in half a dozen scrapes with authorities. No longer were they disciplinary cases or candidates for reform school.

The "impractical" principle of reshaping young minds and souls through love was paying off.

He could not guess the future, but he sensed it was full of promise. Already he was planning for it. Here, during those first months in the German-American Home, were started, in primitive fashion, many of the programs which have become world-famous as part of the techniques of reconstruction of modern-day Boys Town.

The athletic program, for example. On a playing field behind the new home the boys were taught almost every type of sport—not only baseball and football, but track competition, boxing (although they had only two sets of boxing gloves in the home), and basketball.

They played only among themselves, dividing into teams of "Blues" and "Whites." But the spirit of competition was high, and they were learning to play hard, to be good winners and good losers.

During the first summer they started also their first band. Father Flanagan made a call upon the Musicians' Union in Omaha. Didn't they have some instruments too far gone for further professional use? Would they be willing to sell them to his home for boys?

The musicians of those pre-Petrillo days donated the instruments —a pile of tarnished bugles, one slightly dented French horn, and a bass drum. Furthermore, an Omaha music teacher volunteered to give them instruction, and under his teaching they learned; harsh discords began to turn into a remote species of harmony and the pace took on the brisk and stirring tempo of band music.

The day came when Father Flanagan sent them forth on the first "tour" ever made by his boys.

What he wanted was to show the public the kind of boys he had in his home, and the work of which they were capable. The band, such as it was, visited and played in church concerts at a number of Middle Western cities. High light of this trip was a climactic concert before the inmates of Leavenworth Penitentiary. If the concert brought no huzzahs from critics, it did bring cheers from men behind bars.

Another part of the program launched at the German-American place was the first farm operation. This began in wholly unorthodox fashion when a farmer in a truck showed up at the front door one morning. Demanding to see Father Flanagan, he opened the back of the truck and led forth a cow.

"Can't afford money," he told Father Flanagan. "Figured I'd let you and the boys have Lucy."

They kept Lucy in the back yard. There was great argument at first about who was to be allowed to do the milking, but Father's decision was that all were to learn, taking turns. Many at the home were farm boys who should, he thought, return to the soil when they left the home. That began his planning for scientific agriculture that today makes Boys Town the equal of a state agricultural college; it started here, in a very small way.

A small plot was cleared for a vegetable garden and planted with the high hopes born of seed catalogues. But there were no crops. The young farmers, under Father Flanagan's direction, did everything they were supposed to do, watering and weeding and watching with great anticipation for the first sprouts, but still nothing came up. Nor was the mystery ever solved; they just went at it again the next year—and this time they got results.

In the chicken-raising program they fared better. Friends gave them starting chicks, and these they raised, layers, broilers, and roasters.

With more than a hundred boys now, there was also the increasing problem of paper work. And the job of keeping books, records of boys in the home, and filing of the correspondence was a burden. In addition, fund-raising letters, letting the public know about the work of the home, had to be sent out regularly if the contributions needed to keep the home going were to continue. Yet there were no funds for secretarial help.

What to do? Pray and beg was Father Flanagan's answer, and soon a group of young men and women in the neighborhood volunteered to give their spare hours to the cause. Many were men and women who worked as clerks and stenographers in Omaha. During evenings and over week ends they came to the home and got out the letters.

And then, to his great relief, he was allowed to take on an assistant—Patrick Norton, his nephew, from the old country. That was the beginning of a most important and lifetime association. Norton became not only Father Flanagan's chief aid but also his closest friend. They were together throughout years of struggle and growth, sharing many uncertain adventures of the early days. In later years Norton became business manager of Boys Town, a post which he still holds. It was Pat Norton who was with Father Flanagan when he died.

With Norton and the volunteers, the paper-work question was partially solved. But paper work was not the most troublesome of worries; a hundred boys had to be fed and clothed and some attempt made to keep them clean. It was too much for too few Sisters. Again the neighbors lent a hand. This time housewives and mothers, grand-mothers and aunts volunteered; women who understood the diffi-culties involved in bringing up even a few children—and knew what it was to love a child.

Not long after Father Flanagan took over the German-American building, the women of the neighborhood held a meeting to discuss how they could help. A delegation informed him of the creation of a "Mothers' Guild" for the sole purpose of helping to care for his boys. They meant it; they washed clothes and ironed them and mended them. There were twenty in the group, and their work quickly eased the operation of the home. It was also a way of spread-ing the story of what was being done here; the women became evangelists. Through their friends and their clubs they were letting the town know.

Father Flanagan was beginning to realize how important it was that the story be told. The public must know that these despised boys were doing well; no relapses into wrongdoing ways; they were lead-ing normal lives, growing up to be good citizens.

With this in mind, he started their first magazine—the *Boys' Home Journal*. It was printed by a shop in Omaha, but was written and edited by Father Flanagan and his boys.

It was no great journalistic achievement, but it narrated events of the home, recorded gifts, and specialized on the back-yard sports. The *Journal* is no longer published, but today at Boys Town they print its direct descendant, the *Boys' Town Times,* a more profes-sional job of editing, and produced on their own power presses.

Another activity of that early time was a misguided experiment in soapmaking. This also was carried on by the boys, in a small factory set up in the yard. When the soap was finished, boys wrapped the cakes in colored tissue paper, while others, constituting their "sales force," peddled it in a door-to-door campaign. Results, how-ever, were so meager, and profits so slight, that Flanagan ordered that any soap made in the future would be for their own exclusive use.

It was a time of experimenting and improvisation, and meanwhile help continued to come, not from wealthy foundations and charities, but from those who had least to spare, from people who would send in at most a one-dollar bill, or gifts of another kind.

The acknowledgments in early issues of the *Boys' Home Journal* tell their own story:

> Two quilts, from Mrs. ——
> One chicken, from Henry ——
> Candy and oranges from Mr. and Mrs. R. ——
> Three blankets from Mr. Richard ——
> Four coats from Mrs. Agnes ——
> Two tablecloths from M. J. ——

These lists would run on sometimes for two columns. Included were some of the town stores which sent out supplies. From an electrical shop a lamp; a shoe store would deliver a dozen pairs. One member of the Mothers' Guild arrived one afternoon carrying a large box of dinner dishes.

She explained she had purchased them especially for Father Flanagan's own use.

"He's been eating off of cracked plates for too long," she said. "A man like him deserves a decent plate for his meal, and a coffee cup that won't leak."

Somehow, month after month, day after day, the money that they needed came in, the help, the clothes, and the food. Nor was Father Flanagan surprised; from the beginning he felt serenely aware that God would take care of him, a hundred boys and all. He continued to go with confidence to his faldstool and his prayers.

II

The boys came now from distant cities and states, but some in Omaha liked the home less and less. These boys had been in serious trouble with the law. Others were destitute orphans. Neither creed nor race had any bearing on whether a boy was admitted, and all were treated equally in the home. There were bitter critics of such tolerance. A few referred to it as Father Flanagan's "Reform School" for young thieves. Others criticized the policy of white, Chinese, and Negro boys living together without segregation.

"If God had intended people to be all the same," one Omaha politician demanded, "why did he make them of different colors?"

"And could you tell me—what is the color of the soul?" was Flanagan's reply. White and yellow and brown, they kept on coming; some without training or education of any kind.

One boy, up from a Southern state, was barefoot as he stepped to the station platform.

"And what did you do with your shoes—dear?"

"Shoes?" The boy looked surprised. "I never got any shoes."

At once Father Flanagan took the newcomer on a shopping tour. The shoes they finally selected were heavy and sturdy, and the boy was vastly pleased with them; he said as much as the priest taught him how to lace them up. Not until they reached the street did the trouble start. The boy simply did not know how to walk with shoes on. He tried hopping, as if he were mounted on some invisible pogo stick. In vain Father tried to show the lad how easy it was to put one foot in front of the other. All the boy could manage was the spasmodic motion of a jumping bean.

The priest accepted the inevitable. Paying no further attention to the glances of passers-by, he led the way, with the boy bouncing up and down the whole way home.

III

Another evening, after dinner, Father Flanagan was told that visitors were waiting in his office. There was a pretty young woman. Like the Wife of Bath, as was later to be learned, she had had several church-door husbands, not including other company in her youth. And in the shadows opposite sat a boy of about eight.

It was the already familiar story of desertion. She didn't know where the boy's father had gone. She couldn't take a job and care for the boy too. Would the home take him?

Father asked a few questions about her home and financial status.

She had little money, but if he would take the boy, she promised to send money for his support whenever she had any to spare.

He glanced at the boy, and pity struck at his heart. The lowered, glittering eyes, the twisting fingers; here was a boy's desire to be brave struggling with a child's instinct to be afraid. He decided to take a gamble on the child; the mother kissed the boy good-by and was gone.

"Stand up now, Tommy. Let's have a look at you!"

But the boy did not move. He said haltingly:

"I'm sorry, Father. I can't——"

The boy was a helpless cripple.

Ordinarily he could not accept crippled children; there were no facilities for special cases. And any boy with a serious physical handicap suffers greatly in everyday competition with normal children. Yet this child's mother had just walked out of his life. And how this half pint needed love!

"It's all right," said Father Flanagan. "You'll have a great time here. One of the bigger boys will carry you up to your room where you'll stay with the other fellows. Would you like that—dear?"

Never again did they hear from the mother. But Biff stayed on. Under medical treatment his condition greatly improved. Today, grown-up and successful in business, Biff walks almost normally, with the aid of a cane.

It w————— his story which served as inspiration for the plaque which has become almost a trademark of Boys Town—a large boy carrying a crippled lad on his back. Beneath the figure is the legend: "He ain't heavy, Father. He's my brother!"

IV

The sheep in his fold were of many kinds. Some were highly talented youngsters. One, for example, had a true gift for music. He could pick up any instrument and play it, although virtually without musical education, and in spite of his declaration that for whistling and singing he had been "spanked as far back as he could remember."

Father Flanagan determined that boys of such talents should be given a chance. Through volunteer aid he made sure that the lad received regular training and kept up his practice. The boy was, of course, the outstanding member of the original band which made its tour of the Middle West. Music was in his blood. Today he is one of America's popular band leaders.

There were youths also with other kinds of talents. Some even had a knack for trouble. Take the two who came to the home following their attempt to invade Mexico.

These lads had resolved to capture the notorious bandit Villa, and theirs had been a conscientious effort. The pair, fourteen and fifteen years old, had actually organized a band of some twenty-five from their town on the banks of the Rio Grande. They had, a little at a time, stolen food, guns, and ammunition from their families and neighbors and from hardware stores. All the supplies were cached away under a livery stable. But other activities of the twenty-five boys had riled the police; they were determined to stem the outbreak of crimes, so the boys decided they dared not delay their "invasion" any longer.

When twilight came to the banks of the river they "borrowed" a motorboat which they renamed the *Buzzard*. Under cover of darkness they loaded their supplies. The night was clear and cold as twenty-five boys crowded on board and finally, in the deep early morning, the would-be conquerors of Villa set sail.

Half an hour later a United States Customs boat drew near and hailed, upon which the two leaders of the "invasion" shot full speed ahead.

The fantastic chase lasted more than an hour. Several times the customs men's bullets sprinkled in the water around them. Finally the boys realized they were being driven out to the open waters of the gulf and decided there was nothing to do but surrender. "We agreed," the two leaders declared later, "to run up the white flag."

Most of the children involved were given suspended sentences and allowed to go home in custody of their parents. But the two leaders, against whom public sentiment ran highest, were headed for real punishment.

Reading about the case in the papers, and checking into the facts,

Father Flanagan sent word to Texas that he would be willing to take the boys into his home.

"I have read," he told them, "that you believe these two boys to be bad. I don't see how you can help them very much, if you think that. They are not bad; they are victims of a fallacy which deceives many older persons—the misguided belief that a good end can justify a bad means. Those lads felt like knights of old—and Villa was the dragon they set out to destroy. And that is true whether they know about knights and dragons or not."

The authorities replied that they were glad indeed to send on the two would-be generalissimos. In fact, the wire added, the two boys were already on their way.

During the months they remained at the home these boys were never in trouble; nor were they afterward. With their own backgrounds re-established, they could, at length, be returned to their families.

"Maybe when we get older," they told Father, "we might join Uncle Sam's army. Until then—we're civilians."

v

Now the schooling of his restless one hundred was a crucial problem for Father Flanagan. While they had been in the Dodge Street house he had sent them to Omaha's public schools. But a boy from the Flanagan Home was of too much special interest in a public school. With the sometimes exquisite cruelty of childhood, youngsters in the class would badger them with taunts that they were criminals and thieves. Many a boy had returned to the Dodge Street home with black eye or cut face after a schoolyard battle. "They started calling us gangsters," the boy would explain. "Flanagan's gangsters."

Furthermore, many boys from broken homes and bad family situations were in need of special instruction, but in public schools such individualized training was hardly possible.

In the first summer of the German-American Home occupancy he started his school. Since most of his boys were in the younger age group, and few had gone higher than fifth grade, he began with primary and grammar-school grades. The "faculty" consisted of the Sisters, Patrick Norton, and Father Flanagan. It was a new kind of school, designed to fit the particular needs of boys whose education had been interrupted or, as in some instances, never begun.

Ever since that summer Boys Town always has had its own school. Today, expanded into a Class-A high and grammar school, it is regarded as an outstanding educational center, with a faculty to match that of any in the best preparatory schools.

In those old, beginning days he established what he called the "story hour," when, gathering younger boys around him, he would read aloud some of the boyhood classics or recount to them some legend of history and literature. He was a natural storyteller, as we were to learn as soon as we sat with him and talked of olden times.

"But what story that I read them or told them could be more wonderful than the ones we were living?" he demanded. "Do you know about those three boys without hats or shoes? They showed up one afternoon during our story hour—and the yarn *that* afternoon never did get finished."

At the entrance to the home the three strangers turned and walked up the path to the porch. The oldest was tall and looked about fifteen; another looked thirteen, and the smallest was no more than nine. All three were dressed in filthy overalls which appeared to be the only clothes they had on their backs; no shoes, no hats! The older boy carried a knapsack tied to a stick over his shoulder. He watched the bundle carefully, as if it were a family heirloom. But, as Father was to say later, it was more like an Arabian Nights treasure.

"We're not beggars, your honor," the oldest boy told Father Flanagan. "We're not asking you to give us anything. We can pay our way and that's what we want to do. Can we come in?"

CHAPTER TWENTY

The Bracelets

For days the brothers had been hiking; meanwhile they had had little to eat except candy bars. Now, with a good meal stowed away, they relaxed and told their real names.

Father Flanagan at once recalled this case; he had been in correspondence with authorities in their home state, and was hoping that they would be sent to him. But the brothers had grown impatient with the law's delays and had set out on their own. The priest studied them with careful eyes. Why couldn't they have waited? And what on earth could be in that knapsack, so tenderly swaddled on the oldest boy's lap?

Leaning forward curiously, Father Flanagan asked: "And what do you have in that bundle—dear? The way you hold it now, you'd think it was full of gold."

The boy nodded.

"It is, Father—just full of gold. Do you want me to show you?" He began to untie the knapsack on the floor.

"It belongs to us three," he announced firmly. "Me and my brothers. We wouldn't have had the nerve to come here, if we didn't have these, so we could pay our own way."

The blue bandanna was untied now and spread out, contents all revealed—golden bracelets, rings and necklaces, with glittering gems in old-fashioned settings; diamonds, emeralds, and rubies. The three boys stood around the glittering pile of jewels, gazing down with admiring eyes. Where had they got this loot? Why, this was their inheritance.

"My father brought it with him from the Caucasus," the older boy explained. "It all belonged to his mother. But now she is dead

—and you know about our pop—so the whole business belongs to us. It's our protection, and it's all we got, Father."

He knew how much horror there had been in their lives. Many times he was to cite their case as an outstanding example of the helplessness of children, of their inability to escape from evil if their parents are involved.

The brothers had lived on a ranch with father and mother. The man had not been able to afford much help and life for the boys was a routine of hard work, which they accepted, knowing nothing else. But mother longed for bright lights and music. She began to take "vacations" from the ranch, going off on trips alone, visiting friends only vaguely identified. As the boys grew older her "vacations" became longer and more frequent.

She had been gone for several weeks on one of these trips, when the father became seriously ill. For several days he lay in bed, with high fever. The boys were getting him a meal, late one afternoon, when the wife unexpectedly returned.

From his sickbed, while the boys watched and listened, the husband began to upbraid her. She flared back, telling him how she hated him and his ranch.

"You can have it here, if you like it so much," she told him. "I'm sick of it. I'm going off tonight and this time I'm not coming back. Do you understand? I'm clearing out for good."

The husband pushed himself up in bed. Still weak and feverish, he grabbed her arm.

"It's no use trying to stop me," she screamed. "It's no use——"

He did not seem to hear. He delicately climbed from bed, walked out of the room, and when he returned he was carrying a harness belt and buckle.

The boys were standing outside the door. The father beckoned to them.

"Come in," he ordered. "I want you to see this."

He lifted the dangling weapon and swung the strap against her face. She screamed as again and again he struck. Before the eyes of his sons he flogged their mother to death. Even after she lay lifeless on the floor, the thudding of the strap kept on.

From the raging and feverish mind of the father, all sense had fled. Exhausted, once he was sure of her death, he swayed with the bloody leather dangling in his hands. It was a long time before he could speak; he muttered to the boys to fetch some water. But the water was of no use. She was dead. Terror swept through the fevered man; he began to murmur to himself that the sheriff would come and get him. They would hang him for having murdered her. His three sons would be the eyewitnesses against him. They better not!

He would have to think of something pretty quick. But what? Well, the woman was known by everybody to go off on vacations. No one ever knew where she went. No one had seen her come home this dark afternoon. Why couldn't they say she had not come back, if anyone asked questions?

He commanded the boys to go with him, out to a nearby field where they kept the hogs. Here all four started to dig. Later that night, under cover of darkness, the father and the three terrified boys buried the mother's body. They shoveled back the earth and all stood on it and stamped it down.

Back in the house, he told them they must put the thing out of their minds forever: "All you know is that your mother went away."

No one knew the truth, he thought, except himself and the boys, and they would be too frightened to tell. No one, he was sure, ever would know.

But, of course, he was wrong. People *had* seen her come back to the farm. No one had seen her leave. There was talk. And then the thing the killer had feared came upon him; the local sheriff came out to ask a few routine questions. The father tried to hide his nervousness, but the suspicious law agent searched the grounds, and found her.

For weeks the crime on the lonely ranch caused excitement in the community. But after the man was shipped off to prison for life, the excitement died down, and people forgot. *It is a matter of verified fact that no one in that community bothered to ask one question about what was going to happen to the three boys.*

They stayed at the ranch, attempting to go on housekeeping, and farming, by themselves, with the older boy taking charge. Always in the back of the oldest boy's mind was the realization: "If things go

Gateway to a new life for thousands of boys.

The new entrance: The Administration Building is to the left.

A Boys Town classroom.

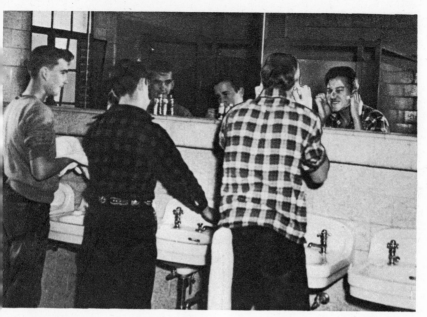

Cleaning up.

Turkey for two.

Bread for today—a trade for tomorrow.

Student barber and customer.

too wrong, if we do run out of food and money, we've still got the jewelry. That's worth enough for us to eat on forever."

He had told no one of that secret treasure. Wrapped in the blue bandanna handkerchief, it was kept in the back of the bureau drawer.

But at last somebody began to wonder about the three brothers. A reporter from a paper in a nearby town set out to get for himself a "human-interest" story. His story of three boys living alone on a big ranch, mother murdered and father in prison, did arouse the community. Not that anybody offered to take them. But they did write to Father Flanagan, a thousand miles away. The town fathers heartily approved of that idea; if the priest would take the boys off their hands, it would be a great saving to the county. Even so, the correspondence lagged until the three youngsters took matters into their own hands and hiked to Omaha, treasure and all.

"We don't come as beggars, Father," the oldest boy reported proudly. "We've got these jewels. We can pay our way and we want to!"

From that day on the three brothers were immersed in work and study, sports and recreations. The nightmare of the past began to fade. Today all three are successful. The oldest became owner of a farm, the second is a barber, and the third has an executive job with a factory. Not long ago the second oldest returned, to introduce his bride to Father Flanagan.

"We still have the jewelry, you know," she smiled. "We have our share and the brothers have theirs. After keeping it all tucked away so carefully here at the home and then all these years afterward, they'd never want to sell those valuables now, even considering the way prices have gone up for old jewelry."

Father smiled, as De Maupassant must have smiled once upon a time. From the first glance he had known that the treasures they thought so priceless were actually garish imitations, brass and glass.

"But if we tell the story, Father," we reminded him, "they will read it and know the truth."

"Good! They're entitled to it. Only, I never had the heart to tell them. But it's time they knew!"

CHAPTER TWENTY-ONE

The Girl in Boys Town

The return of the young barber to present his bride to Father was no remarkable circumstance. Return of former boys, often with wives and children, has become an almost weekly occurrence at Boys Town.

From the first the concept of Father Flanagan was that his place must be a true home, to which the boys could always feel they "belonged." So real did this concept become that many, entering service in World War II, listed Father Flanagan as their "next of kin."

Father himself continued to write to hundreds of his boys after they had gone out from his home. Today his staff carries on this practice. Scores of letters go out each week to members of this "family," scattered in every part of the world.

It is a "family" which today numbers more than six thousand young men—and one young woman!

The story of the only girl in all the files of Boys Town extended over twenty years before the case could be written off as "satisfactorily solved."

It began when two young brothers were sent to the German-American Home from a juvenile court. They were very young boys and had done no wrong. The court had found they were suffering from neglect; the parents were drinking and giving the children no proper care.

Some time after their arrival Father Flanagan received a phone call, late one winter evening, from their mother.

"Father," she began excitedly, "I'm calling from Union Station. I'm leaving town and I'm not coming back. I'm ditching my husband."

"And why call me to tell me these terrible things at this time of night?" the priest asked, a quaver creeping into his voice. "If you must go——"

"Because we've got *another* baby, Father," she said. "I'm leaving it with an old woman, in the basement of a building over at Twenty-fourth and Douglas. If you want my baby, Father—you can have it!"

The woman gave him the precise address and slammed up the phone.

By that time Father had acquired a Model-T Ford, "gift of a friend." He drove out alone to the building; no lights were to be seen, but there were basement steps, and at the bottom, through the glass of a door, he could make out a dim glow. He knocked and pushed the door open.

By the light of a coal-oil lamp burning on a table he made out a crone—"just like the hag Azucena in *Il Trovatore*," Father told us. She was holding the baby in her arms and rocking back and forth, refusing to give it up.

"The mother's coming back for it," the hag insisted. She was surly, persistently rude and ill-humored. "She told me so. I'm only minding the child."

"She won't return," Flanagan said slowly. "She told me so. She's run out on you—and on this poor infant."

Still the old woman shook her head. Father Flanagan had to produce a police badge he had recently been given by the grateful Omaha police commissioner. Now was the first and last time he ever used it; he showed it to the old witch, and it did the trick. He took the baby from her. He wrapped it in a stinking blanket and a few minutes later he was on his way back to the home in his Model T. The baby was sleeping peacefully by his side on the front seat.

He called two astounded Sisters into his office and presented them with the baby, and from them he learned the truth. It was a girl!

That night the waif slept in an improvised crib in the Sisters' quarters. Not far away, in the dormitories, slumbered the baby's older brothers, who did not even know they had a sister.

Because of the upset conditions they had lived through, and of circumstances which might arise in the future, the priest decided not to tell them right away. Next morning he took the baby to the home of a childless husband and wife who, like many others, had often told him they wished for a daughter. The couple readily agreed; only three weeks later the husband and wife began court action to adopt the little girl.

When they grew older the two boys were also adopted, by different families. The background out of which they had come seemed a part of the past which would stay dead forever. Occasionally Father Flanagan would hear from the boys. And although he made no attempt to see the girl, he kept track of her.

The war came, and many former Boys Towners were going into service. The older of the two brothers enlisted in the army and was sent overseas. And now the soldier began to ask questions about his background. Sometime later, perhaps, Father Flanagan responded, he would be able to trace all the facts for him.

Then one day he received the telephone call. It was a woman's voice, and the moment she gave her name he knew. The very grown-up young lady calling was the baby he had taken from the arms of an old hag twenty-one years before.

"I'm calling, Father," she was saying over the telephone, "because I have to know who I really am."

Married now, she had been trying to obtain a war job, but needed a birth certificate. In her search she had discovered that her origin was a mystery. There was no longer any point in withholding the facts. Father Flanagan told her her own life story:

"Those two boys—your brothers—have grown into fine men," he concluded. "One is overseas now, in the army."

There was silence at the other end of the telephone. After a second he asked:

"Is anything the matter?"

He heard her screams of happy laughter.

"I'm still here," she said. "It's only—you just don't find yourself with two brand-new brothers every day in the week."

There began a series of crisscrossing letters. The younger brother had not been heard from for some years. But the older boy in the army was writing regularly, and now the priest was able to reveal the facts the youth had been so anxious to know.

"Your own sister is now happily married," he wrote. "I am sending you her letter and address. I am writing her today telling her I have done this. I am also sending her the little record you sent to me for Christmas. I am sure she can get some machine to hear your voice. And you are going to see her again, please God."

At once brother and sister began writing to each other. But after a while the letters from overseas stopped coming and the sister began to wonder. It was five-thirty one morning when her doorbell sounded. Standing on the steps was a good-looking young soldier. As she opened the door he threw his arms around her.

"Don't you know your own brother," he was demanding, "after all these years?"

Later Father Flanagan was able to reach the younger brother and to bring all three together. All are married now, with children of their own, but every little while they meet in reunion, these three who started life with almost every break against them, except that they were lucky enough to come within the loving ambit of this indefatigable priest.

CHAPTER TWENTY-TWO

One of the Least of These

The storehouse of Father Flanagan's memories of those early days in *old* Boys Town was an embarrassment of riches. Literally he had a story for every lad in the place; it was not easy to pick and choose. But certainly the story of Henry Sutti belongs among the indispensables, especially since it demonstrates some of Father's most controversial ideas.

As far back as that second home on South Thirteenth Street, there were types of experts—distinguished by a cold, hostile frenzy toward religion, as much as by anything—who said the tall, blue-eyed priest with the long stride and the deep voice was pursuing a chimera. You just simply could not run a home for derelict boys on such superficial ideas as he cherished under his black-brimmed hat.

Love was not enough. It might be good Christian dogma—but boys off the streets and out of reformatories would never understand that dogma.

With the perverseness of such boys, however, they did understand. And they were influenced by Father Flanagan's bland approach, where others, scientifically trained, failed miserably. From the earliest days of his Home for Boys, Flanagan lived in the midst of triumphant proof of Christian philosophy. His most persistent critics could not but see the fruits of the credo of love. It was from that disputatious era that there came Henry Sutti, known in the Central American world today as the "priest of the jungles."

Henry was just one more boy at the home. Yet in the wilds of British Honduras, because of the works of Father Henry Sutti, late of Boys Town, the children of native *chicleros* and mahogany cutters are now attending high school and preparing themselves to be leaders of the community, for the first time in the history of that tropical land of poverty and superstition.

It was a part of Father Flanagan's credo that every personality is divine and you never can tell which of the group will be chosen by Heaven to do some outstanding task. As was the case with Henry.

Back at the start of the 1920s, Henry Sutti was a twelve-year-old boy who seemed to have every break against him. His parents having died in New York City when he was an infant, he had been placed in a foundling home. At four years of age he had been adopted by a farmer and his wife in the Middle West. Then, when the boy was twelve, the farmer and his wife, who had been mother and father to him, suddenly died, leaving him homeless a second time—without a single living relative.

It was a farm neighbor who appealed for the boy to Father Flanagan at the former German-American Home. When Henry finally reached Omaha, the equipment he had with him was about standard for candidates: one suit, very patched; two shirts, one tie, one pair of shoes, three pairs of socks, one harmonica.

But from the first Henry fitted easily into life with the hundred and twenty-five other boys. He had a talent for music and played in the band. He was good at sports. Only in his marks was he different; from his very first month Henry's marks were up in front of Abou Ben Adhem.

Here, Father Flanagan promptly realized, was the most brilliant scholar who yet had come into his home.

"Have you any idea what you want to do when you grow up?" he asked Henry.

The dark-haired boy nodded unhesitatingly; he wanted to be a priest. And Father Flanagan recalled the long-ago day when he had made the same profession; remembered the long and tortuous road before he reached his goal.

There was the question of money; he would have to find the funds to finance the long education for the church.

For nearly a year he did not speak to Henry about it again, not until the end of high school. The brilliant marks had never fallen; the scholastic record showed for Henry Sutti not a single grade below ninety. With a record like that, a scholarship was not hard to obtain. The twice-orphaned young man came back to Boys Town fifteen years later as the Jesuit Father Sutti and celebrated his first Solemn High Mass with Father Flanagan as assistant.

Later new word of this Boys Town graduate came to Nebraska; he was working in the Negro slums of St. Louis.

"He helps the woman who must have her children watched while she goes to the hospital; he teaches a family to budget and to cook economically, advises a youngster who has a problem, handles a stabbing case. I call him another Flanagan!"

In 1943, Father Sutti was given an even greater chance; Jesuit Headquarters in Belize, British Honduras, needed a priest. It meant exile from his own country, probably for the rest of his life, but Sutti had taken a vow of poverty, chastity, and obedience. His new work was chiefly with the natives of inland villages. He made his rounds on horseback, through jungles so thick he sometimes had to cut his way with a machete, step by step. And he had to learn to live as did the people of this bushland, to eat their food, sleep in their huts, and speak their language, and establish jungle missionary stations. In the thatched huts which served as church he must celebrate not only morning Mass but special regional services of early evening.

"It is another beautiful custom," he wrote to Father Flanagan, "that they have novena services every night the padre is with them. Afterward, I hear confessions; then I look about for a place to sleep. One family offers me a place in their little hut. It is a crowded place tonight, and there are but three rooms. The padre, the family, consisting of the mother and father and three children, and even the pigs, turkeys, and chickens all use the hut to sleep in tonight."

Like Father Flanagan before him, Father Sutti already saw that it was the children who needed the most help.

Delinquency as Americans know it scarcely existed in this jungle world. But the people were poor, and none, except children of wealthy planters or government officials, had a chance to go beyond elementary grades. At a very young age a child was sent into the fields, starting a round of labors which would keep on, without hope or chance of improvement, until he died.

One day Father Sutti was reading a magazine article by Father

Flanagan endorsing the idea of farm co-operatives. Why not try out this idea in the jungles?

He began as Father Flanagan had done, with boys; native altar boys, from impoverished homes. They earned a few pennies for work after school hours. Now Father Sutti proposed that each boy save one penny a week.

If they did this, he promised them, somehow he would provide the means for them, when they were ready, to go to high school.

At the end of the first week the total capital amounted to seventeen cents. But soon the idea caught on; other boys came in, and by the end of the year they had amassed twenty dollars. Each member carried a "passbook" with his savings listed. By late 1945, four hundred and fifty children carried books; they had a thousand dollars in their bank. With this sum of money all of them could get through high school.

As a result, grownups asked him to start a plan for them; a "Parish Credit Union" was launched under his direction by three young women whose first deposits amounted to seventy-five cents. But a year later assets totaled ten thousand dollars. Fifteen similar clubs have since been formed on the same pattern throughout Honduras. In every case they are working to improve living conditions; children of the jungle going to high school, learning history and geography, mathematics and finance, while grownups go to night school—and all working together to improve their lives. They praise Sutti, but he tells them about Father Flanagan in Omaha, Nebraska, in an ex-German home full of boys from other kinds of jungles. Who could have told, in those early days, what one more boy in the home would mean to the helpless children of Honduras?

II

By 1919, without spectacular benefactions or the visible help of miracles, Boys Town was on an even financial keel.

That was a stirring time on the great backdrop of the world. The Czar of all the Russias, with his wife and children, had been ignominiously shot to death in a cellar at Ekaterinburg by Bolshevik soldiers. The Peace Conference had begun at Versailles. The Comintern was organized in Moscow. More and more birdmen were flying across the Atlantic. Prohibition was in the law, and soon, as never before, crime would be organized, while uncared-for children would be surrounded by incredible new perils. Theodore Roosevelt, idol of strong American youth, had lain down to sleep and died in his dreams.

Father Flanagan's Home for Boys grew slowly, but with resistless vigor.

Support still came chiefly from small gifts sent in by increasing hundreds of donors, augmented by sums earned through the sale of the *Boys' Home Journal*. Some of the clothing came in gift boxes, invariably secondhand, repaired on the spot by the ladies of the Mothers' Guild. Much of the food was donated by local tradespeople; so with shoes and shirts. A shoe store would send out a crate of shoes of assorted sizes. Or a department store would ship out several gross of shirts. The school, conducted by the Sisters, already, in its curricula and results, surpassed the requirements of Nebraska educational laws. Classes in those days were limited to grammar grades.

Not long before, in 1918, with his home established and growing, Father Flanagan had become a naturalized citizen of the United States of America. In the winter of 1920 the home was incorporated, with the Bishop of Omaha as ex-officio president; first being Archbishop Jeremiah J. Harty, who had given the authorization to launch the home.

There had been no national publicity, but a great deal of talk among lawyers and judges, doctors and social workers. At first visitors were extremely professional; later came tourists and sightseers, believing that bad boys were turned into good here by some sort of pontifical abracadabra. Congressmen, foreign statesmen, business executives, even movie stars, were among the callers at the sprawling old house on the hilly street.

By September 1, 1921, they had sheltered in the home a total of 1,251 boys, and while the greater part of these had come from Omaha, a large number were from sixteen other states, as far east as Ohio and as far west as Washington.

Many would stay only a few months and would then be returned
to their families, ready for a fresh start. Or they would be adopted
by good families, stringently scrutinized by Father Flanagan before
he let them have one of his boys.

And again, week by week, the old German-American house became more crowded. There had to be another physical expansion of
his factory for souls, as someone had called it. Not only for more
additions; Flanagan needed land. The failure of that plot in the
back yard to grow even a single bean he had never quite forgiven.
They wanted land where they could grow their own food, keep their
own animals.

First they tried a stopgap plan. Friends joined to help his purchase of a place known as Seven Oaks Farm, on the northern outskirts of Omaha in a section called Florence. The farm became part
of the property of the home.

Here the second agricultural program was launched, although
it had to be directed mainly by remote control. A tenant farmer
did most of the work, but the boys were brought out on week ends
to help in planting and harvesting, and to bring sacks of corn or
fresh vegetables back to the home.

But even though the beans and corn did at least come up, the
yield was still not enough, nor were the boys learning enough. So
Father Flanagan eventually sold the place, and with the money he
got for it he purchased another farm in the same area, known as
Forty Acres. Here the harvest was larger and the boys helped out
more, and yet it remained an exasperation—never the right thing,
doing nothing of what he visioned in his daydreaming. He felt at
sixes and sevens, not only about the farm but about the home, which
he began to think of as a sardine can, jam-packed. The simple fact
was that Father Flanagan's Home for Boys had again outgrown its
britches!

III

Once more the priest set out in quest of a new home.

It was when he started on this latest search that the "silent op-

position," as he called it, the objections of people who said he was
running a resort for young criminals who ought to be in reformatories, began to raise an influential clamor. No neighborhood wanted
them, so it seemed.

For a time he thought of building on the Forty Acres farm. But
there were many who let him know that his home would not be
considered a welcome addition to the flowering suburb of Florence.
Find some place else!

In Omaha proper he had his eye on a building previously used
as a school. It was large enough, and those in charge of the property
were anxious to sell.

Then came the protests. Not loud, not vociferous; discreet and
polite, with all the violence of firm politeness and influence. Some
residents in the neighborhood, both Catholic and Protestant, were
unshakable in their opposition. One resolution, voted in protest,
described the home as a "reformatory for delinquent and incorrigible boys" which would do great harm in a neighborhood where
residents were trying to build "the right sort of moral environment."
By that time the whole fight was in the open, and a new note had
crept into Father Flanagan's voice.

"These objectors undoubtedly are conscientious," Father Flanagan told reporters the day after the resolution was passed. "But
they are protesting against something they know nothing about.
They call my school a reformatory. It is not. There is only one reformatory in the state, at Kearney. My boys' home is a home in
every sense, as well-regulated and well-disciplined as any Christian
home in Omaha."

Then he tried to explain to the newspapermen the need for such
a home.

"Only two weeks ago I was called to Sixteenth and S streets at
midnight, to care for a little lad who had crawled into a clay bank
for shelter. His father was serving time in a state penitentiary for
murdering his mother. If he had been left in that clay bank that
night, he would have been picked up a frozen corpse the next morning."

He told them, too, about the boys themselves.

"They aren't bad boys," he reiterated. "They are simply misunderstood. When they come into contact with those who understand them, they are as plastic as boys in the best Omaha homes."

But it was not enough merely to answer objectors. In his heart he knew it would be wrong to throw his boys into any environment where they were unwanted. Being unwanted was the reason many of them were in his home.

It was then he remembered a rolling farmland west of Omaha, on the crest of a hill from which you could see the fields sprawling out on all sides.

It was land away from any built-up community, far enough removed so that no one could protest against what they thought of as contaminating influence. And there was space in it to grow. Space not just for one building but for many. Space, if they ever needed, for a whole town of boys.

IV

Joseph O'Keefe, the real-estate man, thought it might be possible to buy that land. Together they made a tour of the grounds and the buildings which constituted the ninety-four acres of what was then called Overlook Farm.

The farmhouses would, of course, have to house his boys. They were chicken coops and barns mostly; one small garage and a one-story house in which dwelt the tenant farmer, one Daniel Cattlett.

But it was possible, Father Flanagan was thinking as they trudged over the fields, that he could put up temporary housing. Later they would assuredly raise the money to build a permanent building, large enough to serve their needs; a fine one!

O'Keefe was a kindly man, quite interested in the work of Father Flanagan. But he was also a practical man of business.

"The cost of Overlook Farm," he said, "will run into many thousands of dollars. I don't want to dishearten you—but do you have that kind of money, Father?"

The priest smiled sadly. He did have a few thousand in actual cash in the bank, he explained. Money he had been putting aside as a building fund for a new home. And in addition he had his forty acres of land.

"But altogether your holdings are hardly worth a fifth of what this place would cost. How can you even think about purchasing Overlook?"

"Because we will get the money," Flanagan declared, and then, observing the incredulity of the real-estate man, he hastened on: "Our gifts come in slowly but steadily. That is real capital, you see. The good will of people who know about our work and contribute. If we can have time——"

O'Keefe could only gasp at the man's audacity. He had not had the heart to be specific and tell him that Overlook was worth close to a hundred thousand. And this amiable priest's idea was to purchase the farm in exchange for forty acres of second-rate farmland, a few thousand in cash, and the rest in time payments—to be obtained out of contributions they hoped to receive someday!

The owners of the property, O'Keefe disclosed, were David Baum and his wife. Baum was a highly successful Omaha businessman.

"He is a good and warmhearted man," O'Keefe remarked slowly. "But he is also a man of sound business judgment."

v

David Baum sat in stony silence as the tall priest before him outlined the blueprint of a dream.

"The gifts will come in, you see," Father Flanagan promised, "as they always have come in. People are good, and when they know what we are doing, they send in their small gifts and it all mounts up."

David Baum, having listened attentively to what seemed a most unrealistic business deal, then gave his answer:

"You are a good priest, Father, but I am a good businessman. If you should fail, no one would blame you. But I have associates and interests and responsibilities. I must think of them and what they might suffer from heavy loss."

"But is it not a good investment, Mr. Baum—these boys who will grow, because of what we can give them, into good Americans?"

"It is a gamble," the businessman insisted. "A business gamble you want me to make on an experiment with a crop of bad boys."

"Bad boys!" Father Flanagan almost shouted the words. "Mr. Baum—there *are* no bad boys. How can they be bad boys? They are just children—God's children!"

He wiped his brow. He had intended to make no such emotional outburst. This meeting was strictly business.

"I'm sorry, Mr. Baum," he said. "I speak in this way only because I know what wonderful boys they are. I realize I have very few assets——"

"Your greatest business asset," Mr. Baum replied, "is your faith."

Even then Father Flanagan did not realize that his outburst had carried the day. But Baum continued in unhurried voice:

"I will take the forty acres as down payment. The remainder will be paid in installments to be arranged—in the future."

VI

Without question, it was a fantastic business transaction, a gamble involving thousands of dollars, on the dream of a priest. Baum refused the cash.

"It might endanger your plan," he said. "You'll need every cent you can get to build paths out there, and roads, and your temporary housing."

As he walked to the street, thanking God for Mr. Baum, the priest was recalling those words he had used as if Heaven had put them into his mouth:

There are no bad boys.

The shortness of the phrase pleased him; it said everything.

In the years to come Father Flanagan's name was to be indissolubly connected with that simple statement. It happens that at least one other worker among boys has used the same phrase and states that he used it first. But it does seem to the authors that it began back there in the fields of the Leabeg farm. In any case, it was Father Flanagan who drove home the meaning of that phrase to the conscience of the people.

He had never said it in quite that way before. In his faith, of course, all humans were born in sin. But that was not what people meant when they spoke of bad boys. They meant that poor, homeless children were more sinful, more heavily touched with evil, than those who had homes.

And they were wrong. They were wrong because God would not blame mere children for being mistreated, misguided, and unloved by those in whose care He had placed them, to be reared and taught in His light.

In this moment of triumph, aware that he was making a great new step forward, the start of a new phase in the growth of his home, the priest knew also that what he had told David Baum was close to the heart of what he believed.

There *were* no bad boys. There were only bad parents, bad environment, bad example. That would be his credo, in full focus at last, from henceforth. No bad boys. None!

Book Three

CHAPTER TWENTY-THREE

Mother Comes Home

The fields of Overlook Farm rolled along one side of a thin ribbon of road, a highway twisting past this fertile, hilly section of land which lies almost exactly midway between the Atlantic and Pacific coasts.

Today it is the four-lane, super-speed Lincoln Highway. A new kind of city was to spring up here, at the side of the road, a haven for the fugitive and frightened, a new kind of "home town." Many such children, Father Flanagan surmised, would come in to him off this highway. And he was right. Stubby from the boxcar was a composite symbol of many others. Like the one about whom came a letter recently, typical of many that arrive at the Boys Town Post Office from out of the past.

The letter told about a young man who, back in the years of the depression, had become involved with racketeers and bootleggers siphoning illicit liquor into New York City speakeasies. He had begun to carry a gun and to think of himself as a "tough guy." Then authorities began to close in on his gang and the youth took flight.

After weeks of hitchhiking, he found himself, broke and hungry, along that twisting highway, and saw the sign: *Father Flanagan's Boys Home*. Though he had never heard of the place before, he walked in and asked to see Father Flanagan. The priest asked no questions; gave him food and a bed.

Now Father Flanagan had his suspicions about the young traveler. For one thing, the lad looked him too straight in the eye. It is a long-outmoded illusion that crooks have shifty eyes. Experience had taught Father Flanagan that the first thing young lawbreakers learn is to look at you with clear, untroubled ease; a technique of juvenile deception.

The fugitive stayed only a short time. He rested and joined the others in sports and he listened to the priest who talked about God as a loving Father who was ready to help His children. Then he left the home, "hitting the highway" once more. But this time he was heading back east. Privately, he had made an extraordinary compact with himself.

Back in New York, he joined the CCC. Later he found a factory job. When war broke out he served in Africa and Europe as an army sergeant. When the war was over he went back to the factory, and it was then a letter came to Father Flanagan.

"Today," the letter writer stated, "that man is an executive in junior capacity in a large retail chain of department stores. He owed this to the philosophy he learned at Boys Town.

"You can print this—it's true. It's me."

II

Excitement among the boys was at fever pitch when they heard about moving out to Overlook. Every one of them clamored for a chance to go out there first, to help in the preliminary activities. All during that summer Father Flanagan led them out in small groups to watch the roads being laid and the construction started on the "temporary housing."

These houses were one-story structures similar to soldiers' barracks, arranged in a quadrangle. In these buildings, by careful juggling of space, he was housing school, dormitories, chapel, dining room and recreation hall, and one building for the teaching of mechanical trades.

"Moving Day" was October 22, with the boys jammed into trucks, each toting his few personal belongings. Father Flanagan and Carlo, the dog, joined the last "load." Only Carlo seemed reluctant to go along. But he went.

First order of business, naturally, was to explore. The boys scattered wildly—but they were back at the temporary quadrangle by mealtime. The enthusiasm for the new place was boisterous. This was their first freedom to wander over fields where no policeman could chase them off. And Father loped along with them, feeling immensely proud that, in spite of debts, he was the somewhat battered suzerain of this vast new domain, invested with paramount authority over many delightful acres. He gazed upon those acres with delight.

It was the first time, too, that Father Flanagan had a "residence" of his own: a one-story garage, without basement. He converted it into a dwelling of two small rooms—office and bedchamber.

During the summer some of his boys assisted Dan Cattlett, the tenant farmer, who had been kept on to direct farming operations. He set up a vegetable garden for the boys. All of them wanted to be farmers, but there were other jobs to be done: setting up a baseball diamond and a running track. Soon they had a field, full-sized, for football and baseball.

But long before that the school program was going full blast; the Sisters, too, had not been idle. The one really new addition to the educational program was the "trades school." All they were able to begin with was a carpenter shop. The first trade at the home was that of Joseph, foster father of Jesus. Before long, under the tutelage of a master carpenter, teaching on part time and for the rest kept busy on jobs around the place, the boys were able to make tables and lamps and bookcases, all very much needed in the four temporary houses.

At this time, too, Father Flanagan, who had only recently enunciated his passionate credo, came to another spiritual decision: There would be no walls around the farm, no locks on the doors!

"I am not building a prison," he informed alarmed Omaha residents. "This is a home. You do not wall in members of your family."

But even some of Father Flanagan's own family were beginning to be worried. The tremendous labors of the priest, the moving, the reorganizing, the keeping on with his program, all began to leave a mark. He needed rest.

And when he roundly declared there was no time for vacation, Nora, his mother, decided to go to Overlook.

III

It was, he said, like being in Leabeg again. Mother was back on a farm, but with a much larger family to care for. She supervised cleaning and sweeping and cooking, but particularly she was watching over that two-room garage where her son lived.

Nora Flanagan was to become a curious force in Boys Town, a link between the children themselves and the childhood of Father Flanagan. She treated them all as she would have treated her own sons. And it promptly became an honor to be chosen as the boy whose "charge" of the week was to assist her.

Father Flanagan used to say her popularity was due either to her charm or to her cookies, and she would answer that it was certainly both.

These were times when he would grow disturbed at some sporadic outlawry among his youngsters.

"That poor Tommy," he would mourn. "He took apples from the next farm, you know. And he's done it before. The farmer is very angry with me. What am I going to do with that Tommy now?"

"And I suppose you never took apples yourself from a neighbor's orchard when you were a boy?" Nora Flanagan, who had a long memory for Leabeg, would demand.

He remembered. He often remembered the apples of his early temptation—and applied the recollection to the understanding of these children, who had never known such love as had been in the house at Leabeg. They would adopt any stratagem, any desire for obtaining advantage, getting something for their hearts or bodies, which had known so little. And over him again would sweep, as so often they did, some favorite lines by Sir Walter Raleigh— lines about justice and mercy in the Kingdom of God:

> For there Christ is the King's Attorney,
> Who pleads for all without degrees,
> And He hath angels, but no fees.
> And when the grand twelve-million jury
> Of our sins, with direful fury,

Against our souls black verdicts give,
Christ pleads His death, and then we live.

Be Thou my speaker, taintless pleader,
Unblotted lawyer, true proceeder!
Thou giv'st salvation even for alms;
Not with a bribèd lawyer's palms.

Meanwhile, Nora Flanagan moved among her son's adopted ones, and understood them as she had understood him.

IV

They were still crowded. New boys were seeking admittance at an increasing rate. Youngsters straggling in off the highway. Some would have a note with them—or just a card tied to a collar: "Father Flanagan, please to take in this boy, because I can no longer do for him."

The writers seldom, if ever, signed their names. He would take them in, learn enough to trace down the parents and the story. Then he would decide. But none was ever allowed to go back to a home that was no home—to parents or relatives who did not want the child.

Other cases were offered by telephone and letter and personal appeals of judges, probation officers, welfare agencies, even neighbors.

He could not accept them all. They had more space here at Overlook, but not the quarters they needed, the facilities, the money, to take care of all who wanted to come.

Sometimes there were cases brought in by the parents themselves. One father showed up with a boy who gripped a trombone. The mother deserted the home. The father was not earning enough to pay for anyone to look after the youngster while he was at work. In the garage office the father stood, squeezing the despondent boy's hand and proudly boasting of the lad's talent for music.

"I can't afford a teacher, you understand. He found the trombone —and taught himself——"

"He will like it here," Father predicted. "We've got a real band now. A band just for boys, you know. But we still need musicians."

"I'll never like it here," the young trombonist announced bitterly. "I want my home. I want my father. And I want my mother."

Nevertheless, when in 1925 he was graduated, Father Flanagan gave him a going-away present of two glittering trombones. And some years later he came back to Boys Town as a famous trombonist and a member of one of the "big-name" bands. With him came a young lady. He had brought her along because he wanted Father, rather than anyone else in the world, to perform their wedding ceremony.

v

When they moved to Overlook the plan had been to make these temporary quarters serve until they could square all their other financial obligations and accumulate enough funds to start on the big enterprise of building a main house.

But as the parade of newcomers kept streaming in, it was plain, almost before they were settled, that they would have to find a way of increasing facilities immediately.

Already they numbered nearly two hundred, and overburdened welfare agencies and charities poured in their appeals for others. Word of this plight quickly spread in Omaha, and just before Thanksgiving a group of leading citizens called a meeting. Topic for discussion: How can we help Father Flanagan's home?

"We all know what he really needs," one speaker declared. "He needs a big house."

"But the kind he wants would cost hundreds of thousands to build."

"All right, then! Let's raise hundreds of thousands!"

That night they launched a campaign to raise two hundred thousand dollars to erect a great new building at Overlook Farm, big enough to hold a school and a gym and dormitories and workshops —the first permanent building of Boys Town.

VI

It began as a campaign for what nearly everyone now agreed was a worthy cause. But it turned into a crusade which virtually turned the city upside down.

The start was not auspicious. Before they actually got under way, several well-meaning sympathizers decided it might be smart to bring in professional fund raisers. Unfortunately, these professionals did not realize that this cause was something different. To them, it was just one more charity. And their approach to the people of Omaha was just as it had been in a hundred other high-pressure drives. Their approach was no good in Omaha. To the people of the city, Father Flanagan, once criticized, now almost universally applauded, was a personal possession. They were having no part of strangers collecting funds in his name with a flock of stereotyped phrases.

By the end of the first week it was clear that the drive was a failure. The fund raisers were sent home. And some who had started the campaign were also ready to give up.

But there were other enthusiasts who urged a new approach. Why shouldn't the people right here in Omaha run the drive? Not professional money diggers, but men and women who were part of the community life.

The man to whom all eventually turned was J. D. Davidson. Tall and lean and young, Davidson, later to become president of the Nebraska Power Company, was already an active figure. Only a few months before he had successfully managed a campaign for a civic sport and recreation center known in Omaha as Ak-sar-ben. When Davidson heard the story of the failure, he agreed to take up this challenge. He was prominent in Protestant activities and in the Masonic order, and when he accepted the chairmanship he gained at once the support of a great majority of his friends, people of all creeds. The objectors soon faded away as the drive was resumed. In years to come Davidson, while potentate of the Mystic Shrine, was at the same time to serve as a director on the Boys Town Board of Trustees.

The men who conducted that fund-raising campaign under the leadership of Davidson were, in their way, as much a composite of America as the boys in the home itself.

There was Morris Jacobs, publicity and advertising man, who was one day to head an agency with branch offices in many cities. There were Henry Monsky, who was to become president of B'nai B'rith. And Francis Matthews, who would be Supreme Knight of the Knights of Columbus.

An oddly assorted group to run a campaign for a Catholic priest. One Catholic, one Protestant, and two Jews. The campaign they launched is remembered to this day.

Davidson and the others agreed the main thing was to get the public's interest at once, even if they had to set off firecrackers in the city streets. They did not go quite that far. But they did go down to the railroad yards and buy up a batch of signal flares. They started out for their first meeting at night, parading dark streets, with their freight-yard torches. Crowds would follow them to a corner; there would be a few songs, a few very short talks. Then the main speaker of the night would stand up—tall Father Flanagan.

"Hundreds of homeless boys have come to us, right from Omaha," he would say. "You should see these poor little fellows, their clothes ragged and their faces thin and pale. If you have a boy of your own in a good home, think of these unfortunate children who have no homes."

And then the collection!

Another star campaigner was Charles Kenworthy, a boy from the home itself. His efforts on behalf of the home during the drive won him the title of "Boy Orator" of Father Flanagan's home. The "Boy Orator" spoke at many meetings, composed of people accustomed to all sorts of appeals to their emotions, but nothing had touched them as did this boy and his words:

"Three boys a day are turned away from Overlook Farm, our home, because we have no room for them. I tell you, gentlemen, many a time I have wept as I saw a boy turned away, carrying his grip, his head bent low, beginning his journey back—to where?

"He has no home, he has no friends; his home has to be the streets and alleys and unclean hovels where criminals are made.

"I come to you as a salesman, for I have something to sell. The love of a homeless waif is for sale and it is my business to sell it to you. There are two things in this life greater than money, and they are faith in God and love toward your fellowman. You might have millions, but if you do not have these things, your life has been lived for naught.

"We do not want to develop into bad men. We want to be good citizens. On the farm we have cows, chickens, horses, everything; and we only need a building to make it a boy's paradise."

Sentimental tear-jerking, Hollywood style? Yes, no doubt. But those who listened saw a living exhibit of what the priest was doing. Many an audience, having heard the "Boy Orator," rose and cheered and then emptied their pockets.

Nevertheless they still needed nearly two hundred thousand dollars, and they had nowhere near that amount as the campaign drew toward its close, and they might never have raised it if the women hadn't stepped to the fore.

Directing the women's part of the drive was Mrs. Arthur Mullen, for some years head of the Catholic Daughters of America. Her husband was floor leader for Franklin Roosevelt in the Democratic presidential convention of 1932.

It was Mrs. Mullen who organized the "Women's Bucket Brigade," for a whirlwind finish. Omaha had never seen anything to equal it. The women brought buckets from their homes, for use as collection "plates."

They organized themselves into platoons of five or six. They divided the city into sections, with the determination to cover every home and apartment, every store and business, every family and adult in Greater Omaha.

Downtown they invaded restaurants, stores, night clubs, poolrooms, even speakeasies. Bootleggers and gamblers, bums and crooks in the backwash of Omaha's business section threw their coins and dollar bills into the buckets.

With this last-days help from the ladies, Davidson and his aides —Monsky, Jacobs, and Matthews—had won the victory. They had raised over $215,000.

In March of 1922, less than a year after they had moved to Overlook, ground was broken for the new five-story main building. Father Flanagan was jubilant. No prophet still, he could not guess that the darkest hour lay just ahead.

CHAPTER TWENTY-FOUR

The Circus of Father Flanagan

It was a sore and embarrassing trial that he could not get credit from tradesmen for his running expenses, while the cash raised in the drive went straight to the building contractors. Even as the din of hammers and saws filled the air and the new five-story building began to rise, Father Flanagan was again, or still, in a financial crisis. Extra contributions as well were taken by the builders—and payments owed on the land had to be met, so that very little was left for food and clothes and fuel. As bills from grocers and dairies began to pile up, the distrustful stores would send out truckmen with stern orders not to unload until Father Flanagan paid in cash.

"The food is all in the truck, Father," a deliveryman would state. "But I'm not taking out one loaf of bread until you fork up the money. You know how it is—a lot of people think this whole scheme will crash and you never will be able to pay."

More than once the food would have to be taken back. The situation called for a drastic remedy.

Presently the harassed Father Flanagan thought he had devised a solution—a new way to carry his case to a new public. In the front yard a crowd was watching a dancing Negro youth, boy spectators singing and clapping hands. Other boys in the home also sang or danced, Father Flanagan reflected, and there were lads with various talents, including that young juggler. Why couldn't he put together a group of performers and take them out on the road, a band of juvenile minstrels and vaudevillians, a show dramatizing the story of the home and its needs?

As he danced in the twilight the Negro boy could not have guessed that he was the inspiration for a fabulous troupe, and one of the strangest adventures in the saga of Boys Town.

Once before Father Flanagan had sent out the band on a brief trip, but then they had traveled by train. Now railroad travel would cost too much, and so the bemused man of God had another flash: why not use horse-drawn wagons, gilded and red, like a circus?

As it turned out, there was a factory in Omaha that constructed such wagons for carnivals. From that establishment, secondhand, Father Flanagan obtained, cheaply enough, circus wagons and horses. But when word leaked out of what garish new preparations were going on at the home, there were many conservatives in Omaha who mumbled in their beards: What kind of new tomfoolery was Flanagan up to now, with his household of young desperadoes?

Unperturbed, Father Flanagan went on to organize his exhibition. The first step was to start his talent hunt. There must be an interval before tryouts and rehearsals when, in spare time, boys could practice specialties: one trying to yodel, another endlessly repeating a trumpet solo, a third doing cart wheels outside the dining hall. The home for neglected boys began to sound like a rehearsal hall off Broadway.

Those not lucky enough to win a spot in the program competed for the less glamorous job of repainting the circus wagons with coats of red and gilt. Across the sides of each of these wagons glittered the words: FATHER FLANAGAN'S BOYS' SHOW—WORLD'S GREATEST JUVENILE ACTORS.

As the wagons started off the entire population of the home gathered to cheer a noisy send-off. The wagons glittered in the sun and the brightly polished harness of the horses jangled as they pulled through the gate.

An amateur advance agent, hired by Father Flanagan, meanwhile was arranging bookings: first stop Fremont, west of Omaha. The tour was to be under the direction of Pat Norton, but Father Flanagan decided to go along as far as the first stop. He could not miss opening night.

At Fremont the advance agent had done a good job; there were stories in the local paper and a half-page advertisement:

Father Flanagan's Boys' Shows! Hear the sixteen-piece Boys' Band! See Humpty-Dumpty's Fall! Orators, Dancers, Actors, Soloists, Comedians, Choruses. Adults, fifty cents. Children, twenty-five cents. More enjoyment and entertainment than ever before offered for the price of admission.

Somewhat overenthusiastic, perhaps, but it had the desired effect. The town auditorium was jammed. Everybody in town turned out, and they saw a good show. Keyed up after weeks of preparation, the band played at its loudest and most harmonious and the specialty performers went through dance routines, skits, and monologues with inspired precision and élan. One boy sang "Mother Machree" and another "If I Only Had a Home, Sweet Home," and the weeping of the spectators was ecstatic and wholly enjoyable.

From the wings Father Flanagan watched nervously, as worried about the show as any Broadway producer at a première; and, like such professionals, frightened most of all that the audience might laugh and applaud in the wrong places. But, as act followed act, applause grew louder; by the last curtain, people were cheering. The show—and the boys—were a hit, a palpable hit. Convinced that they had only clear sailing ahead, Father Flanagan left the show in command of Pat Norton.

Everything went along smoothly for the next few weeks. Night after night they would play a town, then pack the show back into the wagons and start off for the next town, jogging slowly over the Nebraska roads. As they neared a town, local boys would gather en masse to welcome them, and later would march behind the departing wagons as they rolled away. Many were the lads who wanted to "run away with the circus," until Pat Norton gave them a little talk about how lucky they were to have a home of their own.

But the enterprise was not making a profit, and that was its object, although it was also a "friendship tour," which would produce contributions in the future. Meanwhile the shows they gave just about covered expenses and paid off the original investment. But business fell off as the excitement of the performers began to die down; everything, even travel, became routine, and the company were in a kind of doldrums.

Then, like many another show troupe before them, they ran into sudden, unexpected disaster. It struck in a little town, which shall be nameless, three hundred miles west of Omaha.

II

As they rode into the village there were no boys at the edge of town; no one came out to greet them. This was unusual, because in all other towns officials had cordially received them.

Pat Norton climbed out of the lead wagon to investigate. It did not take long to piece together the bad news. No booking had been made for them in this town, and no auditorium was available for them. Worse, from what he could gather, they had no bookings beyond this town. Because of Ku Kluxian prejudice, the advance agent had run into booking troubles and had departed for parts unknown without informing them. In all their red-and-gold glory the troupe was stranded.

Pat Norton telephoned Father Flanagan that they were almost broke; only a few dollars left, just about enough for one more meal.

"Stay put in the village," ordered Father Flanagan. "Let the boys sleep, as usual, in the wagons. Tell them not to be alarmed. It will be all right. I'll be on my way, first train out."

It was a downcast group he found waiting when he arrived. But he refused to be heavyhearted. He had brought along some extra money; the cost of running the wagon troupe was low, and if they were careful, they could work their way back to Omaha, playing concerts in the open and passing the hat. He would stay with them all the way.

The emergency plans seemed to work for a time, but they took in less than they spent; little by little, funds were running out. By the time the wagons arrived on the outskirts of the city of Lincoln, all money was gone; there was not a nickel left. It was afternoon, and none had eaten since breakfast. The only prospect before them was a dismal one: the towers of the penitentiary. As Father Flanagan looked at those gaunt bastions, he smiled feebly.

"You know," he told Pat Norton, "the warden is a friend of mine. I think he may be having unexpected company."

Shaping unhardened clay.

Shoemaker's shop.

Learning to swim.

Boys Town teams in all sports compete with the best in the country—

but informal play is important too.

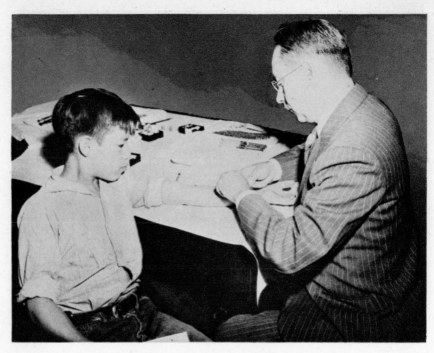

Boys get the best in medical care.

School's out.

The red-and-gold wagons rumbled in toward the prison gates. On the towers, guards trained machine guns down at the strange caravan. The same guns, swinging slowly, followed the hungry priest as he informed the entrance guard that his boys were very anxious to meet the warden. Only a short wait and the warden was greeting Father Flanagan like a lost brother. The priest was apologetic. He realized he and his boys were dropping in unannounced. But as long as they were passing, he thought he ought to stop in and say hello.

"Of course!" the warden exclaimed with an acuminous wink. "Why, this is wonderful. Say, Father, now that you're here, I've got a favor to ask of you. Would you let your boys give a show for our men?"

So it was all settled, as hoped. Naturally the warden entreated them to stay to dinner, since the show would be in the evening. And there was a place outside the walls where the wagons could bivouac for the night.

That prison executive was of Scotch descent and perhaps he had second sight. He said to Father Flanagan:

"You've come too late for lunch; there's no way I could take care of you for that. Except one thing, Father: there's a cantaloupe patch over yonder. The melons are just coming ripe. Think maybe your boys would like to sample them?"

"Those melons were the most unforgettable cantaloupes we ever met," Father Flanagan told us.

They gave a good show that night, and when it was over, the convicts yelled for more.

"But they've done all they know," Flanagan expostulated.

"Couldn't they all sing a little?" the warden suggested.

Well, back home they had sung hymns; they would try a few here. The boys by now were real troupers. Sure!

It was no great musical achievement. A group of unfortunate boys singing the Gounod "Ave Maria" before five hundred convicts. Most earnestly they sang, lost in the music. And the criminals, murderers and rapists, underworld creatures of every breed, were deeply stirred by the threnody of young voices lifted in praise of purity and goodness and motherhood.

As he listened, Father Flanagan was also stirred; his mind was running back to Rome and the Vatican choirs; his thoughts also spilled into the future. Someday, he was thinking, there must be a choir in his home. A real choir of a hundred voices. Not an improvised group like this, but a choir so fine it would sing in all the great concert halls of the country. The dream of the Boys Town choir was conceived in the Nebraska State Prison, partly on cantaloupes.

But that dream would be a long time coming to a head. Right at the moment they were broke, and full of music, and glad for this respite in the penitentiary before they started out again the next morning, on the final lap of the retreat to Overlook.

III

Never had there been such gloom in the home. To Father Flanagan it was a bitter defeat. He had planned the tour of one-night stands as a way of winning public support, and in Broadway terminology he had to admit that his show had flopped.

But on that point Father Flanagan was mistaken. They had failed temporarily—but not in the job of winning help. Messages from new friends began to reach the home: letters from fathers and mothers, from town officials and teachers of the towns where they had played. Some enclosed checks, others greenbacks; all said about the same thing: they were glad to have seen how fine were his boys; not cowed little lickspittle inmates, but buoyant, cheerful young citizens, deserving of help.

Confronted with such friendliness, Father Flanagan revived. He called in Norton and others; the idea of the traveling show, he told them, had worked better than they had dared to hope. He was going to try it again.

From a banker in Omaha he borrowed additional capital. But this time he wasn't having any circus wagons. The boys would go by train. They would travel into nearby states, where the home was just starting to be known. And for the new tour they hired a professional advance man of wide experience.

Results of this tour dazed Father Flanagan. What he had not realized was that the story of the stranded circus wagons had spread throughout the Middle West. People had resented the bigotry that finally blocked the tour; had smiled and wept over the show in the penitentiary. Already the story had become a legend. Everyone knew about the boys and everyone wanted a chance to cheer them along. This time there was no doubt about their success. They played to packed houses at night and kept up their studies every morning. Just before Christmas they returned home with a real profit. They had won new friends and the boys themselves had widened their horizons.

This was a bright time for Father Flanagan. The main building was finished in late fall, and the boys had already moved in. They had weathered the storm, the bills were paid on the building and the land, and contributions were increasing. Father Flanagan could look to the future now with high hopes—and confidence.

IV

In the next few years he sent many troupes out during summer months, touring the West and South, and staging a completely new show each "season." Eventually the boys traveled in their own private car, across which was displayed a glittering sign, "Father Flanagan's Boys Shows." Living in the car was a great advantage. They were safe from the cold, and the gusts and blasts of prairie winds. The boys cooked their own meals, sure of getting proper food, and they saved on hotel bills. Sister Nellie went along on some of the trips, serving as mother, confidante, and friend to the boys.

Not always were they greeted with smiles in those days when the Ku Klux Klan rose to its greatest power. There were occasionally "incidents." In one town a group of frowning men warned Pat Norton that the boys had better not show up for the evening performance.

"If they do, there's going to be trouble," the leader promised. "Somebody's going to get hurt."

Norton stood his ground. He could not call off the show; the tickets were all sold, the people were coming. And what harm could there be in the performance?

The harm, it appeared, was the fact that they were from Father Flanagan's home. Anxious to avoid trouble, Norton finally had to agree that the name of Father Flanagan would not be mentioned. The boys would simply be introduced as from Overlook Farm. That seemed to appease the prejudice of the community, and the performance was given without mentioning the name of the priest.

Sometimes there was trouble, too, because the troupe included boys of all races and religions. One day they were lunching in a hotel, while the train kitchen was being repaired, when Norton discovered that one of his boys was missing. Search revealed that the woman who ran the little hotel had forced the Negro child into the kitchen, to eat his dinner alone.

Norton told her emphatically that the boys always ate together and that there must be a place for him at the dinner table.

There was a place set for him, all right. And the dinner was in the kitchen, ready to be served. But the mistress of the inn had disappeared; she preferred to spend the night elsewhere.

Norton did not let her disappearance upset their plans; in spite of her vanishing act, they would not be forced to leave; they would still sleep the night in her untended hotel. After the meal Norton went behind the desk and passed out room keys. To the Negro boy he assigned the best suite in the hotel.

Often couples in the audience would remain to ask if they could adopt a boy.

"Why, if I were to let people take my boys," Father Flanagan would reply, "I'd come home with no boys at all."

No one was ever allowed to adopt a boy directly out of the show. But there were cases where they were adopted later by applicants out of the audience, after investigation.

There was also the everlasting problem of boys who wanted to join the troupe.

One night a small boy, ragged and dirty, marched himself into the private car. He was about ten years old, and he wanted to know: "Can I go on the train with you, Father?"

Even as he asked the question he was frightened to a point where he was trembling. Gradually Father Flanagan calmed his fears and drew out his story. His name was Hans; he had no idea where his parents were; "They're orphans," was all that he would say. He lived with another boy in a shack. He sold newspapers to buy food. The next morning a checkup showed that the boy's story was true; the ten-year-old had been living for months in a filthy shack.

Most of the townspeople, Father Flanagan learned, had known nothing about the case; now that he was taking the child with him by authority of a local judge, everyone was anxious to help. When he took Hans down Main Street on a shopping tour, the merchants treated the ragged child as a celebrity. They gave him shirts, socks, shoes, two new suits.

"None of which would have been necessary," Father pointed out, "if anyone in that town had loved the child in the first place."

Road tours of seven years served as one way of bringing to the people the needs of his boys. But it was a long road from the first group of boys singing hymns in the state prison to the world-famous Boys Town choir of today.

v

Father Flanagan's faith in the therapeutic value of music deepened over the years. He had never forgotten that long-ago conversation in the High Alps. Music, and especially singing, was an outlet for the energies of youngsters, a way of letting off emotional steam, of special value to the maladjusted. "I have seldom known of a boy who could sing and loved to sing who turned out bad," Father Flanagan once declared.

During the late twenties and the thirties the tours of his troupes were abandoned. Music and singing were confined to activities around Boys Town itself. The band played at games and gave informal concerts, and there was a loosely formed choir, solely for chapel services. But Father had not given up the dream of a traveling choir. Tenaciously he had held onto that dream, and finally, in

1941, he brought to the home a tall young priest, ordained only a few months before, Father Francis Schmitt.

"I want you to build the finest choir of boys in the country," Father Flanagan commanded with a grin. "I think we've the material to do it."

Father Schmitt, organist as well as singer, had given many years to the study of harmony and composition, continuing his musical training all the time he was preparing for priesthood. For two weeks he put volunteers through their trials. Incredible falsettos and premature basso profundos could be heard all over the place.

Once having chosen the most likely prospects, he moved them all into one apartment house. "They live like any of the other fellows," Father Schmitt explains, "but we do try to keep them from yelling themselves hoarse in some free-for-all just before a concert."

On the top floor he installed a library of records and sheet music. Here the boys come to listen to the classics. Light operatic music, spirituals, and folk songs are included, but no jazz, no swing.

"Once they get a chance to hear real music for a little while," Father Schmitt argues, perhaps naïvely, "they don't hanker for jazz. Some won't even listen to it on the radio. At least that has been my experience."

The choir grew slowly as he taught the vocalists an understanding of harmony, of musical forms, even the biographies of the composers whose works they sang. And presently the work began to take on importance in the home; to belong to the choir was almost as slick an honor as making the football team. There was even a "second-string" choir for those not making "the first squad."

The first major choir concert was in the Joselyn Memorial Museum in Omaha. Few of those who came anticipated a real concert. They were prepared for amateurish efforts, which they would feel bound to applaud—but, oh, shucks! What they heard astounded them: a magnificently trained and disciplined choir, capable of holding its own with anything similar in the nation. Cheers rose that night for a new musical group of real distinction, which had thrilled its first audience. Until the war's end in 1945 the boys sang at bond rallies and in army camps. With travel restrictions lifted, they started on their first real tour in 1946. Forty boys, in a train heading forth to sing in great concert halls. First the vast Municipal Auditorium in St. Paul. Again, on the opening night, Father Flanagan was in the wings, but the audience he peered out at was no mere few hundred, as once long before in Fremont; tonight the boys were singing to nine thousand people.

It was an ambitious program, highlighted by Faurés "Requiem" and the "Ave Maria." Encore after encore was demanded; when the boys woke up the next morning they found themselves and Father Schmitt hailed by the music critics for a brilliant achievement.

Wherever they went it was the same story. Symphony Hall in Boston, Carnegie in New York, and Constitution Hall in Washington; Pittsburgh, Peoria, Cincinnati, and St. Louis. Throughout America the fame of the choir from Father Flanagan's Boys Town began to grow. Immediate profits were not great, because of high overhead and operating expenses. But contributions from impressed auditors provided real dividends.

It was hard for strangers, hearing the singing of these boys, to realize that any of them had ever been in trouble. How could you look at those uplifted faces, as they sang the "Ave Maria," and believe that some had only recently been on the road to being hardened criminals? Skeptics indignantly charged that the choir was not a real cross section, that it was a hand-picked group of the "better type" of boy. One woman reporter interviewing Father Flanagan pointed to a lad in the tenor section and demanded: "Are you going to tell me that sweet-faced boy was ever in any trouble with the police?"

Father Flanagan did not reply, although a mordant answer, a biting and pungent rebuke, was on the tip of his tongue. He would not violate his sacerdotal trust by revealing the story of a boy whose name could be identified on the program. But the "sweet-faced" boy she picked had an interesting background. While less than 20 per cent of Boys Town citizens have police records, the "sweet-faced" boy was one of them. "He was an example," Father told us, "of how crime flies!" His parents had been divorced when he was hardly more than an infant. For a time he had been taken care of by an aunt, who later sent him to an orphanage. Finally he had gone to live with his father and a new stepmother, a lady of brittle beauty and frangible temper.

He had not liked his new family life, and not long after he arrived he ran away, only to be arrested. He had skulked back to the orphanage and tried to induce other boys to run off with him and form a gang. Three months later he was arrested again, this time for theft. Police found he had been practicing burglary ever since he had been returned to his father's home; the "loot" included fountain pens, cameras, bullets, and rifles and oranges. One social worker called him an "oaf."

Police had no legal choice about what to do with this twelve-year-old thief. From his cell in the jail he wrote to his father:

". . . I was glad in a way that they caught me and in a way I was not, because it was my last chance. I have to go to reform school . . . I want to see you but I cannot because I am going to reform school for eleven months . . . Please don't tell anybody about me being in jail . . ."

Father Flanagan was able to have the boy sent to him. From that day on there was no more trouble. Grateful for a new chance, the boy became one of the outstanding citizens, a leader in the classroom and in scouting activities, and in the choir.

The choir is no "showcase unit," no display window of carefully selected items. Behind every lad in Boys Town there is some story of tragedy, mostly of homelessness and neglect, of parents who walked out or who lacked the love, sometimes the means, to make a home for their child.

How do such boys react to the publicity, their pictures in the paper and all the fuss made over them wherever they sing? Father Schmitt says they take it in their stride. They are constantly reminded that the publicity is not for them personally but for the whole choir, and for Boys Town.

They have occasional racial problems, on tour, even today. In one Southern city the choir was offered the use of the municipal pool in the morning, before it was opened to the public. But when the boys showed up the keeper informed them that Negro members of the choir could not contaminate the water.

Father Schmitt promptly decided that none would use the pool.

But the Negro boys protested: "It's not right for the other guys to lose a swim on account of us." So the white boys swam. But the pool still was polluted, Father Schmitt adds triumphantly, because some were Negro boys, light enough to pass for white.

Long experience confirmed Father Flanagan's belief that music is a therapeutic agent of tremendous value, particularly in dealing with youngsters emotionally disturbed. There was the case of Enrique, a Mexican youth, who had been in difficulties at home; everyone had hoped he would straighten out under the Boys Town program. Instead he ran away repeatedly. Over a period of months this boy ran away fifteen times.

At last the Boys Town psychologists reached what they thought was the root of his problem: the boy felt he had no talents; he did nothing very well. There was no field in which he excelled as other boys.

The trick was to find some field in which he might be able to become a champion.

Inquiry disclosed that although Enrique had no voice, he nevertheless did sing at times when he believed he was alone. Always off key, sad to say, but in spite of that the psychologists called in Father Schmitt. Would he make an attempt to teach the boy to sing?

For weeks Father Schmitt tried to bring Enrique to a point where he would stay on key with the others. At first the boy took little interest. He would laugh when his mistakes were shown to him. Even so, gradually, he began to improve a little. He stopped laughing and began to take his work more seriously. The one hopeful fact was that for three weeks he had not attempted to run away.

After three months Father Schmitt was able to turn in an amazing report. Once this boy had gotten over his original feelings of inferiority, and desired actually to learn how to sing, he improved, so greatly that now he was good enough, Father Schmitt declared, to be a member of the choir. Not the second team—but the "first squad," the choir that would go on tour.

From the moment Enrique heard that news he became a new person. His whole outlook on life changed. His work and deportment blossomed, and of course the runaway problem was cured.

Some months after the whilom runaway had been graduated

from Boys Town, Father Schmitt received a letter from him. Over the radio Enrique had been listening to the world-famed Vatican Choir.

"It was good," he wrote. "But you know, I did think some of the phrasing was just a bit sloppy."

CHAPTER TWENTY-FIVE

The Boy They Wanted to Kill

With the passing of the years, troubles changed in kind, not in degree. Father Flanagan once declared he always felt snugly at home in hot water. When finances were no longer the most galling problem, his difficulties became those of boys he wanted to help. He had to fight for them, to fight even for the opportunity to help them.

Often it would have been easier to avoid publicity on the unpopular side, merely by staying clear of some case. That was when Father Flanagan would almost certainly move in, uninvited and often enough not wanted. He had an old-fashioned respect for authority, but he waged battle whenever he felt police and judges were wrong about a boy, as in the case of one "killer," nine years old.

It began when a mother and little boy of moonlike face walked into Father's office.

"I have brought my little boy, Pudge, here," the mother announced, "because they want to kill him!"

"Who wants to kill Pudge?"

"Lynchers. Neighbors in our own town. They say he's to be made an example of."

With Pudge sent off on a sight-seeing tour with a commissioner, the mother told the story.

The parents had been divorced when the boy was three. The mother had eventually remarried. Stepfather was a good man but the boy was his wife's child and he felt it was her sole problem to discipline him and guide him. As hard times came along the mother had to work out, and it was not long before Pudge was running around with older boys. One afternoon they found a bottle of whisky and all drank of it.

Staggering and half blind, Pudge had come home; the physician declared he had been poisoned by bad liquor. Pudge, only eight at the time, was saved, but two of the older boys died.

After that his mother tried to keep a closer watch on Pudge. But he and other youngsters used to play "gangsters against police," in which they would shoot each other "dead" with make-believe guns. One afternoon Pudge and another boy found a torn old coat, and in one of the pockets, a gun.

It was an old gun, rusty and worn, swell for playing. Pudge had never touched a real pistol before. To him this was was just like the toys he had always played with. He pointed the muzzle at his comrade.

"I'm a gangster," he said.

Before the other boy could move, the finger of this nine-year-old pressed the trigger. The other boy screeched in pain, toppled forward on his face.

The nine-year-old stared in befuddlement. This was not the way the game was supposed to go. The blood spurting over the asphalt was real. Practical, in spite of his panic, Pudge hoisted up his victim, slinging him over his back, and carried the bleeding victim down two blocks and up steps to a doctor's office. But there was nothing the doctor could do. The boy was dead.

When this killing became known, rage spread through town like an epidemic. It had been deliberate murder, a cold-blooded deed of violence by a precocious nine-year-old criminal who already had a record as a drunkard! In this rapacious rising generation something was needed to put these devil-ridden street brats in their place.

Why not lynch the kid? Once and for all, that act of public anger would teach juvenile delinquents a lesson they would never forget. This madness spread like a prairie fire, even though a coroner's jury unanimously agreed that the killing was accidental.

On two afternoons a threatening crowd gathered outside the home. Mother, stepfather, and Pudge barricaded themselves in, well aware that they might all be stoned or shot or burned to death. For two days the siege lasted, until a welfare worker got into the house late at night and pleaded with the mother to send the boy to Father Flanagan's home. Under cover of darkness she carried Pudge from the house—and here they were.

Hearing all this, Father Flanagan set the mother's chief worry at rest by assuring her immediately that the boy could stay. However, there might be further legal action brought, in spite of the coroner's verdict. County officials might still be determined to send Pudge to reform school. But Father Flanagan promised her he would resist them.

While he did anticipate some trouble, he expected nothing like the hostility and bitterness he was to encounter. The county attorney was furious that the woman had spirited "this killer," as he put it, out of the jurisdiction of local courts. So the mother was trying to defeat the ends of justice? He would show her!

Father Flanagan tried to explain that she had run off only to protect the boy from mob violence. He also assured the official that he would bring the boy back for trial. Keeping that promise, they went back together to face the court, priest and boy prisoner.

The courtroom was jammed and the county attorney was on the popular side. The crowd knew that he was going to make sure this nine-year-old did not escape the full weight and penalties of the law. In a long discourse to the court he described the boy as a first-degree murderer, a menace to society. Then, with apparently general disregard of legal procedure, he called Pudge to the witness stand and began to question him, exactly as he might have quizzed some vicious, hardened old slayer. The sharp, lunging questions bewildered the nine-year-old defendant.

After a few moments Father Flanagan jumped to his feet, demanding of the court that the inquisition be halted.

"He's only a baby, your honor," he declared. "This court is sitting as a juvenile court and the interests of this boy are at stake."

He demanded that any further questions be referred to him, since he was there on the boy's behalf. The judge turned to the priest:

"You're here as the boy's representative? Don't you think he's guilty?"

"I am not his judge, but I know he is no murderer," Flanagan declared. "And I know he has been neglected, too. Your honor, I am asking that you let me take this boy into my home. I have had hundreds of boys in my home. I will take the full responsibility that he will be in no trouble again."

Frenziedly the county attorney objected. The facts, he cried, spoke for themselves. The boy was a willful slayer. He should not be allowed to run loose where he could do more damage to other innocent children, even the inmates of Flanagan's place. He deserved no special consideration of any kind.

The Flanagan anger mounted as he listened to the harangue. At last he interrupted:

"You say this boy is a murderer. Then let me ask you this—do murderers carry their victims to the doctor? Don't you know that murderers run from the scene of their crime, that they try to escape and hope they won't be discovered? And isn't it true that willful killers usually have some kind of motive for their deed, beyond the mere playing of a child's game?"

He paused in this elementary lesson and perceived with a lift in his heart the sympathetic expression of the judge.

"Your honor," he lamented, "it's sad and plain to see what happened here. They found a gun and they played as boys will play with things they find. Only this gun was real and tragedy had to be the result. To every father and mother in this room I say an accident of this kind could have happened to their own son, to any boy from any fine home in this town. If such an accident happened to your own son, your honor, and he were nine years old, would you call him a murderer?"

The judge, who was a bachelor, looked shocked.

"Father Flanagan," he said, "I have no son. But I have decided that you may take this boy to your home. He is paroled in your care."

But there was still one more matter which the embattled priest wanted cleared up. Charges had been made that this boy was incorrigible. If the youngster ever returned to the city, no charges, or record of crime, should be left hanging over him.

Because of all the special circumstances of the case, the judge declared, he would allow the priest himself to decide what the record would say. So Father Flanagan wrote the record. It left no black mark against the boy, no statement that he was incorrigible or guilty of any crime. Merely the statement that he was being taken to Father Flanagan's home because the parents did not have the discipline or control over him "that a child of that age should have."

The priest and the boy walked from the courtroom together, heading back to Overlook, for there, as he often quoted to himself: "There the wicked cease from troubling and there the weary be at rest."

Several years later, after the mother had started a new life for herself, the priest, with the permission of the court, allowed the boy to return to her care, and the case of the "accidental killer" was written off the books—completely cleared up.

CHAPTER TWENTY-SIX

The Cinderella Boy

It was about this time that Father Flanagan had to make another major decision. Should he continue to allow boys from his home to be adopted? Or should be proceed on the theory that once they came they were to stay; that the place was truly their home and they were to think of or hope for no other until they were ready to go out into the world and make a home of their own?

Father Flanagan was acutely aware of his own ambivalence on the matter. In the beginning his plan was that most of the boys would remain only a short time under his care, long enough for "repair work" to be done. After that, according to his original concept, they would be adopted into private families, if their original homes could not, meanwhile, be improved, which was seldom.

But, as it turned out, there were unexpected drawbacks and pitfalls in the adoption idea; for instance, the depredations of "boy profiteers," a new kind of skulduggery in his experience. These ghoulish gentry, against whom Father Flanagan waged a bitter campaign during the 1920s, had found a way to use orphans and other homeless boys for their own profit.

The trick was simple. A farmer and his wife would come to the home, all kind little smiles, pleading to be allowed to adopt a boy, experimentally. They would be introduced to a youngster and at once begin to gush. Nicer folks, apparently, were not to be found.

Careful investigation would indicate they were respectable farmers. The boy would be told here was his chance to start a new life, with a new father and mother who would love him as if he were their own.

This usually would happen in the early spring. Anxious to make

good, the youngster would work hard all the summer months, helping the farmer in the fields. But as soon as the harvest was garnered
the atmosphere would change. The whole family became grumpy.
Nothing the boy would do could now please the surly foster parents.
And ultimately the farmer would throw up his hands and take the
boy back to the home from which he came.

Case after case, following this identical pattern, occurred just
after the harvest season ended; all the boys returned as "unsatisfactory."

Naturally the effect on lads who had suffered such experiences
was often disastrous. It weakened their faith not only in society outside the home but also in themselves. And as Father Flanagan took
pains to find out, it was happening in many of the orphanages and
institutions for the homeless in Nebraska; it was a peculiarly heart-
less racket, and he promptly launched a campaign against what he
called "profiteers in boys." It was virtually impossible to eliminate
this evil practice entirely, except on his own home grounds, but his
campaign was successful over the years. Once public opinion was
aroused, reform came quickly.

Not all adoptions were in the racket category; many were highly
successful. To rule them out altogether, as a policy of the home,
would be a serious step. Yet Father Flanagan inclined that way;
there was, even without rackets, a dangerous risk in any adoption; if
nothing else, there was the familiar hazard that an actual parent,
feeling a change of mind or heart, or more likely a whim, returned
to cause trouble.

One mother, for example, abandoned three boys. Father Flanagan took them in and, after a year or so, found fine homes for them,
adoptions by good families. They were growing up, happy and well
adjusted, in their new surroundings.

Then one day the real mother came back. She wanted her children. The priest would not tell her where the boys had been sent.
But the mother found out, anyway, and began to plague her sons,
with letters and phone calls, insisting that they had to return to her
care. The children had known only lack of care and lack of love
when she had them. Now, their emotional life again disturbed, they
wanted to stay with their new families, whom they had learned to

love. But, young and impressionable, they were not certain what was their duty.

Father Flanagan called in the mother and forced her to face the actualities. She agreed finally to leave them alone until they were more settled in their new homes, and went off, promising that she would keep in touch. But neither the priest nor her sons ever heard from her again. There were many similar instances.

It was true also that many of his boys were special cases, with particularly difficult backgrounds and problems which average foster parents, however well-intentioned, were not usually equipped to handle; they lacked spiritual hardihood. This factor led to many failures, and boys would be sent back to the home worse off than ever. As these unhappy experiences multiplied, Father Flanagan began to wonder if adoptions should be any part of his program at all. Would it not be wiser to set a new goal for himself, to build up the home and the grammar school and a full-fledged high school, and give his lads a complete and secure life?

Then came the case which determined his course—the brief excursion of an orphan boy into the world of wealth.

II

The newspapers called him the "Cinderella Boy." His friends called him Snorty. He was twelve years old, and since the age of three he had lived in an assortment of orphanages until he had been brought, when eleven, to Father Flanagan's home.

The adventure in high life began when his picture was published in a magazine article as a typical boy from Father Flanagan's home. The caption declared Snorty had top records for scholarship and deportment.

In a town many miles from Omaha a man of considerable wealth was startled at the sight of Snorty's picture. For a long time he stared with unbelieving eyes at the photograph. He showed the magazine to his wife and she, too, gasped; the photograph so resembled their dead son that Snorty could almost be his double.

People of means and position, they could give this boy a home life he had never dreamed possible.

That afternoon the husband sent a long telegram to Father Flanagan, outlining the facts. And Father Flanagan, once satisfied by investigation, felt that here, for Snorty, was a deserved and unparalleled opportunity. As for Snorty, he jumped up and down in his excitement; it was like a story come true.

From Father Flanagan's point of view, it was unfortunate that word of the adoption, negotiated almost entirely by telegraph, leaked to the newspapers. Naturally it was a story burning with human interest, and it was spread on every front page. Reporters and photographers were at the station in Omaha when the boy said good-by to Father Flanagan. More met him on his arrival, to record the welcome of the new parents and the boy, as the man ran forward and called out, "Hello, son."

The wife wept with joy as they all rode off together in the chauffeur-driven limousine. That was how it began, the world looking on at this real-life fairy tale. But Snorty did not live happily ever after. The "Cinderella Boy"—as the papers called him—did not do very well at the shining palace to which he had come.

Who was at fault? Hard to say, Father Flanagan declared. The simple fact was that the boy was unable to adjust himself. Why was not so simple. Before he had left Boys Town, Snorty had promised he was going to try to make his foster parents love him as their son. "I'm going to tell them about my past, everything I can remember," he had stated. "I'll tell them I wasn't always a good boy. How sometimes I broke rules in the orphanages."

Perhaps that was the trouble; his had always been a world of orphanages and institutions. He had grown used to sleeping in dormitories with forty other boys; to living in a group life, with rules and regulations that must be followed.

He was not used to the freedom belonging to a son in his own home. He was not used, either, to kissing mother good night. He was a little shy about kissing his foster mother, and naturally she wondered if this were a lack of affection.

Snorty talked a lot, too, about the things he had done at Father Flanagan's and at the orphanages where he had stayed, and the father began to wonder if he was trying to tell them that this private home was a bore.

Snorty still looked like their son. But he did not act like him. He could never be like him.

Hardly a month after his flamboyant arrival, Snorty was on his way back to Boys Town. The foster father informed the press that the publicity had gone to the boy's head:

"Nevertheless, we wanted to give him a chance. We knew everything was strange for him. We hoped that in time his attitude would change and he would show some affection for us. But there was no improvement."

III

Snorty told Father Flanagan he didn't know what he had done that was wrong. He had tried as hard as he knew how to make them like him.

"If they gave me another chance," he said, "I'd try harder to show them I was grateful."

The papers, of course, played up this new twist, and a storm of controversy blew night and morning in the editorial columns. Many writers pointed out that a few weeks was hardly enough time for a boy to readjust his entire pattern of living.

Wherever the fault lay, Father Flanagan realized he had been wrong to subject the boy to the experience. But the adventure actually was not finished yet. One afternoon Snorty was called to Father Flanagan's office, where, standing before him, was a tall man, about twenty-two years old, whose face and features, Snorty realized with a shock, were so much like his own they, too, could have been doubles.

"Well," the young man said, "aren't you going to shake hands?"

"He's your real brother," Father Flanagan explained.

"It was like seeing myself," Snorty said afterward. Now he learned that he also had another brother and sister. All three lived together in an apartment in an Eastern city. The two brothers and the sister had spent many years in orphanages themselves. But they had not known where the youngest boy had been sent until they saw his picture in the paper.

"We didn't say anything at first because it seemed such a wonderful chance for you and we didn't want to interfere," the older brother explained. "But when we read what happened, I came on out."

So the "Cinderella Boy" went away again. This time his world did not smash. They did not send Snorty back marked "unsatisfactory." This was different; they loved him, not the memory of another.

That settled the problem for Father Flanagan. No more adoptions.

CHAPTER TWENTY-SEVEN

The Marble Boy

The boom, the depression, the collapse, played scarcely any part at all in the life of Boys Town. The nation was on a binge, heading for smashup, but in the home at Overlook none of this curious madness was felt.

By 1927 more than two thousand graduates had gone out into the world of business or on to high education. Although some of the graduates had once been called "delinquents"—most were just unfortunate children—not a single one had got himself into trouble again with the law after being given his second start.

The home and its director were nationally known now, and many famous persons stopped off to see the work for themselves. The band had played a concert for Calvin Coolidge at his summer residence near Rapid City in the Black Hills, and another for John Philip Sousa at the Omaha railroad station. Eamon De Valera, President of Eire, had dropped in to shake hands with Father Flanagan, formerly of Roscommon. Babe Ruth and Lou Gehrig had talked with the youngsters and autographed baseballs; Tom Mix and his horse had put on a special show in the gym.

Growth continued; new subjects added to the school program, new trades taken up for training, new teachers and new Sisters added to the staff. The facilities of the farm were also increased, and a gradual change to an ultra-scientific farm program was being developed. And just for himself, Father Flanagan was finally compelled to build a home; forced to move out of the converted garage, where he had lived since the first days at Overlook, expelled by an animal invasion. Field mice which infested the garage winter and summer had been the compelling force.

"They were very expensive mice," the director complained. "They cost us fourteen thousand dollars. You see, they were so bold. They would scamper around the floor all night long and made so much noise I couldn't sleep. I had to build a new house to get away from them!"

Time had left more milestones along the road. Some of his older friends who had helped him at the start were gone now. His father had died, as had the discerning old Archbishop Harty, who had given him original authorization to start his home.

For a while his mother had lived at the home. But the strenuous life with so many boys had taxed her strength and she had gone to live her last years with another of her daughters, as Nellie had taken her mother's place in the home. One summer Father Flanagan and Nellie went for a brief vacation trip to Europe. They stopped off at Innsbruck, where he showed his sister the buildings in which he had lived and studied; together they toiled up mountain paths he had climbed years before.

Older now, and thinner, he was beginning to show some of the long strain of running the home. His philosophy in handling the problems of boys had not changed but it had deepened and matured in the light of experience. Love, patience, and understanding remained at the core of all his practices. But he had learned also, over the years, that there were few rules which would apply to all boys and their troubles. The individuality which he sought to develop in each boy called for special consideration, the finding of the one particular remedy.

His deepest worry of those days was the temper of the times, the crass materialism which, flowing down from Haeckel and others, at last permeated the thinking of the people; the breakdown of religious training in the home, the soaring divorce rate, leaving a trail of broken families and children shunted from one indifferent parent to another.

Father Flanagan liked to tell of an episode of that time in the home—a story which symbolized to him a whole fantastic money-worshiping era. Chief figure was Warty, a little boy who stole marbles.

Warty had been in the home about a year. He had never been in much trouble. But one day word reached Father Flanagan that he was suspected of stealing marbles from the lockers of other youngsters. Marbles at that time were the great sport in the home. Everyone played and there were four boys who were recognized "champs," skillfully and consistently winning from all others.

Father Flanagan was well aware of how important marbles can be. He remembered his own boyhood back in Roscommon where he would tear buttons from his coat and trousers to keep in the game after losing his marbles. Now he sent for the infidel Warty.

"Why do you steal marbles—dear?"

It was a long half hour before he got the real answer.

"Because all the other kids take mine. I lose 'em when I play."

It was fear, Father believed; fear that Warty would not be thought of as the other boys, that he would lose the respect of the group if he had no marbles; that was why he stole them. Since he could not be equal to them in actual play, he would get even by stealing. The marbles represented the kind of wealth he felt he had to have if he was to hold up his head.

Dismissing Warty, Father Flanagan sent for the champion marble players.

"I've got a chap who loses at marbles," he began slowly. "In fact, the kid loses every marble he gets."

"We all lose sometimes," one of them ventured.

"But this boy steals marbles too."

"We know who it is, Father."

The priest was thoughtful a moment.

"They tell me you fellows have lots of marbles," he said finally.

"We've got thousands, Father. Maybe millions."

"Millions, is it?" He laughed. "And where do you keep them all?"

"The Sisters keep them for us. We got 'em in boxes and crates and bags. The Sisters put 'em away for us."

"Would you be willing to give those marbles to me? All of them? Every single marble you've got?"

He had to have them, he explained, to use in solving the problem of the boy who stole. That afternoon the marbles began coming in. It took several hours to complete the job. Boxes and barrels and crates were lugged in, until Father Flanagan's office was piled up with more marbles than the priest had ever thought existed.

"There were millions of marbles," the priest used to say. And he would smile and add, "Well, maybe I do exaggerate a little. I didn't count them myself. But there must have been a hundred thousand anyway."

The next morning he summoned Warty and showed him the open boxes and barrels, piled high with marbles.

"They're all yours, dear," the priest said slowly. "They all belong to you. You said you wanted marbles."

"All mine?" gasped Warty.

"Every last one. Now take them away. You've got to get them all out of here today."

All day long the boy stuck to this task. Father Flanagan had never imagined he would complete the job, but he did. By nightfall he had lugged away every one of the boxes and crates of marbles and had found some place to stow them. It was nearly dinnertime when he carried out the last box. Then he came back and stood in front of the desk.

"Father," he said, "I want to ask you one more thing."

"What is it—dear?"

"Do you think I could ever learn to be good enough maybe to win some marbles on my own?"

That was the moment Father Flanagan was waiting for. In man-to-boy straight talk he explained the difference between a game and a prize. Not whether you won or lost, but how you played, was the important thing. Failure was nothing to be ashamed of; it was a part of the process of success. Suppose a baby learning to walk gave up after a few hard falls? He would never learn to walk. Marbles were nothing; the fun and the growing expertness, these were the real rewards. All of this sudden avalanche of material wealth still left Warty empty-handed, whereas he would have been rich with one marble won from or lost to the other fellows. Those marbles built for him a new set of values.

And as he watched Warty trudge off in the twilight that evening, the priest could not escape the symbolism that episode held for him.

For a whole nation, like this boy, was running after a different kind of marble, setting its sights on false goals, on material wealth and get-rich-quick schemes, forgetting entirely the things of the spirit.

Someday, he realized, they would surely learn, in smashup, how little the glittering marbles really meant.

CHAPTER TWENTY-EIGHT

A Lost Cause

Like echoes from the long past, now, voices of physicians again warned him to slow up. As of yore, he was driving himself too hard through the grim closing years of the twenties, once more heading for serious illness. He would not heed the warnings. The home was growing too fast. There was too much to be done.

By now Boys Town had grown into a sizable plant. Assets in buildings and land were reckoned at more than half a million dollars. Cost of maintaining the plant was high, but most of the operating expenses were paid out of small gifts, a few dollars each, from all over the nation. To this day small gifts are the main support of Boys Town.

But donations, he knew, would not continue to come in unless people were kept informed about what went on in the home. Part of Father Flanagan's job was to keep the public enthusiastically behind his work, and that responsibility meant hundreds of talks every year, made in all parts of the country. Speeches and the necessary travel took a heavy tax from his strength. And managing the home was still a one-man job.

Even with a growing staff, he supervised a large amount of detail. A boy needs an operation? Father Flanagan personally arranges for the surgeon and watches at the hospital door like an actual father. Another lad runs away? Father Flanagan himself will square it with the police and bring back the runaway by the hand, ready for a second chance. Administrative problems also increased; by 1929 many of the activities were overflowing from the main building into new temporary structures. As time and time before, so now, again, the need for expansion was daily growing greater.

The director decided to take action, and the building program which he laid out involved a new fund-raising campaign for another quarter of a million dollars. There were to be five new buildings, all brick structures and fireproof: a gymnasium with a swimming pool, a trades-school building, a faculty residence, a dry-cleaning plant, and a combination laundry and boilerhouse.

Work on the new buildings was begun in September of 1929, less than a month before the Wall Street crash wiped out millions of dollars in paper profits and started the country on the short toboggan ride to depression.

Many felt, after the stock-market collapse, that the building program should be called off. But Father Flanagan stubbornly said no. He would see it through somehow; he who had ridden out many more desperate storms than this, with faith as his only compass. So the building program kept on, through the very depth of the depression. Somehow the money to pay the bills did come in, even in that time of spreading ruin.

By the fall of 1930 the buildings were finished. The dedication ceremony was one of the great moments of Father's life. Gathered at the home were leaders of the church, of city and state governments, notables from every walk of life.

The governor, Arthur J. Weaver, made a speech in which he said the state of Nebraska was a better place now because of the home which Father Flanagan had founded there. The mayor of Omaha, and its bishop, the most Reverend Joseph F. Rummel, and Rabbi Frederick Cohn also of Omaha—Jews, Protestants, Catholics joined in praise. Many remarked it hardly seemed possible that only a few years before there had been a mere handful of ragged boys and a priest in a crowded little house on Dodge Street.

Another honor came in the spring of 1931, when the American Legion pronounced him Omaha's First Citizen, at a meeting attended by nearly a thousand of the city's leaders.

With Father Flanagan at that gala affair sat his mother. She was eighty years old now, a weary but sedate old lady in black. She had not understood about the award to be given that night to her son, and she was startled at the tremendous ovation which went up when they entered the hall.

"What is it now, Father Edward?" she asked him over the cheers. "Is this yelling all for you?"

"No," he answered with a grin straight from Leabeg House. "It's for us, Mother. For you and me both."

The newspaper reports stated that Mrs. Flanagan received almost as many cheers and congratulations that night as did her famous son. But some of the reporters noted also that Father Flanagan looked a little thin and that he coughed quite a bit during the evening.

The doctors continued to warn him that he was heading for a breakdown, and they were right. One afternoon in the spring of 1931 he slumped over his desk. He managed to push himself up finally, to stagger out of the administration office over to his residence.

He assured Nellie he was all right—all he needed was a little rest. After she got him into bed Nellie brought him a hot potion and called the doctor. That night physicians held a consultation about Father Flanagan's condition. Their final report was a staggering blow. The patient was indeed suffering from the breakdown they had predicted. His lungs were in danger of being affected. He must have at least six months' complete rest in a sanitarium.

II

This time there was no argument. His life depended on whether or not he followed orders.

Arrangements were made for him to stay in a sanitarium in Denver. And his brother, Father P. A., agreed to take over as acting director of the home until Father Flanagan returned.

All the boys lined up at the gates to shake his hand the day he left. He smiled and told them he would soon be back. Smiling, he waved as he was driven off; they could not guess how lonely and despondent he was at that moment.

But illness was not to crush his spirit long. It was, in fact, only a few months later, from the hospital bed, that he was to engage in the bitterest free-for-all of his stormy career—to save a twelve-year-old boy from a life of solitary hell.

A losing battle—or so they say!

It began one afternoon when Father Flanagan suddenly rang the bell for the nurse. A young Irish girl, she stood at the foot of the bed, wondering what it was to be this time. She was growing used to this unpredictable patient, who on one occasion, in spite of all her vigilance, had skulked out of the hospital to see a heavyweight prize fight.

"What is it now, Father?"

"I want you please to take a telegram," he told her. He gave her the name of two attorneys in Seattle, Washington, and began dictating the message:

"Have read convicting of twelve-year-old murderer and his probable commitment to penitentiary for life. Judging from background, I feel this boy has never had a chance. Would you ask the court that this boy be given such a chance now? I will take him to my home and be responsible for him.

"Have cared for three thousand neglected and homeless boys during past fourteen years. My home is at Omaha, Nebraska, known as Father Flanagan's Boys Home. Answer me here, Mercy Hospital."

He told the nurse to get it off as quickly as she could, but it was already too late. The message arrived one hour after the boy had been sentenced to prison for life.

Newspapers were calling the crime the "Barefoot Boy" killing, because the slayer, when arrested, had neither shoes nor stockings. For days the crime had been splashed on the front page. The prisoner, as Father Flanagan learned, had been in trouble from the age of six. Fourth child in a family of nine, he had been caught several times stealing money from his teacher's purse. At eight his mother had placed him with a Children's Aid Society. A year later a family had taken him in but had been forced to return him to the society when his petty thieving continued.

At ten he had tried in vain to persuade another boy to join him in robbing the safe at the society's home. Afraid the other boy might report him, the youngster next ran off in a stolen automobile. After wrecking the auto, he came back to the home on a tricycle, also stolen.

He was sent to a state reform school for a few months, then paroled to his grandmother, but soon he was in trouble again and sent back to the reform school to finish out his term. Finally, when at last released, having no other kinsfolk, he went with the grandmother to live in a small town.

One afternoon he got hold of a gun. How does not appear. He walked the streets of this town, trying to decide what to do with himself and his revolver. The hours ticked on toward midnight. He was growing hungry. He had no money. But he did have that gun. That was how to get food. He could get anything he wanted with that gun.

It was one-thirty in the morning when he broke into the town's general store; he was grabbing anything edible he could lay his hands on when a door opened and dark figures advanced upon him.

The boy ducked down behind the counter. He reached for the gun in his pocket. This was like something in a movie, he thought. Then he heard a man's voice calling out: "Whoever's behind that counter, stick 'em up."

The boy raised his gun and squeezed the trigger. There was a flash, a deafening roar, and a groan; the thud of a fallen body.

Others in the room quickly closed in on the boy. Within a few seconds they had his gun; his hands were in steel bracelets behind his back. He stared down at the body. Yes, he knew this man he had shot. It was the sheriff. He and his satraps had come to investigate reports that someone had broken into the store.

III

Those were uncontrovertible facts. "But," as Father Flanagan declared, quoting from the folk wisdom of ages, "nothing on earth can be so fallacious as a fact—except a table of statistics!" In this case there were other facts, palliating facts—and Flanagan could always find them. For one thing, the father of the boy had been committed to an asylum for the criminally insane when the boy was very young. Certainly that was one ponderable circumstance. Ever since, the boy's mother had let him run free. He had been allowed to go out and come in as he pleased, picking up meals where and as he could. No one had seemed to care what happened to him. That was the worst of it; no one had ever, ever loved this child. Such had been the pattern of his life, except for the brief period when he was with a foster family. But by that time he needed corrective measures.

When his mother had died, his father still in the asylum, the boy was left with his grandmother, too old and tired to control him. The fact that a boy of twelve was roaming the streets barefoot at one-thirty in the morning, with no one bothering about where he might be, was a most significant fact; the sordid, wicked background of neglect with which Father Flanagan had long become only too familiar. Not life in prison, but proper training and love were called for here—even now it was not too late, no matter how desperate seemed the crime.

The first hint of how bitter the struggle over the prisoner would grow appeared in local newspapers. Included with the story of the offer to take the child convict into Boys Town was a statement by Kenneth Mackintosh, member of the Wickersham Crime Commission, nationally famous at that period. This former justice of the Washington Supreme Court denounced the life sentence as too lenient:

"The boy will always be a criminal, a continued menace to society . . . It is reasonable to expect that at some future time he will again be at liberty. A life sentence under our present system means only a few years in the penitentiary. He should have been hanged."

Father Flanagan read this flapdoodle and gasped. The statement seemed to reflect a society gone insensate, brutish, mad, thirsty for a child's death. It summed up, at least for him, all the maladroit blundering of the ages. A cat knew how to take care of a whole boxful of its kittens better than some human mothers, fathers, relatives, social workers, judges, and members of National Commissions knew how to deal with one child, though it possess an immortal soul. He called in the nurse once more and dictated a statement of his own for the press, a rebuke of the great lawyer and judge:

"It is a statement without mercy or gentleness. For who is he, or

In addition to his other presents, every boy received one personal gift from Father Flanagan at Christmas.

Informal prom.

Soloists of the Boys Town Choir at practice.

After chapel.

Although no dog ever replaced the original Carlo, pets are still popular. This is one of the many animal pets given by Boys Town friends in recent years.

The farm and part of the herd.

Father Flanagan in Ireland, 1946.

any other human being, to pronounce judgment of death upon a mere child, a victim of society?

"What a travesty of justice to commit a twelve-year-old boy to life imprisonment and to speak of hanging him, when all of the crime commissions, special enforcement societies, and government prosecutors congratulate themselves upon sending such an arch-criminal as Al Capone to jail for eleven years!"

The nurse had grown keenly interested in the case. But she ventured to remind Father Flanagan he could not do much to aid in the battle: "After all, you still have months to remain in the hospital, before you're completely well."

"Perhaps!" he answered softly.

The majesty of the law had already consigned the twelve-year-old to solitary confinement in the state penitentiary. This measure was absolutely necessary, officials insisted, because this was the very youngest convicted murderer in the state, youngest inmate of the prison, too, and they did not want him to come under the malign influence of older criminals.

At this disclosure Father Flanagan, in his sickroom, groaned aloud. In an exchange of letters and wires with attorneys and officials, he learned in the midst of great tergiversation that no official merciful action was likely. The boy was going to be kept indefinitely in solitary confinement.

Next Father Flanagan wrote directly to Governor Roland H. Hartley of Washington:

"It is pathetic that a child so young must meet the fate of the worst of adult criminals . . . Were it not that we have had considerable experience in caring for real problem boys during the past fourteen years, I would not attempt to ask for such a parole. My experience has taught me that through the influence of our home, where kindness, love, and an understanding interest in these boys' problems play such an important part, I am certain our home can bring to this forlorn and dejected boy hope and future success."

No action followed this plea of intercession. But the nurse came upon Father Flanagan at sunset in his room, fully dressed and packing his suitcase. Her shocked remonstrances were of no avail as they bickered in the deep orange light from the western sky.

"I can't just lie here doing nothing," he told her finally.

Even while Father Flanagan was en route to the state of Washington, its governor was warning that his visit would be all in vain. The state of Washington was perfectly capable of dealing with the case of the young slayer without the help of a meddling priest.

"The Chief Executive would be derelict in his duty if he undertook to transfer his responsibilities to an agency of another state," was the self-righteous conclusion of the chief executive.

But the public, too, was aroused, emotions running high. Siding with Father Flanagan and waging a vigorous protest campaign was Mrs. O. F. Lamsom, founder and head of the Seattle Free Parental Clinic. Joining in the fight for the boy also were numerous civic organizations, including the American Legion and the Parent Teachers Association.

Hundreds were at the station to greet Father Flanagan, and hundreds more crowded that night into the meeting called by a local committee to air the maleficent facts and to pass resolutions.

"I'm not here trying to tell you people how to run your affairs," Father Flanagan informed the gathering with gentle sang-froid. "If you have an institution in this state where the boy can be saved for society, he should be sent there. If not—let me have him. The responsibility will be all mine—and if I fail, the burden will be upon my shoulders, but I will *not* fail. That boy *will* respond, as all my boys have, to love. He will develop under responsibility and the right training—and what is vital, he will have the chance to play as all boys should play, in unrestricted freedom.

"Your great governor has a heart and a head, and I feel confident that if I could only lay my proposition before him, man to man, I could win him to my side."

Next day's conference with the governor, however, was brief. The chief executive bluntly announced he already knew all the facts; he was going to take up the matter in the next few days with members of the parole board.

Still weakened from his illness, the priest went down to California, for a few days of sunshine, while he awaited news of the decision of the parole commissioners. The answer was the same as before: No action. The board, in fact, put off any further discussion of the matter until their next session, which would be "sometime in the spring."

Father Flanagan made one more appeal, by telegram to the governor, entreating him—"in the name of all that is sacred and holy in which American citizenship is founded"—to come to the rescue.

The official answer was not received until some days later: it was a scathing denunciation of Father Flanagan, accusing him of injecting himself into the case mainly because he wanted publicity:

"The people, whose sympathies had been stirred by newspaper accounts of the trial, viewed your appeal as an act of mercy . . . These sensational newspapers had almost despaired of keeping the case on the front page until you came to the rescue. What a happy situation—Father Flanagan needed the newspapers as a vehicle to supplement his appeals; the newspapers needed Father Flanagan in the role of humanitarian.

"In my judgment, nothing in recent years has taken place so detrimental to the youth of our land as the melodramatic publicity and exploitation which has attended your trip to the state of Washington and the request to have this boy turned over to your institution."

This vilification, against a man who had risen from a sickbed to fight for a child, was widely published. Father Flanagan was quick to answer.

"The boy's environment, and not heredity," he declared, "prompted him to do the things that led to the tragic day when he pulled the trigger and killed a peace officer. What this boy, who is little more than a baby, did and what he is today is not because of his true heart or mind, but it is the result of poor home environment and bad influences on his first twelve years of life.

"Governor Hartley was within his honored province as Chief Executive of the state of Washington when he denied the parole to the unfortunate twelve-year-old murderer. But when he deplored my efforts and cast insinuations upon my sincere motives in trying to obtain the boy's release he stepped into the gutter of ward politics."

Letters and telegrams poured into the home, most of them in high encouragement. But the twelve-year-old remained in his solitary cell. The strange life of this boy in the penitentiary continued. An instructor came regularly to his cell to teach him through a regular academic course of high-school subjects. In 1938, at the age of nineteen, he was given a high-school certificate in the prison. Three years later, in 1941, he was finally paroled, by a new governor. He was twenty-two.

"He doesn't know yet what he wants to be," the governor stated. "He is going to try his hand as an apprentice machinist, and if it seems to suit his talents, he'll probably work at that trade."

But his release was only a little while before Pearl Harbor Day and the call to arms. The state, which had kept this youth in solitary confinement, would now send him into battle.

The battle at home had perhaps not been entirely in vain. One result of the fight was a change in the law of the state of Washington, brought about by passage of a bill sponsored by Mrs. Lamsom, by which juvenile offenders, even when convicted of murder, are sent to state training schools, not to penitentiaries and solitude by purblind officials.

And the bitter fight had helped a little to awaken the conscience of the people of the nation to the myopic evil of treating a twelve-year-old boy as if he were a grown-up criminal—to the need for revising juvenile laws everywhere and wiping out the concept of vengeance in handling children in trouble.

Book Four

CHAPTER TWENTY-NINE

The Boy Government

The day the post office opened—in the gymnasium, with Pat Norton as postmaster—was a historic moment in the story of the Town. In December 1934 came official recognition by the government of the United States that the place called Boys Town had become an actual municipality, with a postal identity of its own.

The concept of the home as a town, run by boy officials democratically elected, had been in the founder's mind from the beginning. This was a way to teach boys who had seen society at its worst the responsibility of each citizen in a free community.

The first attempt to set up such a change was made as far back as 1926, with a "government" established at Overlook, actually patterned after the system used in Omaha. A mayor and a group of city commissioners, all boys, were elected to serve for a year. However, the boys lost interest soon after the election and the plan had to be dropped. That early failure, Father Flanagan always believed, was due to the fact that Boys Town was *not* an actual town; its government was not real, but its young citizens were all realists. They had been arrested wards of real government; any "pretend" court, any mock commissioners, seemed pallid and phony by comparison with their actual experiences in the world.

But the idea did not die in Father Flanagan's mind. As the home grew and more new buildings were added—power plant, laundry, tailor shop—it became more and more to look like a real town. Meanwhile, for a brief period, in 1929, they experimented with a plan patterned after those in use by military academies. But while Flanagan's boys, with their mixed-up backgrounds, did need discipline, and the self-government idea had seemed to fail, the military experiment was an even greater flop and was dropped. It got in the way of paternal and maternal tenderness, where they were most needed.

With the opening of the post office in 1934, Father Flanagan decided to take another try at boy self-government. In September of 1935 an amendment was made to the Articles of Incorporation naming Boys Town as the place of business of the home—an incorporated village with a population of two hundred and seventy-five. This time there was no make-believe; Boys Town was official, had its own postmark, and the United States Government recognized it as a town. When you have a real town you have to have a real government. They would need a mayor, a city clerk, a commissioner of police, and a commissioner of sanitation, and others.

The election campaign included parades through the dining hall, with banners, placards, and songs. There were whoop-it-up rallies, and speeches by candidates of just-formed rival parties—the "Build Boys Town Party" and the "Help Our Town Party," known as the BBTs and the HOTs.

In the heat of the contest, boy candidates took to making campaign promises, too. Some were assuring the voters that if elected the candidate guaranteed to get the whole school one extra trip a month into town. Others were promising that instead of one movie a week at Boys Town, there would be two.

First mayor under the new setup was Tony Villone, who had come into the home in 1931. Today he has an important job with Metro-Goldwyn-Mayer at Culver City, California.

Violations of town ordinances and laws were punished by the mayor, with his commissioners and councilmen as advisers at the court sessions. Except for rare trouble, so serious that it had to be handled by Father Flanagan or his staff personally, all rule-breaking and disturbances around the home were brought before the boys' own court.

Physical punishment was never allowed. Father Flanagan knew well, from his own investigations, how boys can be brutal to other boys, as in reform-school and jailhouse "kangaroo courts." Every town official had to sign a paper swearing that he would never strike another boy in the carrying out of his official duties. Even so, punishments dreamed up by these adolescent officials were so severe that offenders often said they might have preferred a little old-fashioned brutality.

Grimmest of all sentences—known to the boys as "capital punishment"—was the movie treatment. An offender would be sentenced to attend the weekly movie at Boys Town. Only he would have to stand with his back to the screen throughout the entire picture. And officials were on hand to make sure he did not sneak any looks over the shoulder. To stand with your back to the screen while hundreds of boys screech at an Abbott and Costello farce that you cannot see is quite a trial.

There was also the swimming treatment, given to those who loved the pool. The culprit must go through all the motions of preparing for a swim, undressing, putting on his bathing suit, taking his preliminary shower, and then going down to the rim of the pool.

But he must not go in!

At the edge of the pool he would have to stand, gazing down at the inviting water—and consider the enormity of his offense against his community and fellow citizens.

Although such punishments were a long way from the grueling vengeance of reform schools, Father Flanagan nevertheless decided they were too harsh. They hurt *him* too much, he complained; he informed the commissioners that the penalties came under the heading of "cruel and unusual punishments" forbidden by the United States Constitution. Extra work and extra study-hall assignments became the two main punishments handed out.

With the coming of war in 1941, many of the recreational activities of the home had to be curtailed. The powers of the boy government were sharply limited, and a military training program for older boys, under the control of an army colonel, continued during the war years. Since then the original powers of the Boys Town government have gradually been restored and strengthened. By 1948 "civil authorities" were again in full control.

Today's system has changed little from early times; it is a representative form of elective government patterned after the city government of Omaha. Elected for six-month terms are seventeen commissioners and four councilmen. The mayor is chosen by the boys from the four councilmen, who constitute a board of "elder states-men."

Voting citizens are the youngest participating in any municipal elections in the nation, probably in the world. Sole requirements of a voter are that he be a citizen of Boys Town and be able to read and write his own name. There have been Negro mayors and white, Catholic and Protestant, and many of these were among the most bedraggled and hopeless when they first came to town.

Like Mayor Jackie. When he was ten years old he fainted one day at his desk in public school. Welfare workers found he was suffering from undernourishment and fatigue. Every night for a year he had been on the streets selling newspapers until two in the morning.

Jackie's mother had died and he lived with his father, two sisters, and a brother in the upstairs rooms of a dilapidated two-story house. Here is the picture of that home as reported by a social-agency investigator:

"The house is in a constant state of filth. Little laundrying is accomplished. The children often go without food. The housework is far too heavy for the girls, though they tried to do it. A school nurse visited the sick boy and found he was receiving no care. No doctor had been called although he had a temperature of 102. At this time the only food in the house was a hard loaf of bread. Pieces of carpet were used as bedding."

Such was the "home" out of which came a future mayor of Boys Town. The day Mayor Jackie was graduated the commencement speaker was J. Edgar Hoover, director of the FBI. After talking to the mayor, Mr. Hoover told Father Flanagan: "There's a youth who would make a G-man."

As a result, the mayor got a new job, as a clerk in the Federal Bureau of Investigation. During the war he served in the army and now is studying for a law degree at Creighton University; one day he may become a full-fledged G-man. His wife is also an employee of the bureau.

A more recent Boys Town mayor was a Negro boy whose step-father and mother worked all day and retired at sundown. If the boy failed to show up in time, he found the doors of his home locked. Sometimes he would break in; twice he stole money from his parents for food. But no sooner did Father Flanagan get him into Boys Town than his career became spectacular. He was quarterback on the football team, pitcher on the baseball team, forward on the basketball team, and also won his letter in track; a star athlete.

In addition he achieved high marks in his studies, was a member of the choir, Boys Town's Junior Red Cross representative, and was commissioner and councilman for several terms before being elected mayor in his senior year.

Since graduation he is continuing his education; one of these days he may be a dentist.

The record makes him sound like a modern Frank Merriwell. Yet he started out with two strikes against him; a boy who had to break into his own home, steal money from his parents, to get food.

II

There is a commissioner for each apartment house in Boys Town, and each commissioner is responsible for order in his territory and for the "orientation" of new boys, like the young guide and friend of Stubby from the boxcar. Under the mayor and councilmen, commissioners direct the activities of the boys, seeing that each performs his special chore, his "charge" in the apartment and in maintaining general order.

These commissioners live with their fellow citizens in the same apartment. They soon know which lads are prone to be "breakers of the peace." Because they are elected by the boys themselves, the commissioners are respected and obeyed.

At the trial courts the mayor presides, with the city clerk at his side to assist and the commissioners ready to give advice and information about the various defendants.

A boy rises to answer the charge that he was smoking. He protests he was merely consorting with another boy who simply gave him the cigarette to hold, just for a minute. That is a bewhiskered alibi and the town officials are not gulled by it. But they don't argue. Instead the mayor considers a moment and then asks:

"Didn't you have the intention of smoking the cigarette, anyhow, when the boy gave it to you?"

"Yes, sir, I did," the boy admits.

Then even if the boy were not guilty of smoking, he certainly had the intention of being guilty. His sentence: a week in the Workers' Crew, a group assigned extra hours of drudgery from their free time.

The next boy is accused of being "out of bounds." In the hayloft on the farm, to be exact. The commissioner from his apartment tells the mayor the defendant has been improving in his conduct. The mayor lets the lad off with a light sentence.

A third boy is accused of neglecting his "charge": disposal of incinerator ashes. The city clerk explains that this boy, in charge of the incinerator, has recently been given a helper. "But now the helper does all the work and he lets his part slide." The boy gets ten days' extra duty cleaning up around the incinerator. In addition he must take care of the ashes every day.

III

Some few cases are more serious. There was, for example, the boy who had the apparently incurable habit, whenever he lost his temper, of throwing knives in the dining room. After being sentenced to eat his meals for a month without knife or fork, he was cured for good and all.

Another was brought in for accepting tips from visitors who came by hundreds and thousands to see Boys Town. The little chiseler was compelled to do extra work until he had "earned" the money taken in and turned it over to the Town treasury.

It is a weird flow of troubles which these juvenile officials—many of whom were in desperate trouble themselves only a brief time before—must hearken to and solve. For the mayor and his advisers and the defendants brought in, the courts are classrooms of another kind. Each boy is learning to live in a community which is, so far as possible, a self-controlled democratic world.

Small wonder, then, that in 1939, when the Variety Clubs International established their first Humanitarian Award, they chose Father Flanagan as the first to be honored.

CHAPTER THIRTY

The Way It Happens

What is the usual pattern by which a boy in trouble comes to be a citizen of Flanagan town?

The average boy will not be a delinquent. Like 80 per cent of youngsters who come to Boys Town, he will simply be without proper family care or love, without what could soberly be called a home. But he is living under conditions which may lead, if continued, to delinquency.

In any community hundreds of such cases can be found. Some make headlines when they are discovered, if they have a dramatic "angle": a mother chaining a child to a bed while she goes out nights, or a moron clubbing his eight-year-old daughter. For every case you read about there are a hundred which never make headlines.

An average boy—call him Joe—is one who does not get his name in the papers. His mother is dead; his father has deserted him. The boy is taken in by his uncle Nat.

Joe's uncle Nat drinks too much and plays the horses. He says he wants to do what is right, but it is obvious he is not able to give the boy proper guidance or supervision. Already Joe is playing hooky from school, getting into minor scrapes. And already the uncle is worried. He reluctantly tries giving Joe a thrashing with his belt. But physical pain does not help little Joe.

Outside the home the boy begins to "pick on" other youngsters, is turning into a bully. Parents of other boys grow anxious and say Joe ought to be sent away.

The next-door neighbor is an old woman, a grandmother; no student of juvenile problems, but she knows about the care a child

ought to have. From time to time over the years this grandmother
has contributed a few dollars to Boys Town. Here, she decides, is
a case where its care might help. She takes it on herself to write to
Father Flanagan.

That is not an unusual way; often he would hear about boys in
trouble because neighbors would write him, or a priest, a rabbi, or
a social worker. Occasionally, as we have seen, Father Flanagan
would "move in" on a case uninvited. Clipping files were kept of
cases that got into the papers, a plan continued today by the staff,
under Monsignor Wegner, the new director. If they decide to make
their own investigation of a case in the newspapers, a definite routine
is set into motion. Trained workers of the Boys Town Welfare Department acquire detailed information.

In a case like that of little Joe, the neighborhood bully, first information consisted merely of a few unsubstantiated statements in a
grandmother's letter. A request for a full report is sent to a welfare
agency near the boy's home. Since the welfare agency is publicly
supported, such investigations are made without charge. Often officials are glad to be informed of a case in their area about which they
may have known nothing and which they are able to solve through
local facilities.

A good report from a field worker will contain not only Joe's brief
history but the history of his parents; it will also give a full picture
of the uncle and his attitude. It will tell not only of economic conditions under which Joe lives, but also the emotional and psychological
conditions, and the moral and religious training he has—or doesn't
have.

From this survey the staff at Boys Town will determine if Joe is
the kind of lad the Boys Town program can help. It is not possible,
of course, to accept any and all. Seldom, if ever, is a physically dis-
abled or mentally unsound boy accepted. One with a physical handicap is at real disadvantage in a home of normal boys, and the
mentally ill boy might himself cause great harm to others. Borderline
cases are most perplexing problems.

Early in 1948, just before he left on his last trip, Father Flanagan
was asked if he would accept a twelve-year-old murderer on trial in
Chicago for the slaying of a playmate.

Father Flanagan, who happened to be in Chicago for a lecture, interviewed the prisoner. But the boy was having none of Father Flanagan. His answers to questions were laconic and noncommittal. After a brief session the boy said coolly: "Sir, I prefer not to discuss this case with you any longer."

Yet this boy was not actually rejected. Facts of the case clearly showed he needed psychiatric attention. Father Flanagan informed Chicago authorities that while Boys Town could not accept him at the time, he would reconsider the case after the boy had been given a year's psychiatric treatment.

More than four thousand applications for admission to the home come in every year. Boys Town would have to be four times its present size to accommodate this number. The great majority must be rejected.

But little Joe, budding neighborhood bully, is one Father Flanagan believed they could help.

Here, as always, he would try, if possible, to find someone who would pay a small part of the expense. This contribution might be as small as five dollars a month. Even such a pittance does much; if nothing else, it makes the boy feel that he is not a charity case; his way is being at least partly paid for.

No doubt Joe's uncle Nat is willing to pay a few dollars toward Joe's support. But if he does not, no matter; once the staff has decided Joe can be helped, he will be taken into the home.

While the staff is waiting for his arrival, conferences are held at which the case is discussed and a tentative program outlined. This preliminary program will be followed until teachers have had a chance to watch Joe and analyze his special needs.

Usually a boy will come by train. If he were a court case, he might be accompanied by a social worker. In most instances the Boys Town staff prefers the boy to travel alone. A member of the staff is at the Omaha station to meet him.

For a while the custom was to put the boy right into an apartment with "old" boys, so that he could start immediately on his adjustment to group life. Recently, however, a plan has been evolved for a "reception" center where new boys stay for anywhere from two to six weeks, while psychological and medical tests are made. This gives the newcomer a chance to adjust gradually to his new life before he is moved into one of the apartment-house "dorms."

This study of the individual is paramount at Boys Town. Apartment houses and cottages are divided into groups, with each group watched over by a dean who is a priest. By dividing the buildings into groups, the individualized training continues, no matter how large this magic city grows.

Each dean is responsible for a hundred boys. As more priests are trained and made available, the "case load" will be lowered. A dean has under his general direction four civilian "counselors," each of whom is in charge of an apartment or cottage with from twenty to twenty-five boys.

Joe meets his dean and his counselor when he moves into his apartment. The counselor will introduce him to one of the Boys Town commissioners, who becomes Joe's pal and helps him "learn the ropes."

Meanwhile, during these first weeks, staff members hold several meetings about Joe. His problems are debated, his examinations and reports studied, and a new program devised.

From that time on, Joe is a full-fledged citizen of Boys Town. Quarterly progress reports are drawn up for his record and, if he has anyone outside who is interested in his progress, a copy of the report is sent to that person. Regularly twice a month he has interviews with his dean and with his counselor. He may talk with them at any other time he wants to do so.

The boy's schedule or program may be frequently shifted around if his progress is faulty. Often the program is specially contrived to solve some particular trouble.

One boy, for instance, had an uncontrollable temper yet was a good athlete. Father Flanagan suggested he go out for boxing. In the ring he proved highly capable—until he lost his temper. Then he would invariably wade right in with fists flying furiously. A trained opponent could stand back and let the enraged antagonist have it neatly with both gloves. The coaches began pointing out the simple fact that whenever he lost his temper, he lost the fight. Because he wanted to win, he learned to control that temper, to preserve complete coolness under difficulties. Eventually he became an expert boxer, winning high honors in a state competition.

Little Joe's problem is different. He is a bully. But the Boys Town staff, having studied the case, knows Joe is not actually sadistic. The reason he picks on smaller boys is to get attention, the one thing Joe has lacked most of his life. So they invent a special assignment for him: to watch over a class of smaller boys in the home. He is to keep older boys from "picking on" any of those smaller kids.

Joe walks with his shoulders thrown back. He is somebody now! He's got himself an assignment—protecting little fellows. He is no longer a bully when he becomes the protector of weaker kids—against bullying.

In senior year at Boys Town High, Joe begins to concentrate on plans for his future. This starts with more staff conferences, at which teachers and deans discuss with him what he wants to do, and what financial backing, if any, he may need to realize his ambition.

Joe has been specializing in auto mechanics. His big idea is some-day to own and operate his own repair shop. Now they know how to help Joe. The graduation from Boys Town is quite an event. The neighboring grandmother who wrote that first letter may well be there in the crowd. Even the Uncle Nats often show up. Through a welfare agency back in Joe's home town, where he wants to live again, a job has been lined up for him in an auto-repair shop. So Joe goes back, to the town where he was known as a hopeless case. The boy the neighbors wanted to condemn to reform school now takes the dents out of their fenders on Monday, after praying with them in the same church at Sunday-morning service.

II

There was another fellow, fifteen years old, who could neither read nor write. His mental development was lower than that of a pupil in the third grade. His I.Q. rating reduced him to a "moronic level."

But Father Flanagan and the teachers, the deans, and directors at Boys Town knew the background of this boy, his story of home-lessness and the fact that he had been in school only a few weeks in all his fifteen years.

They suspected that the "moronic level" indicated in oral and written tests was not a true reflection of actual mental abilities. So the fifteen-year-old was placed in a special "ungraded" class at Boys Town, where boys of all ages study together to make up lost schoolwork with expert assistance. As a result of work in the ungraded class, the fifteen-year-old "moron" in one year's time was ready for the eighth grade of grammar school, achieving marks high enough to indicate he will continue a complete education successfully.

The school which solved his problem is one of the most unusual—and one of the finest—of American educational institutions; not the product of any half-baked theories or scholastic schemes, but an evolution over years of persistence and prayer.

At the outset Father Flanagan had realized that scarcely any of his boys would fit into any average school program. There were too many gaps in their background. In the days of the Dodge Street home he had seen how his boys suffered under petty cruelties of classmates in the public schools.

Since the days at the German-American Home he had always run his own school for the boys, and from the start he had insisted that the curricula must rigidly follow the educational requirements established by law for Nebraska public schools.

But that, he figured, was not enough. One thing more was needed above everything else: individualization. Each one of his boys he knew to be a special case. The program almost invariably had to be adjusted to fit each pupil's special requirements. Education at Boys Town could not be on a mass-production basis.

They had started out with Sisters as teachers, their numbers growing over the years. In 1939, the year when the Boys Town High School was accredited by the Nebraska Department of Public Instruction, some De La Salle Christian Brothers were brought in for the high school. The Brothers remained in charge until 1944. Since that time the teaching has been turned over to a lay faculty, composed of men and women of all faiths but chosen with greatest care because of the special understanding needed in these classrooms.

The instructor at Boys Town is far more important in the life of his pupils than is the teacher of children who have their own homes and parents and friends to counsel them outside of school hours. Moreover, it takes a specially sympathetic person to help remove blot and stigma from young minds. In this work, women teachers are better than men; one of the few ways the boys have of knowing a feminine influence is through women teachers. Manners, courtesy are by-products of that influence.

One requirement is that the teacher, man or woman, however well qualified, must have lived a normal life, come from an average background. This type is best for work with boys who have suffered under many abnormal conditions. Most of the teachers live in Omaha. Some of the school officials live with their families in houses on the grounds or close to Boys Town itself. Often they entertain the boys in their homes.

In some institutions that deal with juvenile problems it is considered poor technique for instructors ever to be informed about the background of their pupils. To know too much may prejudice a teacher and cause him to be "looking for trouble."

Father Flanagan scouted this theory. Teachers at Boys Town are given a complete picture of every boy under their care, and they participate in conferences with the Welfare Department over the progress being made.

The grammar school—until the postwar building program was launched—began with the fifth grade. Except in rare cases, no boy under twelve was taken into the home, or no one incapable of doing fifth-grade work. But with the new buildings, added space, Boys Town is now taking in younger citizens. Eventually the grammar school will cover all grades, first to the eighth.

High-school courses, taught mainly by men teachers, parallel those in any Class-A high school. They include courses in English, two years of high-school mathematics, history and government, and at least one laboratory science. But Father Flanagan insisted that spelling be a required subject for all students in all grades through high school; he said he had read too many misspelled communications from district attorneys bent on convicting children.

Religious training is a regular part of the high-school work. Each Catholic boy has two periods a week of religious education.

Protestant boys have two periods a week of character training and biblical studies under a Protestant minister. Jewish boys are taken into Omaha for religious services Friday night and Saturday morning.

Physical education is another must, in addition to sports: two periods a week of exercise, gymnasium, swimming, and track. Boys who fail their courses must attend special summer school: no one is allowed to fall behind. Classes are kept small, about eighteen boys, and they are quite like any classes in any school in the world. There is just as much chattering and mischief, including cartoons of teachers drawn on the blackboard, portraits all unsigned. Just as many boys have to be sent to the principal's office or kept after school. But they are getting more character education than most.

Father Flanagan used to tell the story of the boy whose destructive fingers wanted to smash everything he could lay hands on. Father decided to take a gamble—to let this boy work in the ceramic shop, with its hundreds of pieces of fragile pottery. His very first assignment in the ceramic shop was to help glaze copies of the Blue Madonna, the same lovely statue which stood behind the founder's desk. A strange thing happened there: for the first time in his life the smasher realized that his hands could be used for creating as well as for destroying. He who had broken so much stood off and admired his finished figure. He even warned others to handle it carefully.

From the start boys were prepared for careers in trades, business, and the professions. The devil finds mischief not only for the idle— but even more for untrained hands. Each student is placed in one of three general programs—college preparatory, vocational, or farming. Trades and farm students spent half of each day in their specialized field. College-preparatory pupils devote full time to academic courses.

The trades-school program is considered the finest trades school in Nebraska and one of the finest in the nation. In the magnificent new trades-school building the boy has a choice of subjects—ceramics, printing, sheet-metal working, baking, carpentering, barbering, tailoring, electricity in various branches, radio, automotive work, shoe repairing—with expert teachers and latest equipment. Graduates have little trouble finding jobs; the staff maintains close relationship with businessmen and union officials. Some industrialists even send advance information on their future needs so that boys can prepare themselves.

One large baking firm has agreed to hire any Boys Towners graduated from the baking school. Not long ago they sent word that there was a shortage of pastry cooks. Could Boys Town help? The staff in the baking school set to work specializing in pastry experiments. By spring Boys Town was able to graduate six trained pastry cooks who walked into good-paying jobs.

Such achievements are unspectacular, but sound. Not average boys from average homes, these graduates came from the alleys and slums, from courtrooms, reform schools, jails, miserable hovels. They start out on their own careers with clean slates and well equipped in training and in character attitudes.

Nor are their horizons limited. Occasionally they have lectures on the wide fields of opportunity still open in the world. So they think everything has been invented? Not so! There are fortunes waiting for another young Edison or Ford who can devise a light bulb which will conserve the force now wasted in heat; or find a method to store up the sun's heat in summer and release it in winter; invent a typewriter that will spell correctly, or discover a formula to take the ink out of newspapers so that it can be used again. Colored X-ray pictures, a noiseless airplane motor—there were literally hundreds of opportunities for genius, which, said Father Flanagan, is a combination of talent, faith, and the blessings of God.

The training the boys receive is, in many instances, merely a first step, preliminary instruction for larger careers where some of those great necessities might someday become realities. Who knows?

There is a story of a youngster who wanted to be an architect. He was a boy of high spirits from a low background. At home, when he mentioned the fact that he wanted to be an architect, to build homes for people, everybody laughed. Nobody like him, his relatives said, could ever hope to be an architect. Yet he was so full of it he mentioned his dream at his first interview with Father Flanagan.

"So you're *going* to be an architect!" the priest exclaimed. "You're going to start, right now."

His program was shaped so that he could take courses in mechanical drawing, sciences, and mathematics, any subject offered which could help him toward his goal. He wasn't just going to school because the law said he had to. He was preparing himself to be an architect.

There was never any further trouble with that young dreamer. He was graduated near the top of his class and went on to college— and architectural school, where, in 1948, he was doing well.

III

The farm program has grown into one of the best-equipped scientifically operated farms in the Middle West.

From year to year, as they were financially able, Father Flanagan purchased neighboring farms around Overlook. For one thing, this gave the home protection against roadhouses or other undesirable places being built up near by. More important, there was more land on which to grow food.

Today there are nearly a thousand acres, with six hundred under cultivation. Main crops are corn, oats, wheat, and alfalfa hay. And there is a large herd of milk cows, with from twenty to thirty calves.

All the pork the boys eat is raised on the farm, and about 80 per cent of the beef. They have their own slaughterhouse and refrigerators. They have over six hundred laying hens. In the summer all the vegetables they eat come from these fields, and they "put up" hundreds of cans of corn, beets, beans, and other vegetables in their own cannery.

Products of the farm over a year include three thousand bushels of corn, two thousand bushels of wheat, three thousand bushels of oats, twenty-two thousand bushels of potatoes, and smaller amounts of numerous vegetables.

This whole plant, operated by men of skill and training in scientific farming, is the schoolhouse of boys who want to be farmers themselves. A new program in farm training gives each boy an animal to raise or a few acres of ground to till for the space of one year. Boys Town provides acreage and animals, but each boy borrows the cash he needs, keeps full records of all expenses, including the rent of the land, and equipment. The boy is in complete charge of the project. At the end of the season there is a reckoning. If any profit is obtained from the sale of the animal or the crop, it goes into the boy's bank account.

All money earned by extra "charges" on the farm or in the trade schools—helping to service Boys Town automobiles or to run the barbershop or perform other needed work—is banked to the boy's account. From that fund he can draw seventy-five cents a week for pocket change, to buy "cokes" or stamps or shaving cream at the Boys Town store, which is maintained by the boys themselves.

Many Boys Town graduates own their own farms. Others are managers of large tracts of mechanized farms. Through these main divisions, each youngster's progress is carefully charted; he is not "marking time" in school—he is building for a career.

CHAPTER THIRTY-ONE

Three Who Killed Their Fathers

The anthropologist Lombroso might have had an awakening at the city of juveniles in Overlook. As many well remember, the Italian scientist believed in a "criminal type"; merely by such an indication as the peak of the ears, he thought he could discover a potential lawbreaker. Long outmoded among serious criminologists, this delusion persists in the public mind; people still cherish the notion that forehead, eyes, jaws, and brains of a criminal are different from those of other men. They have yet to learn that there is no criminal type, that in ourselves all of us carry the seeds of violence.

On one visit we talked with a most agreeable Boys Town citizen. He was making a fine record and not for an instant did we suspect the atrocious deed which he had firmly meditated and finally performed. Not too long ago our yellow-haired, green-eyed young football player had taken human life by cautiously and deliberately smearing rat poison in the butter he laid on bread for his father's sandwich lunch.

What possibility for redemption could even Father Flanagan see in such contemplative homicide?

As usual, the facts behind this ten-year-old's deed were more significant than the crime itself. The father was a farmer; the mother was dead. One day the father staggered in from the fields, where he had been injecting poison into gopher holes, and cried to neighbors that he had been poisoned. A few hours later he died in a hospital, and the autopsy showed clearly the cause of his death; the police fixed on the child as his slayer. Everyone considered him beyond redemption, except Father Flanagan. Father traveled to the jail, got the story from the diminutive prisoner, checked the facts with other witnesses, and helped the court-assigned defense attorney to prepare the case. Perhaps no sadder, no more sordid and cruel story was ever told in a courtroom.

From the record of the official interrogation:

Q. Who got the supper?
A. Pop did.
Q. What did he cook?
A. He didn't cook anything. He just ate some crackers and some milk and bread.
Q. Did you have supper there too?
A. He wouldn't give me any supper.
Q. He wouldn't?
A. (Witness nods head.)
Q. Why?
A. I don't know.
Q. Was he mad at you?
A. (Witness nods head.)
Q. Had he been punishing you for something?
A. I don't know. I don't know. (Witness crying.)

He broke down finally, spilling out the truth as Father Flanagan already knew it. The child had always known monstrous, and completely authenticated, hatred and brutality. He had never been allowed to have a toy. If anyone gave him a toy, the father would burn it. He had never tasted ice cream until it was served to him in this jail on Christmas morning.

If he found a pet, the father would destroy that too. Once, in front of the boy, the father laid a plank on two kittens, then jumped up and down on the board until the creatures were mashed to death.

For years father and son lived alone on that bleak little farm. Once, when the man went off on a trip, the boy unearthed forty-five dollars buried in the ground. He hid some of the money for himself and reburied what was left—twenty-eight dollars. Runaway money! Finding the cash gone, the father twisted a rope into a hangman's noose, looped it around his son's neck, and strung him from the bough of an apple tree. He said:

"Good-by! This is the last you'll ever see of me."

"Stop!" choked the child. "I'll show you!"

The father kept the rope about the child's neck, but lowered him, holding the loose end; the other was still around the boy's throat like a halter, and thus the odd pair started toward the chicken house where the loot was hidden. Once he had his money back, the father beat his erring son into unconsciousness. From then on he kept the child in a tiny basement, refusing him food. The boy was allowed to come upstairs only to prepare meals. This regime continued two days. At the second noontime, while fixing lunch, the little prisoner noticed rat poison on a shelf in the kitchen. That was when he mingled the poison with the butter on the sandwiches. All of his story—including the hanging—was verified; Father Flanagan was given the chance to rehabilitate the boy, and the crime is now carried on the state's "secret blotter." If the probationer makes good in three years, the records will be destroyed; otherwise he must stand trial for murder. He had been a citizen of Boys Town only a few months when we met him there. He sings and is out to make the "first string" choir.

II

No sadder or more cruel and sordid tale, we said? But perhaps we were wrong. At least, we had forgotten "Sandy," one of the best football players on the Flanagan team. Many of the crowds, watching Sandy go for a touchdown, remember his real name; only a few years ago it was on all the best front pages.

The original letter to Boys Town had been written by Sandy himself, in pencil, from the cell where he, too, was waiting trial for the murder of his father:

"My father used to say a lot of times that he would like to kill all of the family before he dies: My father stayed in the summertime on a little ranch. . . . When school was out I went up to the ranch to help him all summer.

"My father was all the time mean no matter how much work I made or did. He was always scolding me and lots of times he whipped me. . . . One day he hit me awfully hard with an iron pipe and made me so sick, like if I was dying. That time it came to my mind that I had to kill him, but I couldn't right away.

"I waited maybe that thing would go away from my mind. I walked four days crippled and I couldn't straighten my back and that time I had a lot of fever, but my father made me go to work just the same. He was scolding me every minute and then about the middle of that week one morning I was putting my shoes on, but I couldn't put them on quick like he wanted me to because my back was hurting. He took a frying pan and hit me on the face close to my ear. That time it came to my mind again that I had to kill him."

Shotgun in hand, Sandy lay in wait outside the front door. When his father strode past, Sandy fired and felled him.

From the welfare agency in the boy's home town Father Flanagan obtained the record. Here, once more, was a story of bestiality. The boy had watched the father go after his mother with a knife. Again he had driven the family out of the house at the point of a gun. This was the home in which Sandy grew up. Nevertheless, Sandy was convicted of murder; he was sentenced to a term of from forty to fifty years in the penitentiary. But on the day of sentencing, Father Flanagan was there to plead for him and the sentence was suspended.

When war came to Boys Town, Sandy wanted to join, but now his past caught up with him. It seemed as if the nation had no place for felons, until one day Father Flanagan called the football star into his office and showed him a letter from the governor. Sandy had been granted a pardon, with restoration of all rights. The slate being clean, he could get into the navy, serving overseas with honor. In 1948 he was voluntarily back at Boys Town, working against the day when he could buy a farm of his own.

In the navy, shipmates used to ask Sandy about the scars of those old beatings. He would tell them they were souvenirs of the cleats of overenthusiastic players in football games at Boys Town.

III

The third citizen who killed his father is high on the list of major Flanagan engagements with the law. This lad's name was Paul, and his family had consisted of father and mother, a younger sister, and himself. The father deserted, bespelled by another woman. The mother was hysterical and bitter over the smashup of her marriage, and the boy, unable to watch such dramatic suffering, went to the father and pleaded so eloquently that he solemnly promised to return; they would start life all over again, together.

Sunday midday dinner was the time set for this reunion. Brother and sister decorated the dreary room with a bright crayoned sign in red and green letters: "Welcome home, Dad!" Mother, brother, and sister all went to church together, then drove to a filling station which the father ran. They waited fifteen minutes for him to appear. At last he sauntered up to the car and shook his head at the open window.

"I've changed my mind," he said. "I'm not coming."

On the ride back no one spoke, but once home, the mother again became hysterical. The boy took a rifle and concealed it in the back of the car. He drove to the filling station, climbed out of the car, and walked to the rear window. Inside he could see his father, playing cards with four other men.

The boy took aim through the open window. Inside there were instant cries, but the boy, still pointing the muzzle at the father, waved the others aside. As they edged back, the boy shot his father, who died there and then.

Father Flanagan, armed with these facts, began his battle by writing to the district attorney in charge, pleading that the boy be given consideration because of the unusual provocation. The reply was that the district attorney considered it a case of deliberate, premeditated murder; the boy "should not be acquitted." And in the courtroom he presented so forceful a plea that the jury promptly reached their verdict, which was "Guilty." Now, as so many times before, the priest came forward, flushed with emotion.

"I have come here," Father Flanagan began slowly, "to plead for this convicted boy. In this busy, everyday world, one boy may not be very important. But to me it means more than my own life.

"This boy is no criminal. It wasn't his hand which pulled the trigger of the gun which sent his father to his death—it was the neglect and abuse of his family by a derelict father, a circumstance over which the boy had no control, which pulled the trigger.

"If there is anything unusual at all, it is his great love for his mother. He could not stand by and see that same mother abused further. He had seen the father strike her and break her nose. On another occasion he had seen the mother taken to the hospital with a broken back as a result of a savage beating administered by the father.

"You and I, your honor, with our age and years of experience behind us, would have known how to answer the problem, had we been confronted as this boy was. We would have known the proper sources of law to appeal to. But he is only a boy. He took what seemed to him the only answer to the staggering problem confronting him.

"Four thousand and forty-six boys of all races and colors have already left Boys Town and gone out into the world. All are today successful members of their communities. Not a single one is in jail. If you will trust this boy to my care, I give you my solemn word you will never regret it."

The judge did not look at the district attorney but at the prisoner.

"I'm going to parole you to Father Flanagan," he decided. "The rest is up to you."

Paul was on the first football and basketball teams, sang tenor in the choir, served as a Boys Town commissioner, and excelled in his studies. After receiving a complete pardon, he joined the merchant marine, later transferring to the army. After his discharge he was married. Today Paul and his wife and little girl live in the same community where all of his trouble began. Why he should want to return there always puzzled Father Flanagan—but he admired the spirit of it. The trouble is forgotten now; Paul is successful, respected in the town, yet when Father Flanagan fought for this same Paul he was accused of "maudlin sentimentality."

CHAPTER THIRTY-TWO

Sporting Blood

It delighted the heart of our old friend Bernarr Macfadden, "the Father of Physical Culture," when we told him how much athletic activity and good sportsmanship had to do with the rehabilitation of boys. Those three father-killers were all helped by ardent devotion to sports.

Like other activities, the sports program at Boys Town was a slow development from days when Father Flanagan had a big dream and an almost-empty purse. He lacked equipment, fields, gymnasiums, coaches; it was a great event, six or seven years after he started, when enough boxing gloves of assorted sizes were donated to enable all the boys to box.

Father Flanagan himself was always a sports fan. Back in Roscommon he had played handball, and he loved it all his life. Often he would steal off from Boys Town to Creighton University to play a round on their courts, until 1943, when he underwent a spinal operation at the Mayo Clinic. After that ordeal, no more handball.

But he never lost faith in the restorative powers of sports, in the mind and the heart, as well as in the body.

"It's not the team which wins by the biggest score which gets the most out of the game," he would tell his boys. "It's the team which plays fairly, the team that does not crab or cheat."

Yet he wept when his own team lost!

"And when we first started playing other schools," he told us, "our teams seemed to lose all the time. I used to get up and leave the games. I couldn't stand to watch our fellows lose."

From the start, with a few borrowed bits of equipment, he eventually built for his home an athletes' plant equal to that of many a university. There is a handsome football stadium, and the baseball diamonds are laid out with all the meticulous care of a big-league park. There are swimming pools, cinder tracks, and tennis courts. In the magnificent new field house are half a dozen basketball courts and much besides.

Football is the top sport, and the record shows several undefeated seasons. In the years between 1935 and 1947 inclusive the Boys Town football team won eighty-four games, lost only twenty, and tied eight.

The record is similarly one-sided, particularly in recent years, in basketball and boxing, track and baseball. Under very astute coaching, Boys Town has been turning out champion teams; schedules now include schools in every part of the country. College football scouts keep a close watch, and some of the stars of college teams learned their skill in punting and passing and running while citizens of Boys Town.

Some teams against which they played were not without snobbishness. But now they all have learned that the "urchins" of Boys Town are trained, disciplined, and noted for hard-hitting, smooth-running play.

During a season the Boys Town football team will play to a hundred thousand spectators—an attendance record better than that many colleges manage to achieve. But in sports, as in other activities at Boys Town, teachers and coaches may never forget that these boys have special problems; athletic competition is a part of remedial treatment.

Here is a youth with a bad temper. He's a good athlete but "blows up" when criticized and turns on the coach with a flood of billingsgate back talk. It is more important to teach that boy control than to win games. So there comes a day when the boy flares up once too often, and the coach orders him benched.

When in the third year the boy again makes the team, it is because he has learned to take criticism.

II

Not every boy that came to the home was a glittering success. As time passed, some of the graduates—although very few—fell by the wayside. Not faith or sports or tenderness could reach every one. Nor did Father Flanagan always win in his clashes with ignorance and prejudice. Yet as the forties came on, and he grew older and more tired, he did not lessen his activities; he expanded them.

For example, there was opened at Boys Town a "penitentiary file," now full of hundreds of cases involving grown-up criminals, men and women whom Father Flanagan had helped. He never quite gave up the battle lost in his Omaha hotel for down-and-outers; he still yearned to prove that the bums and criminals were not beyond salvation. Some convicts he helped to obtain paroles; for others he found jobs, and in a few cases he tried to get men pardons. More he helped simply by letters of encouragement and Christian advice.

Many of his fights for older youths—and for criminals too old to bring to Boys Town—were just as bitter as those for younger boys. There was one pathetic instance, unrecognized behind a drama on a radio show of true detective cases. It was a not-unusual story of holdup and murder, a tale of violence, with some brisk detective work by police. They tracked down a girl friend of one of the killers and through her eventually captured the fugitives. The program —in the interest of crime prevention—wound up with a reminder that perhaps if the two boys had belonged to some boys' club, the crime would never have occurred.

As we listened we recalled Father Flanagan's telling us about the case, and his futile efforts to save the two boys from death. There were aspects of the case which the radio drama had omitted. The two had never before been involved in any crime. They came from God-fearing folk, but at a young age both were taken into the armed services and put to work, practicing "commando" methods of quick and silent killing.

Most young men could take such training in stride, but these two were apparently not mature enough to adjust. It was their train-

Miami Beach, 1946.

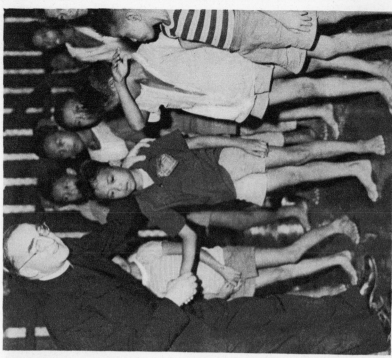

Father Flanagan found these boys "housed" in a Manila

Japanese children besiege him for autographs, 1947

Father Flanagan just before he sailed for Germany and Austria, 1948.

Nellie Flanagan, Father Wegner, Father P. A., and Father Flanagan watching a Boys Town basketball game.

The last picture: Arriving at Tempelhof Airfield, Berlin, May 14, 1948. Father Flanagan was fatally stricken that night and died the next morning.

ing in how to kill—the priest was convinced—which led to the distortion of their thinking and emotions, and their murderous deed.

In a long letter to the governor of the state where the crime occurred, Father Flanagan did not try to excuse their crimes, but:

"Undoubtedly, both of these young men had become depraved by reason of their work, and their youth prevented them from accepting this work in the proper spirit, as older people would have done.

"Your honor, I am not one of those sob-sister types who feels that a man should not die for a crime he has committed in the full possession of his senses and perhaps with premeditation. I think the world is much better off by such men being taken out of it, for they have proven themselves to be unfit and unworthy members of society.

"I do think, however, that these two boys, who had excellent character before entering the services of their country, are very young and the depravity to which they have sunk undoubtedly has been brought on by reason of their youth and environment while engaged in the service of their country."

He went on to urge that the governor give them, instead, life imprisonment at hard labor.

"This would be such a consolation to their respected families who are decent Christian people and who are shocked because of what has happened . . . I shall pray hard that God will inspire you to give these unfortunate boys this chance to live and pray and meditate for the rest of their lives."

The plea was rejected; the governor refused to interfere. A number of letters, moreover, arrived at Boys Town, denouncing Father Flanagan. One lawyer asserted that today's worst crimes were committed by "beardless youths" and society must enforce the laws against them in particular with all its power. So, to the satisfaction of those who hold such views, the two were put to death. But neither the radio authors nor the newspapers knew of two letters which arrived at Boys Town the day after they were put to death.

"Before you receive this," one of them read, "no doubt but what I'll be executed, but I want to thank you for your efforts toward saving my life. I deeply appreciate what you did. Father Flanagan,

I am happy to say that I have made peace with my God. I have no fear of death. In closing, I thank you again."

The other was similarly brief: "When you receive this, I will have been executed. I want to thank you for your efforts in our behalf. We deeply appreciate what you have done, and thank you again. Although I am to die in a few hours, there is no fear in my heart. My creed is not the same as yours, but I feel I am ready for my God's judgment."

III

Some of the cases which the public wrote off as failures were in actuality strange and magnificent triumphs. Most extraordinary of these was the sad misfortune of Willie Francis, a Negro boy whose chief claim to fame was that the electric chair did not work the first time the prison guards strapped him into it.

Willie was fourteen when he committed a holdup murder which netted him a few dollars. They strapped him into the chair and turned on the power. Willie twitched and then a wretched grin came to his lips. The power had failed; Willie was still alive and unharmed.

"It only tickled a little," he said.

The chair that did not work was news throughout the country. Lawyers posed the question of double jeopardy: whether or not he could legally be put to death now for his crime. But in Louisiana, where it happened, it was announced that Willie would be electrocuted again, regardless of such disquieting qualms.

Scores of letters came in to Father Flanagan; couldn't he find some way of saving the black boy's life? At least have the sentence changed to life imprisonment? But all appeals to governor and courts were unsuccessful. The Negro youth was forced to make another trip to the death house. And the second time the chair worked.

Some of the witnesses described Willie's "bravado" as he walked into the death chamber, never guessing that the hour of execution was really for him an hour of triumph. Father Flanagan knew, because he had received a letter from Willie a few days before. The condemned lad wrote that he was willing to pay for his crime, because he knew he couldn't miss his "heavenly goal."

"God's promises are sure," Willie declared. "And Jesus is the only one Who can help us. I think God will make another miracle in my case."

Perhaps he was righter than he knew. For he had not felt or thought like that the first time he went to the chair. All of his new faith he had learned from letters written to him by Father Flanagan and from talks with the prison chaplain. Father Flanagan thoroughly understood when Willie murmured to witnesses: "Everything is going to be all right with me."

IV

There was always tragedy and sorrow in Father Flanagan's work, along with his triumphs. But he knew that the system was right, the foundation was sure; the formula of love surpassed all other remedies. One never knew when the first change would come in the mind and heart of a boy. One had to learn to wait. As in the queer thing that happened one day on the football field.

Time had nearly run out, and the score was tied. Fifteen thousand spectators in the stands were yelling at every play in those closing seconds of the game. At almost the ultimate moment, the coach sent in a substitution. The crowd knew nothing about the second-string fullback who trotted onto the field. They did not know he was the boy who never smiled.

He had been at Boys Town almost a year, brought there after Father Flanagan had heard of his story—a wretched history. He was making out all right now, except that no one had ever seen him smile or heard him laugh. Expressionless and unsmiling as ever, he entered this tense moment of the game. With only a few seconds left to play, the boy who never smiled dropped back to throw a pass, a long, desperate pass, the ball sailing nearly forty yards through the air.

Down the field a Boys Town player was in the clear. The pass was aimed directly at him. The ball spiraled into his arms. But the boy couldn't hold it. The ball bounced up crazily, like a squirming child, seemed actively trying to elude the player's grasp. He stood there, like a juggler putting on an act, while the stands roared and opposing players galloped toward him.

Then, just as the ball seemed about to escape, his fingers closed on it tightly, and he whirled, slithering through would-be tacklers to a touchdown.

In that moment of boisterous triumph, other Boys Towners beheld the second-string fullback who had hurled the pass. The boy who never smiled was laughing; he was laughing so hard the tears rolled down his cheeks. Somehow the throw, the crazy gyrations of the ball, winding up in the catching of the pass and the scoring of the final touchdown, had broken a spell which until that moment had frozen his lips.

"Heaven must have had its eye on that ball," Father Flanagan rejoiced. "That completed forward pass was more than just a pass. It gave him back his faith in himself. That was why he laughed."

CHAPTER THIRTY-THREE

The House without Laughter

The deep-rooted hostility of Father Flanagan toward reform schools was often challenged, but he was uncompromising. Some were better than others, but not many, he insisted, were good enough. A few of them he regarded as survivals of Cro-Magnon brutality and ignorance in an age that called itself enlightened and humane. His famous experience with California's Whittier School, he maintained, was in no sense an extreme exception; it was nearer an incredible norm.

That school, named for a valiant poet and warrior against cruelty, one who sang the sweetness of a barefoot boy, was a prime example of how petty politics can bring hell into the lives of hapless children. Its full name was the Whittier State School for Boys, and it came into sudden limelight when one of its boys was found in a solitary cell hanging by his belt, quite dead.

Even then the case might not have attracted great attention if it had not been the second suicide at the school within a year. The second boy was sixteen years old, the first thirteen. The public outcry was vociferous, and Governor Olson promised a ruthless investigation. He meant it, too, as his subsequent actions proved, but even when public officials promise to see justice done and gross evils remedied, they find unseen obstacles, hidden obstructions, raised by those who fear the light. The shame of Whittier was the shame of so many American municipalities where politics, police, and crime lie in the same bed.

In spite of all Father Flanagan's eloquence, it was hard to believe that anywhere in the world such conditions could prevail as —it was proved conclusively—did exist over a long period in Whittier; hard to believe, too, that in spite of two suicides and a determined inquiry, those who lived on with those horrors struggled to keep the infamous system alive. No one can say, even today, how far from one's own front yard is another Whittier.

Governor Olson appointed a commission, headed by a fiery, bald-headed little juvenile judge, the famous Ben Barr Lindsey. He and his companions were given free hands, and the record they extracted from reluctant witnesses was far worse than anyone had imagined.

The accusations were denied, *in toto*. Officials in charge of state reform institutions, the superintendent of the Whittier School and the guards, all swore that the boys were well treated. A few admitted that they had "slapped" some of the inmates. Making a boy do the "duck walk" was not considered cruel, some testified. Virtually all the officials argued that devices such as the "lost privilege" cottage, solitary confinement, and other stringent methods had to be employed.

But the Lindsey commission obtained testimony of several hundred beatings administered by the guards, and of other brutalities. Then it was to Father Flanagan that they turned, inviting him and two other juvenile experts to study the school and to make recommendations. Father Flanagan accepted, as did Mrs. Helen Mellinkoff of Beverly Hills, California, and Dr. William B. Cox of New York.

It was soon clear to all three that a "cleanup" job had to be done. For the beginning period Father Flanagan offered the services of his assistant, Patrick Norton. Without pay, he took over the post of acting superintendent of Whittier, and the regular superintendent was ousted immediately.

"We are here to help the state of California," Father Flanagan told reporters. "We have been asked for such help in a cause I consider among the greatest on earth. Believe me, I did not come to dictate. But it would be impossible for us to proceed, impossible to achieve results, if the present superintendent remained while we conducted our work. Now we can go ahead. We must teach Whittier boys, as we teach the lads at Boys Town, to appreciate the great country of which they are to be citizens. They cannot appreciate their country if they are subjected to stupid brutalities, if they encounter crass lack of understanding, if they feel that the grownups in charge of them have no interest in their present or future welfare."

The house cleaning carried out by Pat Norton was like a blast of fresh air through the halls of the institution. Thanks to the house-cleaning regime, major evils of the school were eradicated. Finally Father Flanagan and his associates issued a report. They urged that the name of Whittier School be changed because of the odium and terror it evoked in minds of boys. The inmates should be served good, wholesome food. Examinations ought to be held to determine the fitness of staff members to handle problems of children, with no more purely political appointees. Playground facilities should be developed. A full-time physician, a Protestant clergyman, and a Catholic priest should be permanently employed at the school.

Dr. William Cox of the committee was appointed by the governor to take the post as superintendent and to carry out the committee's recommendations.

Probably the school will never become another Boys Town, but as a result of the probe, charges and countercharges, conditions were improved. There have been no more suicides. But to Father Flanagan the greatest good accomplished lay in the exposure of the sordid facts. The people had a chance to see, close up, the vicious-ness in the reform-school system.

"Tell the people what goes on," he entreated in one address. "Keep on telling them—until you awaken public conscience, and this evil against our children is wiped out."

CHAPTER THIRTY-FOUR

A Soldier Takes Off His Ribbons

Nothing did Father Flanagan ever view with gustier satisfaction than the performance of Overlook citizens and graduates in battles on sea and shore.

Hardly had the news of Pearl Harbor resounded over the radio than the boys began clamoring to enlist. They came parading to the residence, not just a few, but the entire home, led by the mayor, a boy who had come originally from Honolulu. Within a few hours of the bombing, Father Flanagan found himself with hundreds of volunteers. A few of the older boys were allowed to enlist immediately. In spring the mayor and others of the graduating classes all joined up. Father Flanagan was named national chaplain of the "American War Dads." Meanwhile he was busy installing a military-training program.

Eventually news began to filter back of one boy after another, wounded, missing in action, or killed. One was named Jimmy. He had come into the home in 1935, with his two brothers. Jimmy's mother had died, and then his father, who had been in combat in the first World War. The case of the three youngsters had been called to the attention of Boys Town by the American Legion.

When the brothers arrived they had carried, with their few belongings, an American flag. They would not give up the flag to anyone. "It was our dad's," they explained.

Just prior to Jimmy's death in battle in 1943, he wrote to Father Flanagan:

"It has been a long time since I have written to you. . . . I have been pretty busy these days . . . At the present time I am in Italy, not very far from enemy lines. I have been wounded once. It was a minor wound and I received the Purple Heart award medal. When I get a chance I will send you the medal to keep for me until I get back to the States.

"I got the wound by strafing planes. I was in my jeep leading a convoy. I was in Sicily when this happened, but I am still kicking . . . Well, so long for now, Father—dear!"

Four days later, Jimmy was killed.

II

Before the war's end more than a thousand former Boys Towners were in service, in every part of the world, and stories of their heroism often filled Father's eyes with tears.

One was of a lad who went ashore in the first days of the battle for Guadalcanal. For days he remained at the front lines, helping wounded marines in a display of bravery under fire which won him a citation for distinguished service from Admiral Halsey.

Richard Tregaskis, in his famous book *Guadalcanal Diary,* mentions the heroism of this boy, tells how he moved forward, heedless of blistering enemy sniper fire on all sides, to save a wounded lieutenant. He did save the officer—and got back safely.

Another story concerned Captain Melvin Dunn of the U. S. Army Air Force, who flew thirty missions over enemy territory in a B-17. A former Boys Towner, Dunn found himself a flyer entirely by accident. He had gone with a friend who was taking an examination to become an aviation cadet. While waiting for the friend, he was mistaken for a candidate, and presently was taking the examination. When the results were announced, the former Boys Towner found he had achieved the third highest mark of those taking the tests. His aviation career was under way.

A year later he was in England, flying with the Eighth Air Force. During months of combat service abroad he earned five battle stars, the Air Medal with four oak-leaf clusters, and the Distinguished Flying Cross. After the war he came back to the States to continue his studies at Purdue University.

III

At Boys Town itself the military-training program, under direction of regular army officers, was in full swing while Father Flanagan, on several bond-speaking tours, helped to raise nearly four million dollars for the nation's war chest. But the aging priest had not thrown aside his enlarging ideas. Someday the war would be over, and already he was formulating his postwar building program, with new cottages and field houses, high school and other buildings which now have virtually doubled the size of the town.

The need for his work, he felt, was going to be deeper than ever. Even then, in the war years, he saw how more homes were breaking up; lives disrupted, normal patterns and standards cast aside, youth left to its own devices. All the factors which produced trouble for children being magnified, it was bound to mean trouble.

Some of the results he began to see at once, in the new boys. This one would have no home life because while the father was in the army, mother was out playing or was sick, perhaps in the hospital. And there were many tragedies of "door-key children," whose parents were too busy working in factories to give them care. It was patriotic to work in war plants. But it was unpatriotic not to care for your children, too.

The case which seemed most clearly to typify what was happening began when three small boys walked into the office one day and asked if they could stay at Boys Town.

Pinned to the coat of one child was a note, from the grandmother. She explained that the boys' father was in the army; the mother had divorced him *in absentia* and remarried. She was traveling around the country now, from army camp to army camp, following her new husband, who was an officer.

The boys had been left with their grandmother, but grandmother had no money to support them. So she was sending them to Boys Town. Would Father Flanagan take them in?

The two older boys were kept at the home, the youngest sent to an orphanage. Meanwhile, through the Red Cross, Father Flanagan learned where the father was stationed and wrote him; the first information the father had had about his sons. The soldier obtained an emergency leave and flew from Africa to Boys Town.

The boys had not seen their father for years. They had forgotten even what he looked like and evinced no interest in seeing him.

"Our mother; next our father," they told Father Flanagan. "We liked her and she ran out on us. How do we know he won't do the same? We'd rather not."

The young father tried to get the boys to talk but he was answered only in monosyllables, as they strolled around the grounds. The only sign of interest was that occasionally they would glance shyly at his military ribbons. Would they like to hear how he got the decorations? Their interest did warm a little as he began to talk of battle-front adventures, winding up by taking off the ribbons and giving them to his youngsters. Perhaps taking off those ribbons was against regulations, but the slight infraction worked like a little leaven, leavening the whole situation. By the time he left, the boys had changed a little; they had a dad who was in the army! He'd been in a lot of battles, too. Won a lot of ribbons. They began telling the other boys about their father and showing off the ribbons.

Back from the war, the father married again, purchased a small farm, and at once took into the home the youngest boy, from the orphanage. But the other two held back. They said they wanted to stay on at Boys Town, and, on Father's advice, they did stay. But at his secret instigation they began to get letters—from the youngest brother—about how wonderful life was on the farm. And how he helped his father take care of the cattle and the crops.

Before long the older boys asked Father Flanagan what he would suggest.

"I think," the priest said, "your father and stepmother and little brother all want to give you love. And boys who have a home of love—with their own family—are very lucky."

They are all together now. They do not hear from their own mother. But in their new home—with father and foster mother—sullen memories have begun to fade.

That was a happy ending. But Father knew that around the world millions of children in war-torn areas had little chance for any such happy ending.

It was to those lost urchins of war that the priest was next to turn his attention.

CHAPTER THIRTY-FIVE

Smoke and Flame

It was now time for an Irish priest, who had become an American in Omaha, after studying in Rome and Innsbruck, to travel to the Far East. The war had left hideous scars on oriental children, as on little ones all over the world, their plight the most pitiful harvest of evil. The problems of homeless youth—always Father Flanagan's special province—had now become a part of world-wide disaster. In Tokyo, General Douglas MacArthur, through the Secretary of War, asked for his help.

Father Flanagan took with him on this trip Byron Reed, one of his close associates at Boys Town for many years. They flew the Pacific, with stop-offs in Honolulu, Guam, and Manila. Perhaps the most thrilling experience of the journey was a visit in Guam with fifteen of his former boys, soldiers, sailors, and marines. They all gathered for a special dinner at the Governor's Mansion; the first reunion of Boys Towners ever held outside continental United States. And it was during dinner that Father's mind was sent scouting through the years, back to a most remarkably difficult problem: one he had given up as insoluble, only to learn that you never can tell.

There had come to the home a tiny Mexican boy, almost a midget, named Pedro. Not a bad sort, he was obedient and studious, except for one intolerable bad habit. Pedro smoked. No matter how eloquently he promised not to, he went right on smoking. No punishment sufficed; he declared he had been using cigarettes since he was four years old, and now, at ten, he was far too old to quit. He was also too shrewd to allow the discipline of Father Flanagan to break the habit for him. For a while the distracted priest lost sleep over Pedro. See that he got no more cigarettes? But that was impossible! Visitors by thousands came to Boys Town and littered the paths with discarded "butts" which Pedro harvested. Solely on Pedro's account, all matches were declared contraband in Boys Town. Overnight it became very difficult even for legitimate smokers to get a light. All felt the ban—except Pedro. He smoked as before and refused obstinately to disclose the source of his fire. Two days passed before Father discovered the mystery; when he followed Pedro into the chapel, he saw him light a cigarette from votive candles near the altar.

Fortunately for all concerned, soon after that an aunt of diminutive Pedro arrived to take him home, and that was the last Father Flanagan had seen of the little fellow until this festive reunion at Guam. The last dinner guest arrived late, when all the others were seated—the door opened and in rolled the smallest seaman in any naval squadron on the seven seas: Pedro in a sailor suit. Father Flanagan greeted him with a yell of rejoicing.

"Pedro!" he exclaimed. "I love the sight of you, fellow!" and, warmed with the glow of forgiving grace, he reached into his pocket and produced a pack of Chesterfields. "Pedro, have a smoke on me!"

But Pedro shook his head.

"No, Father! I haven't had a smoke since I left Boys Town. Thanks just the same."

It was, as Father declared, the greatest example of a "delayed take" he had ever known.

II

By plane they sped on to Manila, and northward to Tokyo, where General MacArthur—"a great Christian gentlemen," Father called him—gave him a free hand. He was to go where he wished, and report his findings and recommendations without fear. This permission Father Flanagan accepted literally.

The conditions he found in Japan, and, later, in Korea, were much worse than he had anticipated. Japan, a nation built around the family unit, had never known juvenile problems before, but now tens of thousands of its children had neither home nor family. Orphanages had been established by people of almost no experience. In one typical institution Father Flanagan found fifty small boys working in a factory a full eight-hour day, six days a week. Products turned out by the children—bicycle lamps, as one example—were being sold at a profit, but the money was not turned back into the orphanages. There were no educational or recreational programs whatever, and no attention at all paid to religion.

The treatment of the helpless, too, he discovered, was much the same the world over. Many of the orphanage shacks were more like prisons than homes, the boys treated as drudges. Five youngsters he found in solitary cells quite like the solitary cells of the Whittier School in California.

"What did these boys do to earn such confinement?" he demanded.

The official replied: "They are new boys and it is necessary to keep them here like this until they become used to the home."

"These boys must be released at once," Father Flanagan stormed.

Later, about to address a general assembly of the boys and staff officials of the institution, he looked carefully around him and failed to see the five children from the solitary cells. Where were they? he inquired. The Japanese officials smiled and bowed and chattered vaguely, but their guest, not to be put off by blandishments, refused to speak until the five were produced. When the officials fetched the five boys to the front row, a cheer went up from the crowd. Here was somebody who seemed to understand.

Many such improvements followed his visits to orphanages, and American officers saw to it that the reforms stuck. In Korea he found several girls thrown in promiscuously with several hundred boys, living in the same quarters. Flanagan lashed out at the officials, told them they would have to get the girls out in an hour. The officials could not comprehend his almost delirious indignation but did send the girls off to another home used solely for women.

Wherever he went amazing crowds gathered. Thousands of children would wait for him at railroad stations. Missionaries had spread the fame of his work among them, and to them he was the greatest hero of the Americans. Local newspapermen also came for interviews, and he tendered them some ideas, including the suggestion that people should love all children and care for them.

"You mean," one skeptical Japanese reporter asked him, "that I should care about what happens to a son of someone I do not even know?"

The visitor told him yes. Every child was important. Every child had to be cared for. Love for the helpless was a natural instinct found in all people. But the scribe insisted that a Japanese could love none but his own. On the windy platform the priest lingered, while he told the reporter how in Tokyo a well-to-do woman had turned her home into an orphanage; she was caring for sixty boys and girls picked up in back streets. Again, in Osaka, a woman was caring for twenty children of leper parents.

"These people must have love in their hearts," he said, "to go to such lengths to care for lost children."

The result was an immediate storm of controversy in the Japanese papers. People now were beginning to be agitated about loving strange children. Because of that interview, a class of adults was formed in Tokyo to study the wider meanings of love.

Archbishop Paul Marella, Apostolic Delegate in Japan, declared that Father Flanagan's visit had advanced Christianity a hundred years in the island world. And when death overtook Father Flanagan, in the midst of a similar job in Austria, there came this message from Giichi Taketa, Minister of Welfare in Tokyo:

"I can hardly find words to express the deep and heartfelt sorrow we now experience. It was just a year ago when Father Flanagan was with us in Japan . . . He visited many child-welfare institutions, giving us helpful suggestions. These suggestions are now bearing fruit. It is our great sorrow to hear this sad news before the happy reports of our developments in the field of child welfare and the passage of our new child-welfare laws could reach him."

"You have reached millions," General MacArthur told Father Flanagan, "where others have reached only thousands. Now recommend what you think should be done."

Back in Omaha, Father Flanagan wrote no "yes-man" report. He called for an official survey in Japan and Korea, to count how many homeless boys and girls there were, provision to be made for everyone. He called for foster homes, founded on the philosophy of love. He pleaded for religious instruction to be given all children; for less regimentation, for trained staffs and medical care, and for keeping boys and girls in separate reformatories. He wrote a new Magna Charta for children of the Orient.

Already many of these proposals have been put into effect. In China a Boys Town has been established near Shanghai. Thanks to one indefatigable man of God, the kids of the Far East are getting a break.

CHAPTER THIRTY-SIX

Who Is There, in the Dark?

This story Father Flanagan told to us on his last day but one in the United States. It was not a finished story and it may never come to the end Father Flanagan hoped for. But a happy ending? "That is quite another matter," he reminded us. "You can judge for yourselves."

And he referred to one of our earlier visits to Boys Town, a Sunday morning when we had hoped to resume a confab that had ended at midnight. But at breakfast table, after Mass, Father was absent; he had flown hundreds of miles to face a Western-state governor, not his own, and plead with him for the "pitchfork boy."

People had stuck the label on the young prisoner not without reason, since it was with that weapon he had murdered his stepfather. The only friend he had in the world was Father Flanagan— he was the aging, wearying priest's last case; the final problem, ending in defeat. Or was it defeat? We were to decide that for ourselves.

"They say the deed was cruel," he began. "No doubt it was, too. But how much more cruel society was to the doer of the deed! Before the crime as well as after. Follow his case with me and see if you don't agree that what happened to the 'pitchfork boy' sums up everything which I argue for and everything that I condemn."

Rapidly he sketched the young man's background: he was seventeen when he committed murder, following an argument at the feeding of the calves. A detailed history seemed to bear out the state's contention of premeditation. The boy had shot the stepfather and then plunged a pitchfork again and again into the prostrate body. The public wanted vengeance.

But Father Flanagan, to whom many had appealed in the boy's behalf, was satisfied, in advance of examination, that in this case, as in all others he had known, some palliative facts must lie in the background. And again, as so often before, local police, prosecuting officer, jail warden, and guards all received him with hostile attitudes, scarcely bothering to conceal contempt, resentment, indifference.

By plaguing them, and going over their heads, the priest from another state was at last allowed to talk with the accused youth. But it was stipulated that a guard must be present, and so it was—a young husky sitting in a rocking chair, which he dragged into the cell, while Father Flanagan, pale and gray, standing for two hours outside the cell, talked through the bars. Under those grim auspices, he tried to get the story of the prisoner, and gradually won his confidence.

Pete—as we may call him—came into the world as a child of depression. When he was born, in 1929, his father had a prosperous farm, but his holdings were soon wiped out. The family moved to a Middle Western city, where the father became a taxi driver. When the boy was eight, the mother went to work as a waitress, and later, in the war boom, changed to a factory. She was a good-looking woman and, with her extra cash, could dress herself stylishly—and did so. At a dance one night she met a German-American who owned a large farm; before long the woman got a divorce and married the farmer.

The young son, now around ten, loved his own father but had no control over his own destiny. He was taken off to live with his mother on the stepfather's farm. Not only because he missed his real father did the boy resent the change; even at his young age he had a quick way with tools; he loved mechanics and he told everyone who would listen to him, as Father Flanagan was later to verify, that he wanted to get an education and become an engineer.

Such talk was, in the mind of the stepfather, now in complete charge of the boy's life, unmitigated nonsense! High School? Bah! College? Nuts! A boy in his position had no right to such ideas; his job was cut out for him: learning to farm, and to do what he was told. The ambition of the boy seemed to provoke a bitter antipathy: that was a lazy and stupid boy, who had to have common sense beat into him. So it was whip and fist; it began when the boy was ten and continued until he was fourteen, four nightmare years. Had he been older, or perhaps a little smarter, he might have appealed to the police. At least he waited too long. On the day before it happened, he had suffered several beatings. Still bruised the next morning, he rebelliously made off alone for an hour of rabbit hunting. On his return he went to the barn to feed the calves. The stepfather came toward him.

"I knew he was going to beat me again," the boy said. "That's why I reached for the rabbit rifle."

The roar of the explosion reverberated through the morning. The farmer fell to the ground, but by now the boy's rage overwhelmed him. He pummeled the dying man's head with the butt end of the gun, then lifted the pitchfork.

II

Yet he did not look like a pitchfork killer. He had wheat-yellow hair and eyes of cornflower blue. He thanked this stranger for taking an interest.

"I hear from my father now," the boy said. "My own father, he's standing by me."

"You love your father?"

"Very much. I never had a chance to see him after the other man took over. If he'd been with us——"

If he only had. Father Flanagan stopped talking through the bars for a spell, while he communed in prayer. Finally he asked: "What's the worst thing about being here in jail?"

"When the lights go out. I'm afraid."

"Why?" the priest asked. "Why does the darkness frighten you?"

"It's so lonely. There's nobody——"

"Nobody? You're wrong!" the priest said. "Didn't you ever hear of your Father in heaven? Don't you know anything about God?"

"God? Sure. Everybody's heard of God."

"What do you know about Him?"

"Not much," the boy admitted slowly.

"Ever go to church?"

"Once or twice."

"But God is your Father; He loves you, and He is with you all the time—even in the darkness. You can't be frightened when you know He is right there with you, and you can talk to Him."

"How do I do that?"

"It's the easiest thing in the world. We call it praying, but all it is is talking to Our Blessed Lord."

"Father," the prisoner said, "tell me about God."

III

As soon as Father Flanagan talked about Pete with the district attorney he realized that hope for clemency was dim indeed. The jury took only a short time to reach its verdict: the sentence, for this seventeen-year-old convict, life in prison. Mercifully, as it seemed at the time, a technical dispute in the courts made the stay of the life sentence mandatory until the issues could be settled by the Supreme Court. That meant the pitchfork boy must be held in jail, rather than in state prison, for at least a year. In this Father Flanagan saw a year of grace and forthwith asked for custody until the last ruling of the court was made known. He wanted the lad for Boys Town, where there were no bars, locks, or gates, a dangerous, unheard-of proposal. Frightened and vengeful society sought to block his purpose; finally the presiding judge required a bond to be posted for twenty-five thousand dollars in cash. And he got it, even though Father Flanagan knew very well he had no authority to put Boys Town funds to any such use, except with approval of the Board of Trustees, which there was not time to obtain. But as he had anticipated, the trustees backed him up enthusiastically, ex post facto.

For one year and four days the pitchfork boy lived at Boys Town. He was a good student, got on well with classmates, and began to think again about being an engineer. During that year and four days he made good. Then the learned justices of the State Supreme Court, ruling on a technicality, found against the boy. He would have to go back to state penitentiary and remain there for the rest of his life.

On the following day Father Flanagan issued a statement to the press:

"It is with reluctance that I return today one of my boys to the penitentiary. It was and is our firm conviction that there were extenuating circumstances in this case and that he did not belong in a penitentiary but needed love, care, and guidance, which we felt we could offer him better than a penitentiary. . . . I had faith in this boy, and not once since he has been at Boys Town has he broken his faith with us. He has been a model both in and out of school. He has not had one single bad mark on his record while at Boys Town.

". . . It is unfortunate that we must return him to prison. We realize, however, that it is the law and we wish to abide by the decision laid down. . . . This does not mean we are giving up our fight on his behalf. We put up a twenty-five-thousand-dollar cash bond so that he could come to Boys Town. We have that kind of faith in this boy. We will leave no stone unturned in our effort to have him returned here."

As he said good-by to the pitchfork boy, the aging servant of the Lord found himself almost in tears. Now it was the youth's turn to play the comforter, as the priest had comforted him when they first met.

"You don't have to worry about me, Father," he said. "You see, I know now: I'm not afraid of the dark any more."

The day after he told us Pete's story Father Flanagan sailed for Europe, never to return alive.

CHAPTER THIRTY-SEVEN

The Final Assignment

The end came so suddenly, so unexpectedly—and yet, if we had taken the hint, if we had followed the clue he gave us at parting, we might not, at the tragic news, have been taken so completely unaware. But we were not to think of that clue again until long afterward. Meanwhile there were questions in our mind.

What was to be the future of Boys Town?

Who would carry on in Father's place?

And would the same policies prevail?

Several months passed before the first and basic question was settled. Then came the announcement made by His Excellency, the Most Reverend Gerald T. Bergan, Archbishop of the Omaha Archdiocese and president of the Boys Town board of trustees. Father Flanagan's successor as director of Boys Town was to be the Right Reverend Monsignor Nicholas H. Wegner, Chancellor of the Omaha Archdiocese.

The announcement was made on September 15, 1948, Father Flanagan having died four months earlier to the day. One of the new director's first statements was a tribute to Father Edmond C. Walsh, who for a short time was assistant to Father Flanagan and who managed the home during the interval between death and the coming of the new director.

In taking over Father Flanagan's desk, with all its memories of Stubby and Warty and Pedro and thousands of others who had stood before it and eaten chocolates with the founder, the new director made it immediately clear that the plan of the home would not be changed. Father Flanagan's ideas will be continued. Said Monsignor Wegner:

"I deem it a singular honor and a great privilege to be appointed the first successor to Monsignor Flanagan. For almost twenty-five years I enjoyed a close personal friendship and association with him.

"In the administration of Boys Town, I will try in every way possible to follow in the footsteps of its founder. And while I look with a great deal of fear and trepidation to the task that lies before me, I feel that with the help and co-operation of the very able staff at Boys Town, and the help of God and the prayers of our friends, the good work so ably begun by Father Flanagan and carried to such glorious height will continue to prosper and meet with success.

"I know I will experience great joy and happiness in working for and with unfortunate boys.

"I earnestly trust and pray that the kindhearted and generous benefactors of Boys Town will continue to support the home and remember the unfortunate boys in their charity. May the memory and work of Father Flanagan never be forgotten in our prayers and generosity."

And in his first talk to the whole assembly of Boys Town citizens, after being presented by Father Walsh, the new director renewed his pledge:

"I am here, as you know, to take on where Monsignor Flanagan left off. If I can do, oh, I suggest, a little bit as well as he did in all these years, I will be very grateful.

"I want to try and make you all happy. I don't want to make anyone unhappy.

"Let's keep this thought in mind: The great founder of Boys Town, Monsignor Flanagan, will always live in spirit here. I will try to follow him in every way possible, to walk in his footsteps. For that I ask your prayers for me. Pray for Monsignor Flanagan that he may watch over you and watch over Boys Town."

Commenting on this statement, the Omaha *World-Herald*, near-at-hand observer of the work, had this to say:

The Catholic Church has chosen one of its most brilliant sons, Msgr. Nicholas H. Wegner, to take over the direction of Boys Town.

As Chancellor of the Archdiocese of Omaha, he has had wide administrative and business experience. He is a lover of sports, which should give him an interest in common with the boys who will be under his care. As a young man he could have been a major-league baseball pitcher, but he chose instead to become a priest.

Operating the multimillion-dollar Boys Town will be a heavy task. And being named successor to the gifted Father Flanagan is enough to give anyone pause. But Monsignor Wegner should measure up to the job. He should be able to count upon all of Boys Town's thousands of friends for help.

A native Nebraskan, Monsignor Wegner studied at the same Gregorian University from which Father Flanagan had to depart; he was ordained at Rome. But more important from the Boys Town point of view was that fact pointed out by the Omaha *World-Herald:* Monsignor Wegner was, in his youth, an expert baseball pitcher and actually turned down two big-league contracts. He has never lost his zest for athletic competition, plays a good game of golf, and was a leader in sports during his long service as director of the St. James Orphanage in Omaha. Honors were thick upon his brow before he reached Overlook. But he considers his appointment to Boys Town his greatest opportunity.

II

The changes at Boys Town were necessary because Father Flanagan died—of a complication of ailments, the principal of which was a broken heart—in the tormented city of Berlin.

The assignment that had taken him there came in the winter of 1948, a request from the War Department that he undertake a survey of youth conditions in Austria and Germany, where the morale of youth was plunging to a new low. He confessed to friends that he did not want to go; in his sixty-second year, he felt mortally tired, but he could not refuse. If ever children were in need of help, it was these children of defeated enemies. Of course the Austria he had known of yore was gone. The warm, lighthearted people of student days at Innsbruck bred a generation brought up as Nazis.

The day Father left Boys Town he called the senior class together.

As he would not be back in time for their graduation, he wanted to say good-by. Eddie Dunn, Negro mayor, recalls how it was: "We seniors in the high school—there were forty-seven of us—gathered in the chapel. Father reminded us of the Christian teachings that we had received at Boys Town, teachings which would prepare us for our future lives. He said he was confident we would all be good citizens for God and country. 'Good-by, Eddie,' he said to me. 'Good luck and God bless you.' "

Pat Norton, close associate since the days of the German-American Home, departed with him. It was just a little after sunset as the priest turned for a last look at the spires of his little town, the girders of the field house and the gleaming roofs of the new cottages he had built for homeless boys.

III

On the day before he sailed, we talked for long hours with Father Flanagan. Over the years his ideas had not changed.

"I can still say that I have never known a really bad boy," he told us. "Only bad parents, bad environments, and bad examples. It's wrong even to call it juvenile delinquency. Why not call it what it generally is—the delinquency of a callous and indifferent society?"

There had been some progress, he conceded.

"People are beginning to realize," he said, "that they must do away with the idea of revenge if they want to make children into good citizens. There's still too much politics. Too many district attorneys who care only about getting themselves re-elected. Too many self-righteous citizens who talk about juvenile criminals that usually are only children. And there is only the one answer: we must love them all. We still need a wholly new type of social worker, with zealous love of God and fellows, especially the kids. They must help to find or make homes for them. They must be social workers who can love, and watch, and pray. Empires fell because home life disintegrated."

We asked him, then, an indiscreet question, but one that had to have an answer, although how urgently we could not suspect. What would happen when he passed on? Was there someone so passionately devoted to children that the work would be carried on?

"God will send," was his answer. "We have already started an endowment fund. Someday in the far, far future that may make us self-supporting. Anyway, the work will continue, you see, whether I am there or not, because it is God's work, not mine."

He was looking forward to seeing Austria again, perhaps a visit to Innsbruck:

"During the war, Hitler used our old college as a barracks for his troopers. I have been warned to expect the worst."

Just before he left he called our family together and gave us his blessing. And we walked with him to the elevator in the hall—which we call our "garden gate," as we wished him Godspeed on his journey. Was there anything we could do for him?

"Thank you—dears," he said. "Maybe, now, you'd like to say one Hail Mary—for my health."

He was smiling as he stepped into the elevator and waved goodby.

IV

Soon he was to see for himself the changes, especially the disintegration of young Austrians. But he was not to lose faith; he never had lost faith in youth.

"Even though the picture seems somewhat gloomy," he stated in a posthumous report, "with bad health and a weakening in morale in some places, Austrian youth for the most part show unexpected energies, tremendous enthusiasm, which proves the youth of Austria still has faith, a Divine faith in Almighty God, and a consequent faith in the future of their country."

Over the radio in Austria he spoke to American service personnel:

"I would like every member of the United States forces to remember that he has a real mission, for which he was chosen by his government. It is the responsibility of every American over here to be a teacher of democracy—Christian democracy—among people who are crying out to live under the blessings of a democratic state. These teachers—in uniform—must always be conscious that their example as teachers is far more important than any mere teaching by precept.

"Instead of using their free time in quest of pleasure, let our men rather consider their free time as their contribution towards teaching the blessings of Christian democracy as they themselves have been privileged to enjoy it from birth in their own country.

"Our men must remember they had been chosen to represent a country that has never abandoned God and the principles of Christianity, by which alone a people can live in peace and tranquillity and redeemable prosperity, with its neighbors and the world."

v

The end of the lifelong journey that had begun in Roscommon was to come amid the rubble of ruined Berlin.

That day of May 14, 1948, according to Pat Norton, had called for a crowded schedule of meetings, interviews, and discussions. He had arrived in Berlin by plane in the morning, flying in from Frankfurt, and got to work at once. All day long there was a series of conferences with representatives of German youth organizations. Father got a good picture of the appalling conditions under which many children of Germany were living. He knew now how deeply the Nazi dogma had infected their minds, and that many were beginning to be poisoned with the equally evil virus of communism. A tremendous job of reconstructing young minds had to be done, if a democratic Germany was to be built. Wherever he turned he saw half-starved waifs living amid ruins.

In talking at length with Conrad, Cardinal von Preysing, in Berlin, he admitted that for all his unfaltering faith, he was heartsick in this shell of a great capital with its miles of wrecked homes and hungry children. At nightfall he had dinner with Pat Norton and a captain from the Signal Corps. For a while they forgot the wreckage around them. Later, at their hotel, Father Flanagan and Pat Norton talked over plans for the next day, when they were to have a meeting with General Clay. First of all, he wanted to discuss with the American commander the Bavarian Concordat, in which the Pope had already expressed interest; secondly, the recommendation that welfare workers be employed by the army in Germany for Youth Centers, and finally a proposal that funds be allotted to provide adult leadership from among the German people to conduct these centers. That was important, he emphasized to Norton, for they would understand far better than any outsiders the problems of their own children.

Around nine-thirty he climbed into bed. About midnight he awakened and called out to Norton: "Pat—I have a pain in my chest. Please get the doctor right away."

It was a heart attack, the physician found out, and at once ordered Father Flanagan to the hospital. He also summoned Father Emmet Walsh, army chaplain. Waiting outside, while Father Walsh heard Father Flanagan's confession, were Pat Norton and Sergeant Patrick Moriarity of the Youth Activities Section, who had helped to carry Father Flanagan to the ambulance.

"After Father Walsh had heard Father's confession," Norton said later, "we were called back into the room, as Father had requested that we be present while the sacrament of extreme unction was being administered.

"While Father Walsh said the prayers for the dead, Father, in his characteristic manner, stroked his bushy eyebrows. As the prayers were finished, Father Flanagan himself concluded the prayer with 'Amen.'

"That was his last word."

The priest had closed his eyes—with that one final breath of prayer, life left him.

VI

At Boys Town, Mayor Eddie Dunn and a few friends were listening to the radio when an announcer broke into the program with the news bulletin about Father Flanagan's death. The whole population went at once to the chapel. A few days later the body of the founder was returned by plane to Boys Town. It was laid to rest in a sarcophagus in the chapel, near to boys every day.

On a marble slab is the golden inscription:

FATHER FLANAGAN—FOUNDER OF BOYS TOWN
LOVER OF CHRIST AND MAN
July 13, 1886–May 15, 1948.

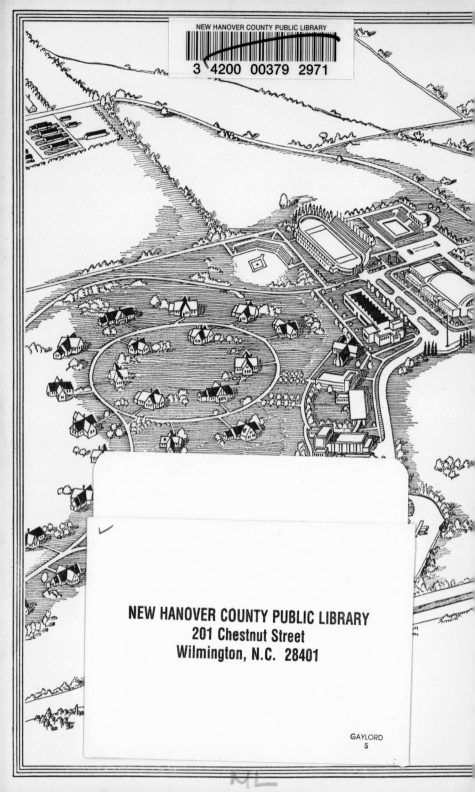